ENDGAMES

ENDGAMES

Questions in Late Modern Political Thought

JOHN GRAY

Polity Press

Copyright © John Gray 1997

The right of John Gray to be identified as author of this work has been asserted in
accordance with the Copyright, Designs and Patents Act 1988.

First published in 1997 by Polity Press in association with Blackwell Publishers Ltd.

Reprinted 2004

2 4 6 8 10 9 7 5 3 1

Editorial office:
Polity Press
65 Bridge Street
Cambridge CB2 1UR, UK

Marketing and production:
Blackwell Publishers Ltd
108 Cowley Road
Oxford OX4 1JF, UK

Published in the USA by
Blackwell Publishers Inc.
Commerce Place
350 Main Street
Malden, MA 02148, USA

ISBN 0–7456–1881–2
ISBN 0–7456–1882–0 (pbk)

A CIP catalogue record for this book is available from the British Library and the Library
of Congress.

Typeset in 11 on 13 pt Sabon
by Ace Filmsetting Ltd, Frome, Somerset
Printed and bound in Great Britain by Marston Book Services Limited, Oxford

This book is printed on acid-free paper.

CONTENTS

FOREWORD

In earlier writings I have argued that our inherited stock of political ideas no longer tracks the world in which we live and strive to flourish. In all western countries, virtually every political tendency embodies some variation on the Enlightenment project of progress towards a universal civilization. Whether neo-liberal or social democrat, the political ideas and movements of western countries are dedicated to the construction of a global society in which western institutions and values are projected worldwide. The Soviet system was an artefact of that Enlightenment project; so are a global free market and universal human rights. All are variations on the modern utopia of a universal civilization in which the local identities that go with cultural difference have been marginalized into the private sphere and are not mirrored in an abiding diversity of political regimes. This modern utopia was the common patrimony of all the political movements spawned by the Enlightenment, liberal as well as Marxist. It continues to animate most currents of political thought in the late modern period. Yet the world in which it seemed to be a real possibility has ceased to exist.

The universal civilization which late modern political thought anachronistically sponsors is modelled on the countries of western Europe and their cultural colonies in North America and elsewhere during the period, lasting from the sixteenth century until only a decade or so ago, in which 'the West' exercised an intellectual, economic and military hegemony over all other societies. Now, whatever it might once have meant, 'the West' in our historical context has become an obsolescent and indeed a substantially contentless notion. In contemporary political discourse, it invokes the backward-looking Enlightenment philosophy of history in which modernization is conflated with westernization and the entirety of humankind is fated to converge on an idealized version of some nineteenth-century western culture. In subscribing to this dreary modern utopia, all contemporary schools of political thought are, in effect, reposing their hopes in a better yesterday. They fail to address the present and its needs. It is not surprising that in many parts of the world, notably the United States and the former Soviet Union, political cultures animated by Enlightenment ideals are at the same time pervaded by fundamentalist and nativist movements which seek to resist the disenchantment of the world wrought by Enlightenment rationalism.

In *Enlightenment's Wake*, I proposed that late modern cultural and political life could be understood in terms of an interplay between the self-undermining Enlightenment project and the fundamentalist project of re-enchanting the world. Most contemporary political and cultural movements are hybrids, combining within themselves incompatible elements from both projects. As Freud observed, it is only in logic that contradictions are forbidden; he might well have added that in politics they are often obligatory. This was certainly true of the New Right, which is the subject of investigation in much of the present volume. The political movements commonly understood as belonging to the New Right were in their economic policies vehicles of an Enlightenment project of the most primitive variety – the free market utopia of palaeo-liberals such as Herbert Spencer and W. G. Sumner, re-invented in our time by neo-liberal ideologues such as Hayek and Friedman. In its rhetoric and social policies, however, the New Right has everywhere tended to cultural and familial fundamentalism. We can discern in the recourse to fundamentalism of New Right governments and parties an electoral strategy, designed to recoup support lost because of the economic failures of the deregulated market; but partly, also, we see an uncomprehending response to the role of the free market in destroying the traditional social forms on which the bourgeois civilization of liberal capitalism in the past depended. The innermost contradiction encrypted within New Right thinking has always been between the free market as an engine of wealth-creation and its role as a destroyer of traditional institutions and cultural forms. The problems for policy and strategy generated by this contradiction remain unresolved, and indeed insoluble, for conservative parties throughout the world.

One of the endgames plotted in this book is that of traditional conservatism. The British right-wing politicians who return from political pilgrimages to the United States clutching laptop computers and babbling of virtual communities and the family values of the fifties are not merely comic figures; they are symptoms of a disabling, even fatal incoherence in conservative thought and policy in the late modern period. In several places in this book, particularly in its first two chapters, I attempt an analysis of the causes of this ongoing debacle of the Old Right. In Britain, the dominant conservatism of the generation after the Second World War, embodied in such figures as R. A. Butler and Iain Macleod, was a subtle and skilful fusion of Tory communitarian and paternalist concerns with liberal values of individual freedom, opportunity and privacy. The effect of the Thatcherite march through British institutions has been to destroy this tradition of conservative practice, just as it has overthrown many of our other traditions. Whatever may happen to the Conservative Party electorally, Tory politics has reached a dead end. If they survive at all, Tory traditions exist now in Britain only as forms of cultural kitsch. They are media artefacts whose distance from any cultural reality is too obvious to carry with it any pathos. The debacle of traditional conservatism in Britain is a narrative, still unfinished as I write, as well as a topic in social and political theory. Accordingly, in chapter 9 I have selected a number of short articles, unaltered except for minor editorial changes, from a series that appeared in the *Guardian*, in which I attempted to give a narrative account of the dissolution of traditional conservatism in Britain as it was unfolding. The upshot of these articles is that there is and can be no coherent form of conservative thought, and no effective mode of conservative political practice, in a late modern culture such as Britain's.

The genuine understanding of enduring human needs which conservative thought once possessed – needs for membership in strong forms of common life, and for a security and stability in economic life – has passed now to other modes of thinking, such as Green theory and, in Britain, New Labour. The enormous difficulty of translating these once conservative concerns into workable policies, in a historical context of increasing economic globalization, assures the Right project of a political future. But the Right will not in any foreseeable future be the party of tradition. Because the free market works to transform or overturn all inherited and traditional social institutions, the Right project cannot now be that of cultural conservation. It must instead be the fundamentalist project of reinventing practices which the free market has dissolved. If free markets, through the demands they make on the mobility of labour, break up families and enhance the individualist culture of ephemeral relationships, then families must be reconstructed by state-enforced social policies; and similarly in other areas of social life. The Right is thereby committed to a politics of utopian social engineering, no less repugnant or absurd because the dystopia of incessant economic change and cultural immobility it projects is too brittle, fragile and stress-ridden a structure ever to be realized in practice. In chapter 7 I consider recent communitarian theory, arguing that in its standard varieties it too is committed to reconstituting forms of social and cultural life that have disappeared irretrievably.

A historical thesis underpinning much of the argument which is developed in this book is the claim that the Soviet collapse was more than the fall of a particular regime. It was also, and more significantly, a setback for the westernizing Enlightenment project, of which Soviet Marxism was only one expression. The Soviet collapse has already had the result, through the enlargement of world market competition which it entailed, of destroying the postwar embodiments of European social democracy. In chapter 2 I consider what a Left project might mean, now that the demise of the Soviet Union has removed socialism as an economic system from the agenda of history and eroded the foundations of social democracy, leaving competition among different species of capitalism as the only remaining form of systemic economic rivalry in the world. In a larger and longer historical perspective, the Soviet collapse may in retrospect be seen as one in a series of countermovements to the global process of westernization. Its significance is then large indeed. Its meaning, however, is very nearly the opposite of that which Francis Fukuyama read into it when he interpreted it as signifying the universal triumph of the western idea and the end of history. One of the endgames plotted in this book is that of the westernizing universalism that has animated the political projects both of the Left and of the Right.

The animating theme of this volume is the meltdown, as yet far from complete, of the ideologies that governed the modern period. In chapter 10, which has been written for this volume, I consider how the illusions of modernity permeate forms of thinking, such as postmodernism and Green thinking, which have set themselves most strongly against the modern world. As I understand it, postmodernism is not a genuine effort to grasp the postmodern condition in which some cultures, notably those of western Europe and perhaps East Asia, really find themselves. It is instead a dying echo of the ruling projects and illusions of the modern age. The postmodern condition is that in which the movement towards universality, which in the modern period was embodied in the Enlightenment project of a single global civilization, is discovered to be groundless, and diversity in culture and worldview is recognized as a historical fate. Yet both postmodernist thought and standard Green theory renew the universalist project by their common commitment to Enlightenment humanism. In postmodernism deconstruction is only the Romantic project of self-creation, a shadow cast by the Enlightenment commitment to universal emancipation. The postmodern liberalism of Richard Rorty, discussed in chapter 4, is a fusion of the modern Romantic ideal of self-creation with the Enlightenment commitment to universal emancipation. In Rorty's thinking, postmodern liberalism amounts to little more than an endorsement of the global reach of American individualist culture – itself a dated artefact of early modernity. Indeed postmodern liberalism's differences from the American liberal conventional wisdom summarized in the thought of John Rawls (which I consider in chapter 3) are slight and ultimately shallow. In Green theory the acceptance of limits on human hopes of progress and emancipation that are entailed by taking seriously ecological conceptions of sustainability is repressed, and the integrity of the environment on which we depend for our survival is believed to be assured by advancing the Enlightenment ideal of progress and emancipation for humankind. In chapter 10 I argue that the humanist commitments of standard Green thinking belong to those parts of modern culture that no longer track our world or our needs.

Late modern thought occurs in an uneasy interregnum between modern hopes that are no longer credible and postmodern realities that many find intolerable. The thought of late moderns is unavoidably post-Nietzschean. It cannot avoid treating as questionable conceptions – such as 'morality', 'science', 'philosophy', 'progress' and 'emancipation' – whose validity was axiomatic during the heyday of the modern period. At the same time late modern thought is distinguished by its anxious and apologetic character. Nostalgia for modernity is a pervasive, and perhaps for that reason a little noted, feature of our age. (The version of the Left project analysed in chapter 5 is best understood as an expression of modernist nostalgia for 'socialism'.) We are probably not far from a time in which the faith of the Enlightenment will be deployed as Pascal tried to deploy the Christianity of his day – as a drug to stupefy the intellect and an antidote to despair. Such a fideism of Enlightenment would be an ironic ending for the Socratic project which the modern age embodied. A fideist cult of reason and humanity remains nonetheless a not unlikely endgame for our time, since it renews intellectual engagements – such as that in 'philosophy', which I interrogate in chapter 8 in the context of a consideration of two of our most arresting recent thinkers – that are primordial in 'western civilization', and thereby central in our contemporary self-image. The dread evoked by an ending of this self-understanding, which sustains so many late modern thinkers in their unflagging labours to save the modern self-image from dissolution, is in truth the principal blockage in our thinking about the present.

The gap between late modern thought and emerging postmodern realities is the space in which the questions that are the subject of this book are put. The thoughts tried out here are throughout experimental and provisional, like the time of transitions that evoked them.

John Gray
Jesus College, Oxford

ACKNOWLEDGEMENTS

'The Strange Death of Tory England' appeared in *Dissent* (Fall 1995), pp. 447–52; 'After Social Democracy' was published by Demos, London (1996); 'Rawls's Anti-Political Liberalism' appeared in the *New York Times Book Review*, 16 May 1993, p. 35; 'Ironies of Liberal Postmodernity' appeared in the *Times Literary Supplement*, 3 November 1995, pp. 4–5; 'Socialism with a Professorial Face' appeared in *New Left Review*, 210 (March/April 1995), pp. 147–52; 'Green Theory Undone?' appeared in the *London Review of Books*, 20 April 1995, pp. 9–10; 'What Community Is Not' appeared in *Renewal: A Journal of Labour Politics* (Summer 1996); 'Berlin, Oakeshott and Enlightenment' appeared in *Common Knowledge* (Spring 1996), pp. 109–20; 'The Tory Endgame' appeared in the *Guardian*; 'Beginnings' was written for this volume and has not hitherto been published.

I

THE STRANGE DEATH OF TORY ENGLAND

The self-destruction of British conservatism by New Right ideology and policies is best interpreted as an exemplification of a central neo-liberal theme – the importance of unintended consequences in social, economic and political life. The radical free market policies implemented in Britain since 1979 have had as one of their principal effects an unravelling of the coalitions of economic interests and the social hierarchies on which pre-Thatcher conservatism depended. In sweeping away the postwar settlement which all major parties endorsed for a generation, Thatcherism demolished the social and economic base on which conservatism in Britain stood, and created several of the necessary conditions for a prolonged period of Labour hegemony. The medium-term effect of neo-liberal Conservative policy in Britain has been to destroy ethos in institutions such as the Civil Service and the National Health Service by remodelling them on contractualist and managerialist lines. In addition to squandering a large part of Britain's patrimony of civilized institutions, this neo-liberal project of refashioning social life on a primitive model of market exchange has speeded the delegitimation of established institutions such as the monarchy and the Church. Further, by stripping democratic local government in Britain of most of its powers and building up the unaccountable institutions of the Quango State – the apparatus of committees appointed by central government to oversee the operation of the newly marketized public services, which is now larger in manpower and in the resources it allocates than democratic local government in Britain – the Conservatives have marginalized their own local party organizations and thereby contributed to the steep and swift decline of the Conservative Party itself. Indeed, the catastrophic performance of the Conservatives in the local council elections of May 1995, in which they suffered their worst electoral rout since the start of the century, suggests that the neo-liberal project of permanent institutional revolution in Britain may well count its political vehicle, the Conservative Party, among its casualties. It is difficult to see how in any near future the Conservatives can recover from the unintended consequences of a neo-liberal project that has hollowed out legitimacy from many British institutions and fractured and dislocated their party machine. Even if, in the normal fortunes of political life in Britain, the Conservative Party is somehow able to renew itself, it will be in a form that cannot presently be foreseen. As for Tory England – that rich network of interlocking interests, social deferences and inherited institutions that Tory statecraft has successfully protected and reproduced for over a century by its skilful adaptation to democratic institutions in Britain – it is now as good as dead.

The self-undermining effect of neo-liberal policy in Britain has been even more cruelly ironic than this brief narrative reveals. Thatcher's principal insight was to perceive that there was, in Britain in 1979, an economic constituency for union-bashing, budget-cutting, low-tax policies – a constituency whose very existence was denied by the patrician Tory 'Wets', but which she made politically visible and electorally decisive from the early eighties onwards. The irony is that it is this group that – aside from the various constituencies of the poor which it has become fashionable to lump together under the American category of the underclass – has lost most in the nineties. For, in a development that verged on an inevitability, the deregulated labour markets engineered by Thatcherism in the eighties undermined in the nineties the job security of the upwardly mobile social group – Essex man and woman – which contained Thatcherism's most electorally significant beneficiaries. The deregulation of financial institutions that in the late eighties flooded the economy with easy money and caused asset values to float to unsustainable heights, at the same time spawned new financial instruments – personal pensions and endowment mortgages – that spelt loss or ruin for millions of households. (An index of the magnitude of the side-effects of financial deregulation in Britain is the fact that during the first five years of the nineties over 300,000 homes have been repossessed – an eviction on a scale that is unparalleled in Britain since the Highland enclosures of the 1740s.)

The very economic constituency that gained most from early Thatcherism has been most savaged by its longer-term effects. At the same time, the Quango State built up in the wake of the Thatcherite attack on democratic local government and the Majorite policy of marketizing public services and intermediary institutions has facilitated the growth of a new class of Tory nomenclaturists, managing vast resources without any form of effective democratic accountability. In its last phase, in one of its crowning ironies, the neo-liberal project in Britain, which began as a response to failing corporatist institutions, has given rise to new economic institutions, which may be termed the institutions of *market corporatism*. These institutions are not only themselves democratically unaccountable; they cannot for long be politically legitimated through democratic institutions. The neo-liberal Corporate State, in Britain as in any other democratic country, is inherently politically unstable.

Neo-liberalism in Britain, for these and many other reasons, has proved a self-limiting project. Yet, contrary to those on the Left – by far the majority – who saw it as a blip on the screen of history, it has transformed irreversibly the social and institutional landscape of Britain, and thereby the terms of political trade. If it has signally failed as the Gramscian project of securing the legitimacy of unfettered market institutions in Britain it was undoubtedly originally conceived to be – if it has failed so completely, in fact, as to destroy for the foreseeable future the electoral prospects of the Conservative Party – neo-liberal conservatism nevertheless has one achievement, unintended and doubtless still uncomprehended by its authors, to its credit – the destruction of Tory England. In the longer perspective of history this role as a brutal and unconscious agent of modernization – including the modernization, and so the return to electability, of the Labour Party – may prove to be Thatcherism's sole historic justification. The cost of this modernization, however, has been not only the near-destruction of much of Britain's institutional inheritance, but also the obliteration of that humane postwar liberal conservatism – embodied in such figures as Butler, Boyle, Macleod and Macmillan – in which Tory paternalist and communitarian traditions were adapted to the conditions of a late modern industrial society.

Any understanding of the history of the neo-liberal project in Britain must begin with the fact that the dissolution of the postwar settlement was underway well before Thatcher's coming to power in 1979.[1] Unlike corporatist institutions in Germany and Austria, which acted as pace-makers for wealth-creation and guarantors of social peace, British corporatism in the sixties and seventies had produced economic stagnation, industrial and social conflict and a fiscal crisis of the state which triggered the intervention of the IMF. The key neo-liberal policy framework of fiscal conservatism and its consequence, the retreat from macro-economic management having full employment as its objective, were accordingly in place in Britain when Margaret Thatcher came to power. The neo-liberal project – the project of reining back the activities of the state, extending the scope of market institutions to the limits of political possibility and securing for unfettered markets an unchallengeable legitimacy in the public culture – was formulated and adopted by the Conservatives during the years between Thatcher's succession to the leadership of the party in 1975 and the Conservative victory in 1979 – the same years in which fiscal conservatism was imposed by the IMF on the Callaghan Labour government (1974–9). It is worth recalling that the earlier Conservative government of Edward Heath (1970–4) had attained power with something akin to a neo-liberal agenda, and that it had come to nothing. The Heath government was elected on a programme of reversing the postwar trend to overextended government in Britain, but it had abandoned this programme long before it suffered electoral defeat in February 1974 as a result of its confrontation with the miners. It was, however, the defeat of the Heath government by the miners which most shaped the early stages of Thatcherite policy.

The first phase of the neo-liberal project, as it was conceived and implemented in the early 1980s, was not an attack on the welfare state, nor the marketization of major social institutions, but instead the abandonment of full employment as an objective of public policy and the development of a stable framework of public finance – both policies which had the effect of diminishing the power of organized labour in Britain, and both of them expressing the anti-corporatist orientation of early Thatcherism. Thatcherite policy in the early eighties was in considerable measure reactive in seeking to break up the triangular relations of collusion between employers, unions and government that sustained the bankrupt British corporatism of the seventies. That it soon became pro-active in attempting to reshape British society and public culture according to the crude abstractions of economic liberalism is to be accounted for by Thatcher's first and most fateful act of privatization – the privatization of policy-making whereby it was removed from the control of the Civil Service and contracted out to right-wing think-tanks.

The New Right thought which these think-tanks – above all, the Institute of Economic Affairs – had incubated during a long sojourn, throughout the fifties and sixties, in the political wilderness at the margins of British public culture, was neither monolithic nor even particularly coherent. It contained a diversity of intellectual trends, of which Chicago economics, Virginia Public Choice theory, and elements of Austrian economics derived from the work of Hayek were the most prominent. Nevertheless, it is true of all of the think-tanks – even the Centre for Policy Studies, set up by Keith Joseph and Margaret Thatcher in 1975 as an explicitly Conservative founda-tion – that their intellectual inspiration was not any kind of conservatism, as that had been traditionally understood in Britain and in other European countries, but classical liberalism. The most distinctive features of New Right ideology in Britain in the 1970s and 1980s – its use of an abstract and rationalistic conception of *homo economicus*, its doctrinaire pursuit of a general theory of minimal government, its individualist and legalist conception of contractual relationships as the basis of economic and social order and its utopian preoccupation with constitutional devices – are all symptomatic of its roots in nineteenth-, or even eighteenth-century classical liberalism, and of the influence upon it of classical liberal-ism's twentieth-century followers. No British or other European conservative thinker has ever supposed that the principle of con-sumer sovereignty, together with institutions designed to prevent the capture of government by producer interests and a constitution protecting individual rights, could frame an adequate political philosophy; yet this thin gruel of economism and legalism was all that the political thought of the New Right had to offer. By contrast, the historicism and cultural relativism of British and European conservative thought, the criticisms of commercial society mounted not only by Disraeli but by Adam Smith and Adam Ferguson, by Carlyle and Ruskin, are noteworthy by their complete absence in New Right political thought. The sharp critique of the Enlighten-ment developed by many conservative thinkers, even Burke, is similarly lacking.[2] The pervasive influences on New Right thought in Britain in the seventies and eighties – by contrast with the United States, where, except in certain varieties of doctrinally libertarian thought, populist and even fundamentalist influences were never altogether absent – were those of classical liberal rationalism, as that has been revised in our time by such thinkers as Popper and Hayek.[3]

New Right thought in Britain, then, was distanced or detached from the larger tradition of European conservative philosophy of which British conservative thought has always been a part. Its distance from its own intellectual and political tradition was enhanced by a further influence – that of the American Right. It is useful to recall that the British New Right achieved its ephemeral hegemony in public discourse during the Cold War, had its political expression in the most unequivocally (and uncritically) pro-American Prime Minister of the postwar period, and coincided with the combination in Reaganite America of a strongly anti-communist foreign policy with an intensely market-oriented domestic policy. This shared historical context made it all the easier for American rightist thought – the thought, that is to say, of neo-conservatives and libertarians of various sorts – to exercise an influence over British conservatism that was decidedly anomalous in terms both of its European intellectual inheritance and of Britain's underlying public culture. The weakness, or virtual absence, in the United States of anything comparable with European conservatism, the near-ubiquity in American intellectual culture of individualist, universalist and Enlightenment themes – the fact, in other words, that in the United States conservative thought is merely an indigenously American variation on classical liberal themes of limited government, individualism and economic progress – made the kinship of the British New Right with the American Right a matter of elective affinity and not merely of historical accident.

This kinship between the classical liberal thought of the British New Right – whose hegemony in the eighties was in the longer and larger history of British conservative thought highly incongruous – with the indigenous American tradition of individualism and universalism was strengthened by the opposition of most on the neo-liberal Right in Britain to European federalism.[4] For many on the New Right in Britain, and certainly for Thatcher, Britain's cultural affinities lay with the United States rather than with the nations of Europe. Thatcher may have had differences with Reagan, over the voodoo economics of self-financing tax cuts and the Panglossian claim that the Strategic Defence Initiative could exorcise the spectre of nuclear war. Yet there is no doubt that she harboured the Churchillian fantasy of a transatlantic Anglo-Saxon civilization. Their ties reinforced by conservative hegemony in both countries,

Britain and the United States would not only renew the 'special relationship' but also follow parallel paths of economic and (presumably) social development, with Britain emulating American individualist market capitalism. In this Thatcher not only misread Britain's strategic situation, which was that of a European power, but misjudged British public culture, which differs from that of the United States in all the most crucially important respects. In Britain, market capitalism has never enjoyed unqualified political legitimacy, being challenged by a powerful socialist culture and accepted by Tories prior to Thatcher only with deep reservations; religion is weak and society substantially post-Christian; and the Enlightenment faith in world-improvement is lacking, or qualified – as all ideological claims are qualified – by an enduring scepticism. More decisively, perhaps, for the fate of the neo-liberal project, Britain remains a far less individualist society than the United States, with attitudes to geographical and occupational mobility, for example, being uniformly far more negative; and the relationship of the British people to the British state remains one of wary trust rather than of suspicion or enmity. It was ignorance of, or perhaps refusal to accept these profound divergences between British and American culture and political life which made the interventions in British public discourse of such American ideologues and publicists as Charles Murray and Michael Novak predictably marginal. If Thatcher's project was that of the Americanization of Britain, these enduring features of British culture – which attest to its greater and deeper affinities with the cultures of continental Europe – foredoomed it to failure.

The remaking of the Conservative Party in the image of the Republican Right, which progressed throughout the eighties with the systematic marginalization of those Tories (such as Chris Patten) who saw its future in convergence with European Christian Democratic parties, cut the Conservatives loose from their moorings in British and European culture and in the history of their own party. At the same time, the long march through British institutions begun by Thatcher and continued by John Major's government has emptied them of much of their ethos and legitimacy, while the pulverizing force of labour market deregulation, which had been applied to the unions in the eighties, has been applied to the professional middle classes in the nineties. The result has been a cataclysmic collapse of Tory support in Scotland and Wales, with the Conservatives there trailing as the third or fourth party. In the Tory heartland of England the permanent revolution of marketization sponsored by neo-liberal Conservative policy has confounded expectations and enhanced economic insecurity among the Conservatives' core supporters, producing a collapse of support on a similar scale.[5] As of May 1995 the Tories did not control a single metropolitan town council and only one county council. The Tories are paying the price of attaching their fortunes to an economic philosophy which recognizes only the human interest in increased income and consumer choice and fails to perceive the weightier interest people have in limiting the personal economic risk to which they are subject. In forgetting the truism of conservative philosophy that most human beings are risk-averse creatures, the Tories have condemned themselves to replicating the fortunes of the western-inspired economic liberals of the post-communist countries, who have been swept from office by social democratic parties which grasp this elementary truth.

In political terms, the strategic situation of the Conservatives is that the most they can hope for in the foreseeable future is to turn impending catastrophe into mere defeat. Either outcome spells displacement for the Tory nomenclatura which mans the institutions of the Quango State, and its members, along with sitting Tory MPs, will use every means at their disposal to limit the spell in opposition which they cannot now avert. Within the British conservative intelligentsia it is not uncommon to find a period of opposition welcomed as a respite from power and an occasion for reflective thought. It is difficult to know, however, what supports the confidence of Conservative thinkers in Britain that the leisure of opposition will allow them to develop the intellectual resources to address the profound changes in British society that Conservative policies have engendered or reinforced. For it is now wholly unclear what, if anything, British conservatism can realistically or coherently set itself to conserve. The hollowing out of the legitimacy of traditional institutions by economic and cultural changes which neo-liberalism has accelerated makes a restorationist or revivalist policy orientation a hopeless dead end – as the farcical flirtation of the Major government with a 'back-to-basics' rhetoric of family values showed vividly. The halcyon England of the fifties conjured up by Major's nostalgist rhetoric, insofar as it has any semblance of historical reality, was an artefact of the Labour-led postwar settlement which the Conservatives have destroyed. Even if it were desirable to recreate it – which is more than doubtful – it is now irretrievable. An American-style stance of cultural fundamentalism has attractions for many British conservative thinkers, nonetheless, because it enables them to avoid confronting the central contradiction in their thought and policy – the contradiction between endorsing the permanent revolution of the global market and the preservation of stable forms of family and community life. If, as is manifestly the case, the effect of unfettered global market institutions is to overthrow settled communities everywhere, to undermine the stability of families by imposing on their members the imperative of unceasing mobility and to dissolve traditional practices and institutions in a flood of novelty, neo-liberal conservatives are compelled to ascribe these changes to factors other than unchecked market forces. The explanation is then sought in antinomian or relativistic doctrines supposedly propagated in schools and universities, in the legacy of sixties libertarianism, in media bias or similarly absurd conjectures. The social – and for that matter economic – failures of market fundamentalism are patched up, or at least obscured, by recourse to the atavistic fantasies of cultural fundamentalism. Only by invoking a conspiratorial elite of liberal intellectuals can the conservative intelligentsia explain to itself why – after seventeen years of neo-liberal hegemony – the ordinary people it claims to speak for in Britain show every sign of consigning to electoral oblivion the party whose policies they continue to support.

The political collapse of the New Right in Britain has many causes, including ones that are highly contingent, such as the adoption of the poll tax (which was one of the occasions of the Tory coup that toppled Thatcher) and the ignorance and hubris which led ephemeral neo-liberal ideologues to proclaim in the eighties that 'Labour will never rule again.' It is still too early to attempt a balanced and comprehensive historical assessment of the conflicts of interest and personality, the errors in policy and the complex interactions of closed ideology and human folly with political power which have brought the neo-liberal experiment in Britain to a close. It is not too early to elicit a couple of lessons from its whimpering debacle. The first is that the pretensions of the New Right to an intellectual hegemony in political discourse were always spurious. The neo-liberal project exercised a transitory *political* hegemony in Britain which it owed to an unrepeatable confluence of fortunate circumstances – the bankruptcy of Labourist corporatism, the disintegration of Soviet institutions, the decline of European social democracy and the trend to economic globalization which weakened organized labour. It contributed nothing significant to conservative political thought. Indeed, its policies have only speeded the obsolescence of conservative thought by illuminating its helplessness before the dominant economic forces of the age.

The second lesson is that there remains, in Britain at least, no historical space for coherent conservative thought. The historical possibility of serious intellectual conservatism has been closed off by the policies of the last decade and a half. To be sure, if history is any guide, the Conservative Party will somehow renew itself, in the normal fortunes of political life in a two-party-system; but Tory England, which it existed to conserve, is already no more than a historical memory. Conservative thought, in this new historical circumstance, is likely to be a mixture of fashionable techno-utopianism – such as the proposition, recently seriously advanced, that the virtual communities of the Internet can replace the local communities that free markets have desolated – and opportunistic fundamentalism. This is not a form of thought from which enlightenment or guidance can reasonably be expected. The enduring human needs which conservative philosophy once acknowledged are not now addressed by conservatives, partly because meeting them entails radical and – for today's conservatives – unwelcome changes in current economic institutions. Meeting these human needs – for deep and strong forms of common life, fulfilling work and a rich public environment – demands re-embedding the market processes which neo-liberal policy has emancipated from any kind of political control or accountability in the cultures and communities they exist to serve. And this is a project, little short of revolutionary in its implications, that no form of conservative thought today is willing to contemplate.

2
AFTER SOCIAL DEMOCRACY

Where we are now

Social democrats have failed to perceive that Thatcherism was a modernizing project with profound and irreversible consequences for political life in Britain. The question cannot now be: How are the remains of social democracy to be salvaged from the ruins of Thatcherism? It must instead be: What is Thatcherism's successor?

Like wet Tories, social democrats did not grasp the radicalism of the Thatcher project in sweeping away old class deferences and hierarchies. Many of them still view it as a blip on the screen of history, to be followed by a return to the 'normal politics' of pre-Thatcher times This is a disabling illusion, especially for the Left. The Thatcher project has certainly been exhausted, and the political energy by which it was animated in the early eighties has evaporated, leaving only the dreary and unmeaning formulae of New Right ideology. Nevertheless, Thatcherism has permanently changed the terms of political trade in Britain in ways that rule out any return either to traditional conservatism on the Right – One Nation Toryism, say – or to social democracy – a species of Croslandism or of Owenism, perhaps – on the Left. Possibly only a handful of observers, including a few perceptive Marxists, have grasped the paradoxical nature of Thatcherism, as a project which failed in all of its positive agenda but which – in conjunction with trends in the world economy which no government directs or controls – transformed British society and public culture so as to render these earlier political projects, along with Thatcherism itself, anachronistic and redundant.

In many respects Thatcherism was a self-undermining project. Those who formulated it did not perceive that the freeing up of markets that drastically diminished the power of organized labour in Britain would have the unintended consequence, over time, of undermining economic security among the social groups who were Thatcherism's initial beneficiaries. It thereby worked to dissolve the electoral coalition of interests that had enabled it to come to power. The aspirational working-class people who perceived in Thatcherite policies the chance of upward social mobility into the middle classes, if they were successful in making the transition, discovered that the life of Middle England had been transformed beyond recognition. They emerged not in the sunlit uplands of bourgeois security but onto a desolate plateau of middle-class pauperdom. The poignant irony of Essex man and woman struggling up the economic escalator only to meet the bedraggled figures of the professional middle classes staggering down it is a narrative of our times that has yet to be properly written. Thatcherism could not act as an instrument of social mobility for its initial supporters because it undid the class structure in terms of which they had framed their aspirations. Thatcherism's capacity to alter the British social landscape profoundly, unpredictably and irreversibly is only a particularly dramatic illustration of the power of unfettered markets to unravel traditional forms of social life.

For all these reasons, those on the New Right who see political salvation – for themselves, if not for Britain – in reviving its lost verities are merely deluding themselves. In our circumstances, a return to Ur-Thatcherism is precluded both by the impact which the policies of the Thatcher and Major governments have had on its initial coalition of supporters and by changes in the public culture of Britain – such as changes in its class culture – for which Thatcherism was itself partly responsible. But to see that we must go beyond Thatcherism is also to see that there is no going back to social democracy.

It is a paradox of British political life that, at a moment in history when social democracy is in retreat everywhere, we are very nearly all social democrats now. In all parties, most of us have converged on a sensible and pragmatic middle ground which in crucial respects already trails behind events. Social democracy was a political project whose stability and even identity depended on the geo-strategic environment of the Cold War. It defined its socialist content by opposition to Soviet communism and sometimes, also, to American individualism. The Soviet collapse has removed this environment and denuded social democracy of the identity a bipolar world conferred on it. The new realities which spell ruin for the social democratic project are the billions of industrious and skilled workers released onto the global market by the communist collapse and the disappearance of any effective barriers to the global mobility of capital. In this changed historical circumstance the central economic programme of social democracy is unworkable and social democracy itself a bankrupt project.

It is true that the new social democratic consensus in Britain represents a real advance on the sterile and atavistic debate between the Old Left and the New Right. Yet it is also a backward-looking perspective that will prove a poor guide to understanding the present and preparing for the future. In this chapter, I aim to clarify and explore the emerging social democratic consensus in British public discourse. My purpose in so doing is not to endorse it. On the contrary, it is to question it. Among the irreversible consequences of the Thatcherite project and its failure in Britain, one of the most neglected is the impossibility of any return to the policies and institutions of social democracy. In part my argument is a historical one. Insofar as it was embodied in a labourist movement which technological and economic change, together with over a decade and a half of neo-liberal policy, has undermined, social democracy is now a political project without a historical agent. The class base of social democratic parties, not only in Britain but throughout Europe, has been eaten away by economic change, at the same time that the powers of national governments, which were the levers of social democratic policy, have been steadily reduced. Though this is a hard truth which practising politicians inevitably find it hard to acknowledge, the new global freedom of financial capital so hems in national governments as to limit severely, or to rule out altogether, traditional social democratic full employment policies. There is a dark historical irony in the fact of the formation of a social democratic consensus at just the moment when both its class base and its political vehicle have been marginalized.

The risk of the emerging consensus is the hardening into a conventional wisdom of a set of assumptions which is as anachronistic as Thatcherism itself. The failure of neo-liberal reforms of the welfare state either to diminish poverty or to control expenditure – both of which have risen inexorably – encourages, as a decent and natural but misguided and unrealistic reaction, the belief that the old

British welfare state can be reinvented in another guise, and the hard choices of real welfare reform avoided. Neo-liberal tolerance of long-term unemployment evokes the illusion that postwar full employment policies can be revived and made effective. The crudity and failure of neo-liberal policies to reduce the size of government – which arose in part because the impact of long-term unemployment on public expenditure was underestimated – obscures perception of the unsustainability of a large and growing state in a period in which neither taxpayers nor lenders can be relied upon to finance public deficits. The absurdity and inhumanity of neo-liberal policies to trim the size of government have produced a social democratic complacency about its growth that is no less costly and dangerous.

The key test of whether we have yet formulated a genuinely post-Thatcherite political outlook is our ability to perceive that, even as it undermined the conditions of its own political viability, Thatcherism at the same time destroyed other political projects – notably One Nation Toryism and social democracy – which had once been its rivals. The end of Thatcherism – which occurred, not suddenly with a bang when Thatcher herself was toppled in 1990, but slowly and with a whimper, during the long interregnum of the Major years – marked not only the political collapse of neo-liberalism in Britain but also the closing of an era in its public culture.

As yet the shape of political life and public culture in Britain in the wake of the Thatcher project remains unclear. Several distinct tendencies are nevertheless already discernible. The fixed points of the social democratic consensus that is now accepted by the majority in all parties are the unacceptable social costs and moral hazards of the unrestrained market individualism of the eighties; the world-wide collapse of central planning institutions, the economic vehicle of classical socialism, and the universal rise – in a wide diversity of forms – of market institutions; and the acceptance that there is no possibility of returning to the corporatist institutions and policies whose failings in Britain – particularly their tendency to act as mechanisms for distributional conflict rather than as means of wealth-creation – were the original political justification and historical rationale of Thatcherite policies. Within this cross-party social democratic consensus, a movement of Tory modernizers currently seeks to apply a right-wing variant of the social market philosophy to the tasks of legitimating the free market in political terms and extending market mechanisms further into the public sector. Within Labour's modernizers, a leading tendency seeks to modernize social democracy itself, by distinguishing between the policies and institutions in which it was embodied in the British postwar settlement and the central values of equality and community which remain constitutive of it as a political morality.

Outwith the social democratic consensus, a group of right-wing radicals around John Redwood, who are no longer recognizably British Tories and who take their cues from American neo-conservative cultural fundamentalists, aims to renew New Right thought in another form. This second wave of New Right thinking rejects the sovereign individual of neo-liberal ideology in favour of a return to 'traditional values', and seeks to buttress the institutions of the unfettered free market with restored forms of traditional family life. It is significant that, whereas in the eighties the New Right worked with the grain of the times, this revised form of New Right thought, while aiming to transcend the primitive market fundamentalism of neo-liberal ideology, works against the culture of Britain in the nineties – a culture that is partly an unintended consequence of the neo-liberal celebration of unrestrained individualism. This newer New Right sets itself against the dominant forces of the times in its denial of the pervasive demand for individual autonomy, its revivalist response to the decay of inherited social forms, and its failure to understand that it is principally the subversive dynamism of market forces that is inexorably dissolving them. Within Labour, a dwindling band of classical socialists stands outside the social democratic consensus, challenging the radical revisionism of the modernizers and rejecting social democracy as an unstable refinement of capitalism rather than a genuine alternative to it. The late Ralph Miliband's *Socialism for a Sceptical Age* may be taken as a statement of the theoretical perspective by which many members of this tendency are informed.

The modernizing tendencies in both major parties need to run very fast simply to avoid being left far behind by events. The aim of this chapter is to sketch a pattern of ideas whose chief merit may be that it is less removed from present circumstances than most of the ideas which inform political discourse. In its theoretical aspect, it advances a communitarian liberal perspective as one which avoids the principal errors of neo-liberalism and enriches standard liberal philosophy with the distinctive insights of communitarian thought. Its claim is that this perspective can aid thought on the central dilemma of the age, which is how revolutionary changes in technology and the economy can be reconciled with the enduring human needs for security and for forms of common life. As it arises in the context of a liberal culture, this dilemma can be expressed as that of balancing the interests in choice and autonomy, which are thought – often mistakenly – to be promoted by free markets, against the benefits, responsibilities and duties of community. In its broadest terms, the communitarian liberal view rejects both the economistic conception of the individual as a sovereign consumer and the legalist view of the individual as above all a rights-bearer. The influence of recent American thought has made a combination of these conceptions the dominant view of the human subject within liberalism, though it was not that of J. S. Mill or Alexis de Tocqueville, any more than it is now that of Berlin or Raz.

Communitarian liberalism differs from standard, individualist liberalisms in that it conceives of choosing individuals as themselves creations of forms of common life. It rejects the libertarian view that individual choice must be always paramount over every other human need and interest – a view embodied in the libertarian misconception of market freedoms as implications of, or derivations from, the basic structure of human rights. It differs from conservative and neo-traditionalist communitarianisms[1] in that it acknowledges the strength and urgency of the need for individual autonomy – the demand people are voicing and acting upon, which is working itself through all of the institutions and practices of contemporary liberal societies, to make their own choices and to be at least part-authors of their own lives. It recognizes the pluralism of such cultures in virtue of which few of us are defined by membership of a single, all-embracing community, and accepts that there is no going back to any simpler, 'organic' way of life. It differs from the political morality of social democracy by rejecting the egalitarian commitment to the imposition of a single conception of justice in all areas of policy and contexts of economic and social life.

The key claim of communitarian liberalism is that individual human flourishing presupposes strong and deep forms of common life. The elements of the communitarian liberal perspective on which I shall focus here are those that are especially salient in our present context, in which the neo-liberal project has all but destroyed itself but has as yet no clear successor. Accordingly I will consider and reject the neo-liberal claim that markets necessarily enhance choice and autonomy, and maintain instead that the liberal value of autonomy can be protected only in the context of a public culture of which market exchange is only a subordinate part. To this extent, the conflict between autonomy and community is superficial. In the last section I shall consider areas of social life and public policy where this conflict is real and difficult. The central application of the communitarian liberal view to public policy is that market freedoms have instrumental value only, as means to individual well-being, and they have this value only when they do not weaken forms of common life without which individual well-being is impoverished or impossible.

To anticipate the sketch I shall advance of this perspective, communitarian liberalism affirms, firstly, that *individual autonomy presupposes a strong public culture in which choice and responsibility go together, and is realizable only as a common good*; secondly, that *market exchange makes no inherent contribution to autonomy, and market competition must be limited in contexts – such as broadcasting and urban development – where its impact on individual autonomy may be disabling rather than enhancing*; and thirdly, that *fairness demands the distribution of goods and responsibilities according to their common social meanings in particular contexts, thereby excluding market forces from domains – the public provision of health care and education, for example – where they violate such common understandings*.

These three claims express the distinctive communitarian political morality in which neither libertarian nor egalitarian principles are fundamental, but rather the renewal and creation of worthwhile social forms. The central insight of communitarian philosophy, as I understand it, is that conceptions of autonomy and fairness are not embodiments of universal principles – principles of justice or rights, say – but instead local understandings, grounded in particular forms of common life. Conceptions of autonomy and of fairness are local notions, both in the sense that they express the ethical life of specific cultures, and because their content varies greatly, depending on the domain of social activity in which they arise in any particular culture. By contrast with social democracy and with rights-based liberalism, the communitarian political morality I defend here interprets our conceptions of autonomy and fairness not as applications of universal principles but as shared understandings arising from common forms of life. In this morality, equality is demanded as a safeguard against exclusion and not, in social democratic terms, as a requirement of any theory of justice. The justice with which communitarian thinking is concerned is not universal; it is the local justice which matches goods to social understandings, as these arise in particular cultures and the specific domains of activity they contain. The autonomy which a communitarian liberalism is concerned to protect and promote is not conceived, as it is in rights-based liberalism, as a claim in justice which has universal authority. Instead it is an element in individual well-being, as that has come to be understood and experienced in individualist cultures such as our own; it is a local virtue. In contrast with neo-liberalism, the communitarian liberal view I advance here seeks to enrich autonomy and not merely to defend negative liberty. In contrast with social democracy, which has extended to social welfare rights the supposedly unconditional claims of negative liberal rights, the communitarian view affirms the dependency of individual autonomy on a strong network of reciprocal obligations.

A fundamental implication of this communitarian liberal perspective is that market institutions are not free-standing but come embedded in the matrices of particular cultures and their histories. Market institutions will be politically legitimate only insofar as they respect and reflect the norms and traditions, including the sense of fairness, of the cultures whose needs they exist to serve. Legitimating the market requires that it be curbed or removed in institutions and areas of social life where common understandings demand that goods be distributed in accord with ethical norms which the market, of necessity, disregards. Public acceptance of a dynamic market economy requires that the ethos of market exchange be excluded from important contexts – contexts in which non-market institutions and practices are protected as a matter of public policy.

These are propositions for whose general truth a reasonable argument can be made out; but they are advanced here, not as elements in some impossible political *philosophia perennis*, but as topical antidotes to the chief dangers and errors of recent opinion and policy. They are meant to apply not universally but locally, in European liberal cultures, particularly that of Britain today.

The bottom-line stance from which this chapter is argued is that of *pluralism*[2] – not the banal pluralism of interest groups celebrated in American democratic theory a generation ago, but a pluralism which perceives and accepts conflicts among fundamental goods, diversity within and between cultures and traditions, and which sees this as – at any rate for us – a permanent condition to be lived with, and enjoyed, not a prelude to some new kind of harmony. The overriding task we confront today is that of preserving, and extending, forms of common life, which highly individualist market institutions threaten to undermine or corrode. A connected task is that of developing common institutions in which practitioners of different cultural traditions can coexist. In both of these cases, we will face conflicts of values, uncombinable goods and choices among evils which are unavoidable.

These conflicts of values compel revisions of some standard positions, liberal, social democratic and communitarian – revisions for which the emerging British consensus, which is shy of admitting radical conflict among fundamental values, is ill prepared. Any species of 'back-to-basics' communitarianism, which seeks a return to 'traditional values' or a restoration of vanished or dying forms of family or communal life, must be rejected as a form of nostalgism, whose fate in political life is likely to be no less farcical than that of the Tory 'back-to-basics' campaign. Any form of social democracy which seeks across-the-board equality and denies or evades the reality of conflicts among equalities – such as that between achievable equality of opportunity and social mobility, and unachievable educational equality which prohibits meritocratic selection in state schools – will in practice sustain an unhealthy symbiosis of a semi-defunct class culture with soft Left anti-elitism. Any liberal view which elevates the interest in individual autonomy above all others risks treating as inherently repressive communities and ways of life in which it is not so valued, such as those of some immigrant groups, and so imposing a monoculturally liberal society rather than building pluralistic common institutions which are genuinely culturally diverse.

The task of the age is that of reconciling the human need for security with the permanent revolution of the market. In our circumstances, this task carries with it two others: protecting common institutions whose ethos is not that of market exchange from the near-hegemony of market values in social life; and balancing the need for common life with the reality of deep cultural diversity. The plural character of our cultural and ethical life means that we cannot recover – if we ever possessed – a common culture that is unified by any single worldview or conception of the good. Nor can we – or should we – seek to reinstate any conception of national identity which expresses an earlier monocultural period of our history. We cannot recapture a 'thick' common culture grounded in a deep consensus on morality and history; but we must, if we are to avoid American balkanization, strengthen and develop a thinner, yet durable and resilient, common culture of shared understandings of fairness and tolerance. We cannot, and should not, hope to revive a 'traditional' form of family life that scarcely any longer exists, and which is in any case only one among a variety of kinds of families our society presently contains; but we cannot either reasonably adopt the fashionable liberal ideal in which government is silent, or neutral, on the central issues of family life. A pluralist state can have few core ethical commitments; but a commitment to the family – in all its legitimate diversity – must be one of them. Government must have, and act upon, a view as to the 'thin' culture of obligations and responsibilities that family life in all its forms presupposes, even as it acts to nurture diversity in the kinds of family a pluralist society properly harbours. Only if it does this can a pluralist state be one in which different forms of common life coexist peacefully in shared common institutions and have a decent chance of renewing itself across the generations.

This reconciliation of diversity with commonality in our culture will require institution-building as well as institution-repair, along with creativity and imaginativeness in the making of public policy. The theorist's task is to engage in preparatory thinking which – with a great deal of luck – might assist the work of those whose political objectives have enough in common with his concerns. It is not to develop policy. At the same time, the historical and theoretical perspective outlined here does have some broad implications for policy. Of these, three may be worth signposting. Firstly, the claim that fairness is local and contextual and has to do with distributing goods according to their common social meanings has a cutting edge on policy in health, where it will be invoked to condemn the commercialization of the National Health Service, and in education, where it supports the argument that forms of meritocratic selection can and should be reintroduced in state schools. Such policies, which restrict or exclude market exchange in the particular contexts of specific institutions and goods, are also mandated by the fundamental insight that, contrary to the claim of neo-liberalism, markets make no inherent contribution to individual autonomy. Secondly, the insight that market institutions unavoidably and desirably reflect and express particular cultures and their histories, which is central in the communitarian liberal perspective, tells against common social democratic proposals for the wholesale grafting onto British economic life of practices which have been successful in other cultural and political contexts, such as those of Germany and Japan, and against the federalist project for European institutions. Thirdly, the historical claim that the traditional social democratic commitment to full employment cannot now be implemented compels urgent consideration of policies in which the human interests that full employment protected can be promoted by other means. In each of these three policy areas, the goal is to protect in new ways the human interests once served by social democracy, and to do so without allowing the task of mediating conflicts among these interests to be distorted by the classical social democratic commitment to overall equality as an end-state desirable in itself.

The sphere of life in which such unavoidable conflicts are negotiated and, always provisionally, resolved, is that of *politics*. The legalist illusion of standard American liberal philosophy, according to which conflicts among rival human interests and among divergent conceptions of the good and their associated forms of common life can be arbitrated by appeal to a theory of justice or rights, finds expression in contemporary social democratic demands for a constitutional revolution in Britain.[3] In the communitarian liberal view I advance, constitutional reform is desirable and even indispensable, insofar as it protects fundamental freedoms by incorporating the European Convention into British law, makes accountable the new magistracy of the Quango State and devolves power to Scotland and Wales. These important measures of constitutional reform can be achieved, however, through existing institutions of parliamentary government in an unfixed constitution, as aspects of the new *political* settlement Britain needs. Of course, national government is not the only, nor always the most important domain of political life; it is imperative that political initiative be devolved to lower levels of government and to non-governmental institutions. But this is, or should be, done as a dispersion of political power and an enhancement of political accountability, not as an attempt to remove issues of public policy from political life and transfer them to the jurisdiction of the courts, as has been tried, with predictably ruinous consequences, in the American culture of legalism.

The most important measure facilitating such a new political settlement is not constitutional but electoral reform. On the pluralist and communitarian view defended here, one of the principal weaknesses of social democratic thought is the constitutionalist illusion that the construction of legal institutions can remove the necessity for recurrent political renegotiation of a balance among competing human interests and of the political pursuit of a *modus vivendi* among different communities. After all necessary constitutional reforms, the real task is the political task of searching for the elusive thread of common life through the labyrinth of intractably conflicting interests and ideals.

What social democracy was

Social democracy was a complex structure of ideas, policies, institutions and objectives which achieved embodiment in recognizable social and political settlements in a number of west European countries during the postwar period up to the end of the eighties. Its intellectual roots were in late nineteenth- and early twentieth-century revisions of classical Marxism and socialism, the most important of which were the rejection – on grounds both of practicability and of their incompatibility with democratic institutions – of nationalization and central planning of the economy. The present period is distinguished not by the dissolution of the classical socialist project, which was recognized within social democracy a century ago, but by the crisis and ongoing decomposition of social democracy, which was classical socialism's successor project. In particular, the social democratic character of European institutions – in which many British social democrats have invested most of their political hopes – has in the past decade and a half been compromised almost to vanishing point, as the European Union has come increasingly to adopt neo-liberal ideology; and distinctively social democratic policies have suffered irreversible setbacks in several European countries, such as France and Sweden. What then was social democracy? And how and why has it ended?

Among central objectives and policies were the pursuit of greater equality of income and wealth through redistributional tax and welfare policies, the promotion of full employment through economic growth as an explicit objective of macro-economic policy, a 'cradle-to-grave' welfare state defended as the social embodiment of citizen rights, and support for and co-operation with a strong labour movement as the principal protector of the rights and interests citizens have as workers. In the postwar period, up to the early seventies, when its decay set in, social democracy was able to appropriate Keynesian thought to provide it with a coherent and viable economic programme, the lack of which during the interwar period had condemned it to paralysis in the face of the Great Depression, and to rout when confronted by Fascism and National

Socialism. In Britain, the decay of social democracy came perhaps to a considerable extent from within, as the triangular collusion of employers, unions and government which typifies corporatism everywhere generated not industrial co-operation and wealth-creation – as it did in postwar Germany and Austria – but conflict and decline; but the constraints of the world market supplemented these internal failings, and brought the corporatist period of the British postwar settlement to a close, when the IMF was called in. These external constraints rule out not only any return to corporatism in Britain but also any reversion to the classic economic policies of social democracy.

Our present – and foreseeable – circumstances are such that the social democratic economic programme – most centrally, promoting full employment by stimulating investment through a policy of deficit financing – has ceased to be sustainable. The aborted Mitterrand expansion in the early eighties, and the comprehensive collapse of the Swedish model in the early nineties, suggest that the power of the international currency and bond markets is now sufficient to interdict any such expansionist policies that might be embarked upon by any sovereign nation-state. In terms of economic theory this is hardly news. It was recognized by both Kalecki and Keynes that the international mobility of financial capital undercuts full employment policy. Yet the practical implications of the power of world markets to constrain national policies are probably more urgent now than ever they were in Keynes's or Kalecki's day. It is no exaggeration to say that the global freedom of capital, which is a distinguishing feature of our current circumstances, effectively demolishes the economic foundations of social democracy.

The underlying political morality of social democracy was eclectic in its origins and contents, and differed in its emphases from country to country and from time to time; more particularly, the relations with trade unions were very different in Germany (partly as a consequence of the institutional clean slate following the Nazi period) from those in Britain. Yet it is fair to characterize the animating ideal of social democracy as a form of society-wide egalitarian community of which the workplace community was conceived to be the germ. Without this animating egalitarian political morality social democracy is nothing. Even though in many countries social democratic parties in government were content to implement policies which merely contained or moderated the economic inequalities thrown up by market capitalism, their ruling ideal remained that of compressing income and wealth inequalities within the narrowest margins, with the objective of approximating a community of equals.

They did not make much progress towards this egalitarian objective, any more than they were successful in eradicating poverty – though in these areas it is arguable that matters would have been even worse in the absence of social democratic policies. In other areas – the housing clearance programmes which shattered working-class street communities, and the education policies which prohibited meritocratic selection – it is arguable that social democratic policies worked against the values they were meant to serve. In regard to poverty, it can be argued that social democratic welfare institutions, like later neo-liberal policies, have had the effect of institutionalizing it rather than removing its causes. In regard to its ideal of equality, social democratic policies have proved mostly futile or counter-productive. It is this central social democratic ideal that our present and foreseeable circumstances render unachievable. Not only the historic policies but also the constitutive morality of social democracy have been rendered utopian by the ruling forces of the age.

A key weakness of social democracy, as of neo-liberalism, is its unwillingness to admit the reality of conflicts between central goods and values insofar as they limit the options for public policy. That the promotion of a more mobile, less stratified and so more equal society might conflict with egalitarian policies in state schools is a discomforting proposition few social democrats are willing to entertain. It implies – what is manifestly true, but also uncomfortable – that equality is not of a piece but complex; worse, that one equality, one demand of justice, may compete with another. On the whole, social democrats are as unwilling to confront the policy dilemmas arising from rival equalities as neo-liberals are to face those coming from competing liberties. As Britain becomes relatively poorer, the luxury of averting our gaze from these painful conflicts is likely to become increasingly costly.

Britain's position as an ill-equipped and deskilled country in a desperately competitive world market would make the political projects of a less straitened past hopeless and unworkable even if Thatcherism had not already seen them off. It is this reality, together with the penny finally dropping among the politically decisive voters of Middle England that on present and past policies they are headed for not-so-genteel poverty, that – just as much as the constraints of global bond and currency markets – rules out a reversion by any future government to the policies that underwrote the postwar settlement. If Keynesian deficit financing is interdicted by the bond markets, any attempt to shore up the Beveridge settlement will be undone by voter resistance to increased taxation. Higher public expenditure in specific institutions of the welfare state – such as the NHS – is in my view highly desirable; but it will be politically sustainable only if reforms in other areas allow it to be incurred without a substantially higher tax burden. These are dilemmas in which the social democratic policies of a decade or a generation ago cannot help us.

For these reasons, the likely turn of public policy in Britain under a Labour government is *not* towards anything resembling the One Nation Toryism of a generation ago *nor* towards the mix of policies identified with British Social Democrats in the eighties. These are obsolete positions, no more available to Labour than primitive neo-liberalism is now to the Conservatives. Labour's likely turn is towards an attempted fusion of the individualist economic culture of liberal capitalism with communitarian concerns about fairness and community. But can such a combination of individualist market institutions with a communitarian social morality be rendered stable? Just such a fusion was envisaged in the 'New Liberalism' of J. A. Hobson and L. T. Hobhouse at the beginning of the twentieth century. The goal of New Liberalism was to harness the wealth-creating dynamism of liberal capitalism while using the powers of the sovereign state to constrain it and temper its impact on social cohesion. It was this New Liberal vision, developed in the interwar period in the Liberal Summer Schools, which informed the Beveridge–Keynes settlement that emerged from the Second World War and endured for a generation into the mid-seventies. At the century's end, the global mobility of capital, and its power to constrain the freedom of action of sovereign states in economic policy, is vastly greater. Keynesian macro-economic policies and the Beveridgean welfare state are pillars of a *status quo ante* that has been destroyed irrecoverably. Can something akin to the New Liberal vision be re-embodied in the *fin-de-siècle* context of swiftly advancing globalization?

Right, Left and globalization

One of the starting-points of my inquiry is a contradiction within neo-liberal policy over the past decade and a half, whose consequences in practice will be inherited by any future British government, Labour or Tory.

The *neo-liberal contradiction* is that arising from support for deregulated markets on the one hand and reliance upon inherited cultural traditions, allegiances and hierarchical forms of social order on the other. Though not predictable in any detailed way, the impact of deregulated markets – in labour, for example – is to alter the relative rewards of different social groups, and thereby to disappoint established expectations; this is one example of the ways in which the free market subverts inherited class hierarchies and deferences. (Of course, technological innovation, and planning decisions in a command economy, will have similar effects; the point is that in present circumstances deregulated market institutions make changes in relative rewards a rapid and continuous process that makes a culture of deference, of the sort embodied in the British class system, for example, dysfunctional and – in the long run – unsustainable.) The marketization of intermediary institutions and professions which have hitherto relied more on ethos and trust than upon contract to regulate their activities has had an analogous impact. Though the tension between freeing up markets and preserving or renewing a tradition-bound social order arises endogenously within nation-states, it is severer in its effects when public policy acts to open domestic economies to global markets.

The neo-liberal contradiction is greater in a context of ongoing globalization partly because it expresses itself in a conception of the state that is incoherent. William Rees-Mogg states the view of the New Right with refreshing candour when he observes: 'The twentieth-century nation-state, taking and often wasting half the citizens' money, is a dying social form.'[4] He does not pause to ask what will replace this dying social form as a focus of citizens' allegiance. In this he is typical of neo-liberal thinking.[5] In the neo-liberal conception, the sovereign nation-state exists to express and support national culture; at the same time it accepts no responsibility for the renewal of cultural traditions, for the protection of citizens from economic risk (apart perhaps from the provision of a subsistence income), or for the survival of distinctive communities and forms of livelihood. (The interest in preserving small-scale and economically inefficient forms of agriculture in Switzerland, which was one of the motives for the Swiss remaining outside the EU, can find no expression in neo-liberal policy. If the free global market so dictates, such livelihoods must go to the wall – along with the communities they support.) The neo-liberal state is minimalist and non-interventionist in economic policy, confining itself ideally to the custody of a regime of rules defining and promoting market competition; but at the same time it acts – through social policies penalizing one-parent families, perhaps, or tight immigration controls – to bolster and renew those traditional institutions and forms of culture on which market institutions themselves may in the past have depended for their effective functioning and popular legitimacy.

What this New Right ideology neglects are the many ways in which promoting market freedoms has necessitated, in Britain and elsewhere, the centralization of power and initiative in strong, often authoritarian, state institutions. The near-destruction of local government in Britain, the denudation of many intermediary institutions of much of their autonomy and distinctive ethos by the creation of internal quasi-markets, together with the construction of the Quango State, are not accidents in the history of the neo-liberal project. They are integral components of it. After all, neo-liberalism was the political expression of the belief that market exchange is the primordial form of human freedom. Political freedom, freedom of voice in autonomous institutions – these were suspect freedoms compared with the freedoms of exchange, and it was wholly legitimate to curb them when market exchange could thereby be extended. It was by this primitive logic that there arose the familiar paradox of market libertarianism, in which it generated a species of authoritarian individualism resting on the political foundation of a centralist state. Macaulay's observation that the gallows and the hangman stand at the back of James Mill's utilitarian state seems premonitory of the neo-liberal minimum state, in which the privatized prison and the Next Steps Agency's accountants fulfil similar functions.

In its applications to intermediary institutions, neo-liberal policy from Thatcher to the present has been one of neo-nationalization. Autonomous institutions of all kinds have been subjected to centralized direction by the imposition on them of a regime of quasi-markets. This squalid regime of market corporatism is the ironic upshot of a project whose original impulse came from a revulsion against the failing corporatism of the seventies. Future historians are likely to be impressed by the speed with which the market Bolshevism of the early eighties generated the Tory managerial nomenclatura of the early nineties. No less ironic is the way a Tory defence of national sovereignty was yoked to a policy of opening up the economy to the full rigours of globalization. Deeper integration into the EU was opposed because it was believed – falsely, on current evidence – that the EU might be protectionist, and thereby inhibit globalization in Britain. In this neo-liberal view, national sovereignty must be defended from the encroachments of European institutions, in order that it may more comprehensively be abandoned through a complete surrender to global market forces. These sorry posturings illustrate the core neo-liberal contradiction – between its commitment to economic globalization and its affirmation of national sovereignty.

The *social democratic contradiction* mirrors the neo-liberal: economic globalization removes, or weakens, the policy levers whereby social democratic governments sought to achieve goals of social solidarity and egalitarian redistribution. Full employment cannot be promoted by policies of aggressive deficit financing since that will now be interdicted by global bond markets (as the Swedish social democrats discovered). Using the tax system to promote goals of income and wealth redistribution is severely constrained by unprecedented international mobility of capital and people. Globalization weakens or undermines the bargaining power of organized labour. Public financing of the welfare state is constrained by dependency on global capital markets, which limit to a narrow range national governments' leverage over interest rates and exchange rates. The magnitudes of these effects of globalization on national economies and governments remain controversial; what is less controversial is the conviction that they will become ever more significant in future.

There is an insoluble contradiction within contemporary social democracy: between commitment to economic globalization and the goals of egalitarian community. It is hyperbolic to claim, as many do, that sovereign states lack any leverage on national economic life; it remains plausible that the inheritance of neo-liberal deregulation, together with ongoing globalization, constrains or removes many of the policy levers on which social democratic governments have hitherto relied. More particularly, they make the distributional goals of social democracy unachievable, at least by traditional social democratic means. Further, the impact on the labour market of neo-liberal deregulation and (though this is as yet probably small) of globalization make the workplace-based conception of community that was traditionally defended by social democrats less practically sustainable, and less centrally relevant to human needs, than ever before.

Globalization undermines both the Left project of egalitarian community and the Right project of reproducing authoritative institutions in a social context of market-generated economic inequalities. This is so however globalization is conceived or measured – by the magnitude of flows of trade, capital or migration, or as a massive extension of processes of marketization of social life that have long been in evidence within national economic cultures. It may well be that meeting the human need for enduring forms of common life will ultimately require the imposition of political limits on aspects of globalization, such as global free trade, which the present consensus will at once reject as both unworkable and dangerously illiberal. However that may be, what is undeniable is that globalization poses fundamental challenges, encompassing novel possibilities both of human servitude and of emancipation, for which contemporary political thought, on all points on the spectrum, is presently very ill prepared.

The diversity of market institutions

Now that the rivalry between the market economy and central planning has been settled decisively on the terrain of history, there is a common perception that systemic competition now goes on between different forms of market institutions. It is of capitalism against capitalism. There is not a single, ideal type of market institution to which all market economies are evolving, but rather a diversity of market institutions, each with its own distinctive achievements and hazards, engaged in a global competition for markets. As far as it goes, this perception is well founded. It rightly rejects the view that there is any model of market institutions – that of American individualist market capitalism, say – to which the whole world is moving inexorably. It embodies the vital insight that there is in the end no such thing as the free market, but rather a variety of cultural institutions and legal devices and instruments through which economic life is mediated. This is indeed the core of the theoretical insights preserved by the 'social market' tradition, for which I have myself in the past argued.[6] The key proposition of social market theory – that 'the market' is not a free-standing institution, the expression of unrestricted human freedom and rationality in the economic realm, but instead an abstraction from an enormous miscellany of practices and institutions having deep roots in social life – remains valid and important.

This is a helpful perspective inasmuch as it frees us from the idea that there is any model of market institutions to which our variety, or any other, will or should approximate. The social market perspective is in this way one that expands our awareness of the range of possibilities for market institutions and their associated economic cultures. It becomes misleading when it is deployed to support policies and reforms aiming to make eclectic borrowings from other market institutions, with a view to enhancing the performance of those we inherit. In truth, the social market perspective works as a theoretical constraint on such eclecticism, inasmuch as it correctly insists upon the embeddedness of market institutions in cultural traditions over which public policy has little leverage. Paradoxically, social democrats who disregard this constraint imposed on policy are at one with neo-liberals in their neglect of the cultural matrices of economic life. They share with neo-liberals a rationalistic and utopian project of harmonizing market institutions according to the requirements of an ideal model.

These social democratic conceptions are expressed in their project for European institutions, which is to extend the Rhine model of capitalism across the European Union, regardless of national cultural differences which have produced different capitalisms in its component countries, including Britain. This project rests on the illusion that there exists presently in continental Europe a viable and functioning model of market institutions that is a feasible alternative to the deformed individualist institutions which we inherit from the Thatcher era. Underlying this, there is the deeper illusion that market institutions are neutral pieces of institutional machinery which can be moved freely around the world and adopted eclectically as elements in public policy. This is a mirage, because market institutions – like political institutions – are not detachable from their histories and parent cultures, but are deeply embedded in them, and remain always integral expressions of them. The ruling error of the Thatcher project was the supposition that American market institutions could be transplanted to Britain – with its vastly different history, its lack of the American culture of mobility, geographical and occupational, and its distinctively European conception of the role of government in civil society. It is imperative that this error of the New Right is not replicated on the Left, by an analogously misconceived and foredoomed attempt to transplant to Britain the market institutions of Germany (or Japan).

There no longer exists a 'European model' which could be replicated in Britain. The truth is that there are no historic models for the future development of market institutions in Britain. It is a particularly dangerous error to suppose that there is any longer such a 'European model'. In continental Europe the social democratic and social market traditions are in long-term retreat and have not solved central problems which we share with other European countries such as structural mass unemployment. There can surely be no more vivid exemplar of this retreat than contemporary Sweden. There, both the active labour policy and the collective wage bargaining policies central to social democracy in that country have suffered such a complete collapse that there is now nothing to which the expression 'Swedish model' could any longer refer. As a consequence, economic life in Sweden is evolving ineluctably towards the neo-liberal norm increasingly dominant in the rest of Europe, with all its costs and hazards. No less striking, if wholly different in its causes, is the precipitate and ignominious implosion of Christian Democracy in Italy.

Recent strategic and geopolitical developments are crucial in accounting for the mounting problems of European institutions. The likelihood must be confronted that, aside from their internal economic problems, and the difficulties they are experiencing in adjusting to global competition, both European social democracy and Christian Democracy belong to an epoch – the Cold War period – that is now a fading memory. Indeed the difficulties European 'social market' economies, including Germany, are having in adapting to global competition are themselves direct consequences of the end of the Cold War, as billions of producers previously shut off from the world economy have now entered it as full participants. It may well be that European social democracy required for its survival a historical niche – the strategic environment of the Cold War – which has now vanished. The intense pressure to adopt neo-liberal policies which exists in all European Union countries may be explicable in part by the new intensity of the competition which those countries face from low-wage but often high-skilled post-communist countries. It is perhaps this altered geopolitical environment, more than any other single factor, that explains the neo-liberal evolution of European policy and institutions. For it greatly reinforces the changes in social structure, and particularly in the relative position of industrial labour, that in continental Europe as much as in Britain have all but destroyed the old class base of social democracy. For all these interrelated reasons, it is a serious mistake for social democrats who despair of neo-liberal hegemony in public policy in Britain to look to European institutions as a *deus ex machina*.

Moreover, German – like Japanese – market institutions are in a process of ongoing evolution. Although this evolution is very unlikely to issue in convergence upon Anglo-Saxon practices, there is now no stable German or Japanese model that could be exported. This is not at all to say that the Rhine model of capitalism (say) is in terminal decline, or is bent on convergence with Anglo-Saxon economic culture. Such prognoses, common as they are among neo-liberals, are extremely implausible. The German achievement in absorbing the East German rustbelt, despite the policy mistakes which accompanied it, is almost certainly beyond the reach of any other economy in the world (aside perhaps from that of Japan); it certainly does not suggest a system in inexorable decline. What the current problems of the German economy do suggest, as David Goodhart observes in his sympathetic examination of the Rhine model, is that 'The future of the social market is certainly not guaranteed.'[7] Even in the likely and highly desirable event that the Rhine model renews itself in a novel form, it will be able to do so in virtue of cultural traditions of consensual-managerial politics which cannot be reproduced in Britain. The Rhine model is sustained by these solidaristic cultural traditions, because it embodies a balance among interests which becomes unstable if any one of them is excluded. The likelihood must be faced that the Rhine model is a historical singularity, owing much to the institutional void arising after the destruction of the Nazi regime. For that and many other reasons, it cannot be replicated anywhere else in Europe.

For different reasons, Japanese market institutions are no less of a singularity. The social contract in contemporary Japan – which, far from being immemorial, emerged from the intense industrial and political conflicts of the immediate postwar period – has succeeded in keeping unemployment levels at uniquely low levels by subsidizing employment practices that are 'economically inefficient'. It is highly probable, and no less desirable, that Japan will resist the importation of western, and more particularly American, employment policies, even if the current forms of lifelong job-holding must of necessity be modified; but the Japanese strategy of reconciling the labour mobility produced by technological innovation and international competition with job security for the majority of the population is not open to us. It depends, among other things, on cultural traditions – in family life and the relations of individuals with communities – which we cannot emulate. The most successful aspects of German and Japanese economic policy seem in fact to be those which are least exportable.[8]

The project of adapting and reforming the individualist market institutions we inherit to meet these enduring human needs is inhibited, not advanced, by the social democratic belief that there exists now, or may come into being in the future, a single European model of market institutions, to which we in Britain may assimilate. French and German capitalism are not subtypes of a single European model with which Anglo-Saxon capitalism can be usefully contrasted. In what respects are the economic cultures of Sweden and Austria, say, similar to those of Greece and Portugal? The objective of 'harmonizing' these market institutions is a utopia of rationalism, since it involves ironing out cultural differences of which diversity in market institutions is a natural expression.

This is not to say that European capitalisms do not possess common features which distinguish them from others – from American capitalism, most importantly, but also from East Asian capitalism and from the anarcho-capitalisms that have emerged in post-communist Russia and China. The manifest foundering of the federalist project for European institutions should facilitate recognition of the truth that the future for distinctively European capitalism is in a diversity of market institutions and not in a single uniform pattern imposed willy-nilly, in the name of harmonization for a single market, on all of Europe's national and regional cultures. The balance of likelihood is that the project of constructing federal institutions in Europe – particularly a single European currency – will come to shipwreck on conflicts of national interest, most crucially between France and Germany. As yet, a post-federalist project for Europe which recognizes these realities has hardly begun to be formulated.[9]

In the longer term, the Gaullist idea of an *Europe des patries* may come to be as obsolescent as European federalism is today, and a

Europe of regions may come into being within something akin to a confederal framework. Nevertheless, for the present, and any future that can be foreseen or guessed at, we may be reasonably certain that the rock on which the European federalist project will run aground is the reality of Europe's sovereign nation-states, and the sometimes conflicting interests they express. However enfeebled national political cultures and institutions have become in recent years, they remain the central forum of democratic political participation. It is because nothing exists that is remotely akin to the germ of a transnational European political culture that we can be certain that attempts to plug the 'democratic deficit' in European institutions will come to nothing. The future which any prudent observer must expect in Europe is not that imagined in the utopian vistas of the federalist imagination, but a Europe of sometimes unstable sovereign states having both common and conflicting interests, whose relations with one another will be governed by the classical logic of the balance of power.

Manifestly, a new European project would entail abandonment of the core project of European federalism, the proposal for a single (as opposed to a common) European currency. From the communitarian standpoint advanced here, the chief argument against such a single currency is that, because of the likelihood that a neo-liberal monetary regime for Europe would be deflationary and would lead to areas of high unemployment, it would be tolerable and workable only if it was combined with an EU-wide labour market with functional (as distinct from formal) mass labour mobility. Such continental labour mobility will be rejected by most Europeans, both electorally and in their own behaviour, as having all the social costs and disruptive consequences for local communities and personal attachments that it has had in the United States. The social democratic project of a single European currency shares with neo-liberal policies a rationalistic disdain for such attachments and communities. Its practical results would be indistinguishable from those associated in Britain with Thatcherite policies. This is perceived by the Right everywhere in Europe apart from Britain. In Sweden, as in other European countries, the Right supports the development of transnational European institutions because it believes, correctly, that they will embody neo-liberal policies, and opposition to them is confined largely to left-wing communitarian nationalists. It is a comment on the parochialism of British political life that social democrats have accepted the Thatcherite claim that opposition to European federalism is the prerogative of the Right.

The social democratic project of extending the Rhine model of capitalism across the European Union is as utopian as the neo-liberal one of harmonizing European economies on an agenda of deregulation and competition. Both evade the reality of diverse national economic cultures in Europe. Both suppress the huge costs, large risks and certain failure of any project of remodelling the varieties of market institutions which Europe contains on any single pattern. The idea that the nations and regions of the European Union can come together in a single economic culture is, in fact, as remote from any historic reality or likelihood as the notion that its institutions contain the makings of a single political culture. Public policy which neglects, or underestimates, the cultural dimensions of market institutions, and the constraints these impose on it, will also fail to perceive and realize genuine possibilities of reforming them so that they are more friendly to human needs.

Welfare, local justice and complex fairness

The variety of market institutions, some of whose implications for policy I have sought to explore, is denied or trivialized in neo-liberal ideology, which shares with vulgar Marxism a commitment to economic reductionism. Tacitly or expressly, neo-liberal thought anticipates and welcomes global convergence on individualist market capitalism on a single pattern – typically, in neo-liberal theory, the American model. It is able to adopt this simplistic position because of its economistic understanding of the relations between market institutions and cultural life. Social life everywhere is understood according to a model of market exchange that is itself an abstraction from one historic variety of market economy – roughly, that of England during the last few centuries, and of countries to which English market institutions were successfully exported. Neo-liberal theory substantially *is* an illicit generalization from the economic history of England in the last few centuries. That flourishing market institutions may be accompanied by, or even depend upon, non-individualist forms of social and moral life is a possibility – in East Asia now a reality – that neo-liberal theory, like the more primitive forms of Marxism, fails to recognize. It was unable to anticipate that among the unintended consequences of its policy of freeing up markets was a fracturing of communities, and a depletion of ethos and trust within institutions, which muted or thwarted the economic renewal which free markets were supposed to generate. Neo-liberal policy on welfare actually reinforced these negative unintended consequences of market reform by applying to welfare institutions the abstract calculus of market exchange.

New Right thought about welfare articulated three cardinal misconceptions. It imagined that the human interest in rising income and increased consumer choice, which the free market supposedly protects and promotes, always outweighs that in the control of economic risk. It understood welfare institutions as mechanisms for income transfer or poverty relief, rather than as devices for security against common risks and the dangers of exclusion; it accordingly favoured forms of selectivity in welfare provision that carried with them huge incentive costs and the moral hazard of creating cultures of dependency where none had existed before. Rejecting the very idea of social justice as being alien to the market freedoms it promoted, and being either indifferent or complacent about the impact of these freedoms on social cohesion, it neglected the vital role of welfare institutions in counteracting the indifference to fairness of unfettered market exchange, and so promoting social solidarity and common citizenship.

All three errors arose from a common cause. This is the neo-liberal *canard* that markets are free-standing social relationships, justifiable – if the need for a justification for them is admitted at all – as embodiments of individual freedom and the human propensity to trade to mutual advantage. It is this fundamental error of neo-liberal thought which accounts for the inability of neo-liberal policy to perceive that markets generate systemic economic risk and a pervasive sense of unfairness even when they produce rising incomes. A dynamic market economy can be politically legitimated, in a democratic regime such as that of contemporary Britain, only insofar as it is complemented by institutions and policies which counteract these hazards, and which remove market competition from some social contexts altogether.

Policies modelled on these neo-liberal errors have been highly counter-productive even in their own terms. In New Zealand, policies based on the conception of welfare institutions as mere income transfer mechanisms, in conjunction with other neo-liberal measures, have managed to create a dependent underclass where none had hitherto existed. They achieved this remarkable result in virtue of a property inseparably connected with all means-tested welfare institutions – their construction of a poverty trap in which perverse incentives imprison welfare recipients in a culture of dependency. Universal welfare institutions – of which the National Health Service prior to the Conservatives' neo-liberal reforms is perhaps the best example – carry no such hazards with them. (Nor do they carry the large administrative costs of targeted systems.) Because neo-liberal thought conceives of welfare institutions solely as devices for poverty relief it cannot avoid remodelling them in forms whose practical effect is the institutionalization of poverty itself.

The counter-productive results of neo-liberal welfare policy are not accidental. They arise from its libertarian political morality, in which any state expenditure apart from that on rigorously public goods is inherently suspect. Welfare expenditures are especially suspect, amongst neo-liberals, because of their allegedly perverse distributional effects, when benefits are extended to those who are not yet poor. The benefits of well-conceived universal schemes in promoting social integration and preventing poverty are not perceived, even when – as with the NHS – such universal schemes are far more cost-effective and less wasteful than targeted schemes in other countries. This fixation of neo-liberal policy on avoiding wasteful redistribution comes directly from its libertarianism, in which market distributions are taken as the norm of justice from which it is wrong to depart. Neo-liberal policy shares with egalitarian social democracy a fixation on such distributional issues. This distributional preoccupation effectively occludes the vital role of welfare institutions in cementing social solidarity in an age in which all forms of common life are challenged by individualism.

Hayekian theory was able to deny the necessity, even the meaningfulness, of social justice, in part because it imagined that the sheer productivity of unfettered markets would preclude any crisis of legitimacy of capitalist institutions. It treated deep-seated and long-standing popular sentiments of fairness, of the sort that were expressed in revulsion against the poll tax, in crassly rationalistic terms, as unfortunate atavisms, which if they do not die out are best stamped out. Like egalitarianism, it conceived social justice in comprehensive and monistic principles, dictating patterns of distribution across the whole of social life and activity. Social democrats have a similar conception, understanding social justice in terms of approximation to some across-the-board principle of equality.[10]

Both neo-liberalism and social democracy understand fairness in simple and global terms, as embodied in libertarian rights or else in a principle of equality. I have argued elsewhere that neither libertarian nor egalitarian principles can be fundamental in a credible political morality.[11] The contents of rights depend on claims about the relative urgency of competing human interests which are inherently controversial. Conceptions of negative rights to liberty, and of a minimum state which protects such rights, are irredeemably indeterminate. Egalitarian principles are no less indeterminate, concealing conflicts among important equalities. Moreover egalitarian principles are implausible in attaching moral importance to purely relational properties, when what has moral importance is well-being. If satiable human needs can be met, no global, overarching principle of distribution is necessary or plausible.[12] This does not mean that distributional principles can be altogether dispensed with. It means that, where issues of distribution unavoidably arise, norms of fairness figure as shared understandings of the meanings of social goods, as these arise in specific domains of activity in particular cultural contexts.

In addition to such philosophical arguments, the central historical thesis argued here is that global freedom of capital – and, to an increasing degree, of labour – restricts radically the leverage of sovereign states in pursuing social democratic egalitarian goals.[13] Yet any government concerned with stability and cohesion in social life will be bound to have regard to the levels of economic inequality produced by its policies. At least some part of the phenomenal growth in economic inequality in the eighties was avoidable, especially the inequality produced by neo-liberal policies, in particular policies which generated or tolerated high levels of unemployment. (It is noteworthy that the only comparable country which suffered a larger increase in economic inequality than Britain in the eighties was New Zealand – in which neo-liberal policies were even more relentlessly and consistently pursued.) Such concern with levels of economic inequality is dictated by concern for common life; but it does not mandate a strategy of equalization – a strategy which the diminished leverage of sovereign states anyway makes probably unworkable.

The unattainability of social democratic ideals of equality does not imply – as neo-liberals like to think – that a stable society can do without norms of fairness. On the contrary, such norms are essential. But they must be local and contextual, not universal or global, and reflect shared social understandings expressed in the common culture.[14] Such shared local understandings are by no means always conservative in their implications for policy. Consider here two salient examples. In Britain, there exists a common understanding of the good of medical care according to which it is unfair that access to decent medical care be restricted by income, or the provision of such care distorted by market forces. This common understanding condemns the neo-liberal commercialization of the NHS, if – as available evidence strongly suggests – the introduction of market mechanisms within it has had the effects of partly decoupling patient care from medical need and making access to care to a significant degree an accident of the policies of the NHS Trust currently in force in one's locality. The social understanding of medical care which still survives in Britain, in which it is allocated according to medical need, demands the reversal of these policies, insofar as they have effects which violate it. (I do not mean to suggest that there is an NHS *status quo* to which we can return. No such *status quo ante* can be recovered in health policy, any more than it can in any other area of policy. A reintegrated NHS would inevitably be very different from that which neo-liberal policy destroyed.) This understanding does not condemn the very existence of private medicine; but it does condemn policies which result in access to decent medical care depending on factors – such as the income of the patient – apart from medical need.

Or consider the social understanding, also still surviving in Britain, according to which the appropriate criteria for allocating educational opportunity are meritocratic. We do not auction places at university, and the American practice of imposing ethnic quotas on university admissions is not on any policy agenda. Moreover, there can be little doubt that the common understanding of fairness in education condemns policies which make access to good school-ing contingent on income. Yet in our circumstances the class inequalities that are reproduced through a large private sector in schooling are reinforced by an egalitarian prohibition on meritocratic policies in state schools. In an international context in which strict limits are imposed on the pursuit of egalitarian goals through the tax system, and widening income inequality allows an increasing per-centage of the middle classes to opt out of the state system, there is an irresolvable conflict between educational egalitarianism and the pursuit of a broader social equality. (I am taking for granted that the freedom to found and patronize private schools cannot be infringed. It is in any case a freedom protected by international treaties to which Britain is a signatory.) This is a conflict of equalities that social democrats are very shy of admitting – and which many deny – but whose reality, on available evidence about parental behaviour and preferences, is not in doubt. If the prospects of egalitarian redistribution through the tax system are now severely limited, growing economic and social inequality can be averted only by an improvement in the primary skills of the most disadvantaged and excluded groups. It is impossible to accept, as many social democrats claim, that a greater commitment of resources to state schools can by itself achieve this objective. The practical result of social democratic opposition to meritocratic policies in state schools can then only be the development of an increasingly stratified society, in which educational privilege and educational egalitarianism coexist in an unhealthy symbiosis. Such an outcome, in which British class culture is guaranteed renewal by the anti-elitism of the soft Left, must be a defeat for the social democratic ideal of equal opportunity.[15] The reintroduction of meritocratic policies in state schools can therefore be defended, in social democratic egalitarian terms, as a vital aid to equal opportunity at a time when widening income inequalities allow growing numbers to opt out of the state system. It can be defended also in communitarian terms, inasmuch as it would diminish the incentives to opt out, and thereby increase the inclusiveness of state schooling. It could achieve these results, most fundamentally, because it accords with the sense of fairness regarding educational opportunity which informs the common culture.

It is no part of my argument here to claim that appealing to shared understandings of fairness in particular social domains or contexts resolves all questions of social justice. Quite the opposite: the claims of local justice may be conflicting. My argument for complex fairness is that there are hard choices to be made which arise from the conflicting demands of fairness, both between and within particular social contexts, and that there is no overarching theory or principle by which such conflicts can be arbitrated. Within health care, there are choices to be made about the relative urgency of different medical needs with which the common understandings of what is fair cannot much help. A beneficial unintended consequence of neo-liberal reform of the NHS is that it has made transparent forms of rationing and prioritization of medical resource allocation that have always existed but have gone unscrutinized and undebated. These hard choices are not greatly assisted by appeal to shared understandings, partly because the development of medical technologies has run far ahead of public awareness and there is nothing akin to moral common sense in regard to many of the possibilities they have opened up. There is another reason why shared contextual understandings cannot resolve all important issues about fairness. In a culture as deeply pluralistic as ours has become, there are contexts in which no common understanding exists, or in which the inherited understanding is strongly contested. Familial and sexual contexts are the most obvious of these, though contexts having to do with the value of human life, or the relations of human beings with other animal species, may be no less important. Many of these hard choices are undecidable by any theory of justice or rights because they are conceived differently by people with different worldviews and conceptions of the good. Religious believers who attach intrinsic and unique worth to human life will understand conflicts of medical priorities involving life-saving differently from those, such as myself, who attach no such moral importance to it. Finally, even where there is cultural consensus on the domains within which goods are properly allocated, they may make conflicting demands on scarce resources which can be resolved only by a collective political decision. In those circumstances, a public conversation is needed, with the aim of generating a sense of fairness that can be shared even by people with very different substantive moral outlooks.

In our historical circumstances, we have no alternative to engaging in ongoing public discourse, in which a provisional settlement is reached, and recurrently renegotiated, on such issues. Forms of liberal thought which imagine that such issues can be resolved by the development of a 'theory of justice', or a 'theory of rights', whether they be neo-liberal and libertarian or social democratic and egalitarian in their commitments, are trading in illusions. Such liberalisms foster a legalist and constitutionalist mirage, in which the delusive certainty of legal principles is preferred to the contingencies and compromises of political practice, where a settlement among communities and ways of life, always temporary, can alone be found. This primacy of the political sphere in the communitarian conception is an insuperable objection to it in all standard forms of liberal thought, including the Rawlsian strand which animates many contemporary British social democrats. It is also a feature of the communitarian view which will be resisted by those who subscribe to fashionable ideas of 'the end of politics'. Yet the intensely politically contested character of policy on education and the family should persuade us that politics has not ended, and cannot be ended, by the liberal legalist attempt to resolve such disputed issues by the entrenchment and interpretation of rights.

The implication of local justice that is most deeply uncongenial to standard liberal thought, however, is that fairness is not only complex but sometimes makes conflicting demands on us. It is the implication that sometimes we cannot avoid injustice – that there is a sort of endemic moral scarcity which runs parallel with the finitude of resources. This is an implication – in my view, a reality – that is deeply at odds with our inherited traditions of moral and political thinking. It illuminates a feature of public policy that is often trivialized by talk of trade-offs and costs and benefits – that it inescapably involves making hard collective choices among genuine goods. Both welfare reform and tax reform encompass such choices. In my view, these hard choices are not adequately captured when it is said – accurately enough, no doubt – that tax and welfare reforms are typically zero-sum changes, at any rate in the short run. The distributional conflicts such choices entail are better understood in terms of the conflicting demands of fairness. Some of these conflicts concern intergenerational fairness – an issue I cannot discuss here, except in passing, despite its clear and growing importance. All of them can be resolved only by collective choices whose proper sphere is that of political practice, not courts of law.[16] And these are not policy decisions which can be settled by appeal to the doctrines of political economy, but political choices informed by ethical judgements.

The demands of fairness are most urgent in the central issue of the post-social democratic period – that of developing a policy for livelihood when the postwar pursuit of full employment is no longer a realistic option. Conventional social democratic thought has relied upon policies combining ambitious reskilling programmes with a resumption of rapid economic growth. This response grasps a vital feature of economic change at present – that incessant change in the division of labour arising from new information technologies is imposing on us not only recurrent changes of job but also changes of occupation.[17] It perceives also that, in an age of unceasing technological innovation, a poor education system guarantees economic failure. The idea that British economic culture can be renewed without fundamental reform of education is plainly an exercise in fantasy. In all these respects the current social democratic emphasis on reskilling is entirely appropriate.

At the same time, it goes against all experience to date to suppose that even lifetime reskilling programmes can move us back to something akin to full employment at a time when technological innovation is displacing human labour to an ever-increasing degree. In fact 'full employment' looks like a policy designed for stabler times, in which occupations were less ephemeral, the division of labour in less of a flux, and the institution of job-holding itself more secure. Moreover the confidence that higher rates of economic growth – even supposing they can be sustainably achieved – will enable rising underlying rates of long-term unemployment to be dented has little in postwar history to support it. No matter how it is measured, economic activity has increased enormously during that period. At least since the early seventies, that expansion has not prevented the core rate of unemployment moving steadily upwards. In this respect, as in others, over-reliance on economic growth as a comprehensive solution for our social dilemmas is likely to prove seriously misguided.

No successor to the social democratic settlement is morally tolerable, or in the long term politically sustainable, which does not contain a credible and meaningful alternative to full employment policy. Even if it has allowed somewhat lower levels of joblessness than our European partners, neo-liberal deregulation of the labour market in Britain has been accompanied by a growth in inequality and the appearance of pathologies – such as marital breakdown, which is commonest in places where labour mobility is high and unemployment low[18] – that are associated with the culture of mobility. It seems necessary, therefore, to look at radical alternatives, however unpromising they may be in immediate fiscal terms. One alternative way of thinking recognizes that the assumptions of full employment policy – including the institution of the job itself – are likely to hold less firmly in future. This view – developed most ambitiously by Jeremy Rifkin in *The End of Work* – sees our inherited culture of work as itself becoming increasingly obsolescent because of technology-driven economic change. Its policy implication is some form of Basic Income scheme.[19] Another view – advocated powerfully by Frank Field MP[20] – favours a state-supervised scheme of compulsory insurance against employment risk (and to fund pensions) in which, unlike the present National Insurance sham, contributions remain the property of individuals. Interestingly, both of these alternatives avoid the moral hazards of means-tested or targeted[21] benefits, and the neo-liberal dependency culture they produce. No less significantly, they each address the interest in autonomy, which it was another of the unintended consequences of the eighties to strengthen.

My concern here is not to decide between such schemes, or to determine how far and in what contexts they might be compatible, but to insist that the political choices we make about them are *ethical and political* and not primarily economic or fiscal in character. There are powerful ethical arguments against the Basic Income approach which give strong support to a policy of self-provision in many areas of welfare. In the first place, Basic Income schemes may be exclusionary in the extra significance they attach to citizenship and in the possibility that the political incentive to reintegrate the excluded will be diminished if they are guaranteed a tolerable minimum. This risk of Basic Income schemes being exclusionary in practice seems to me to be a very considerable one. It is only in late industrial cultures such as our own that the phenomenon of deskilling can occur; in pre-industrial societies poised on the edge of subsistence, or early forms of industrialism not yet rich enough to afford well-developed welfare states, it is an impossibility. In our foreseeable future, however, there is every prospect that a growing proportion of the population will be marginalized, and kept on a miserable subsistence, by the growing productivity of the dwindling working population. A Basic Income scheme could only enhance this risk, since it would make it easier for society to abandon excluded groups with a clear conscience.

There is another objection to Basic Income schemes which I believe to be crucial. It arises from the lack of reciprocal obligation which they institutionalize. Because they are unconditional guarantees of subsistence, Basic or Citizen's Income schemes strengthen the culture of liberty without responsibility, of individual choice without corresponding obligation, which is the least benign moral inheritance of individualism. In regard to the so-called underclass, they reinforce the denial of agency and the lack of mutuality and of a sense of membership which are the most disabling features of the culture of dependency.

The decisive objections to Basic Income schemes are then not fiscal but ethical. (Such schemes might well be cheaper than workfare – which may account for the interest which the newer New Right is taking in them.[22]) They take no account of the strength of ideas of *desert* in the common culture of norms of fairness which Britain still possesses. Indeed they run against the common moral intuition that an unconditional guarantee of subsistence income, regardless of need or merit, is undeserved. They override the shared social understanding of the relationship of subsistence with work which is a central element in local justice in our society. And they go against the grain of much in our moral culture which affirms that, with regard to those who are able-bodied, welfare rights are properly conditional on the discharge of public duties. For all these reasons, Basic Income schemes are no antidote to the culture of dutiless individualism we inherit from the neo-liberal experiment.[23] Insofar as social democrats endorse such schemes, they reveal a basic weakness of social democratic thought in our time, which is that it seeks to cure or palliate the evils of economic individualism by extending the culture of unconditional individual rights within welfare institutions. In most areas of welfare policy, however, the common life is served by attaching duties to rights rather than by making rights unconditional.

These ethical considerations lead me to the conclusion that, whereas welfare reform cannot be the application of any single principle, it should not on the whole go down the Basic Income road, but must instead seek to create the conditions for self-provision for all who are capable of making a productive contribution to society.[24] The ethical basis of self-provision, in this account, is not the neo-liberal ideal of individual choice, but rather the communitarian conception of the reciprocity of rights and obligations. In accepting the conclusion that the future of welfare institutions lies with new forms of self-provision, we are acknowledging that there is no quick fix for the most serious dilemma of a late industrial society such as Britain, which is the growth of forms of unemployment and of poverty whose roots are in deskilling and family breakdown. A new policy agenda on work and the family, replacing the postwar social democratic policy of full employment, cannot promise rapid results or easy solutions. It must confront the evident truth that the growth of an excluded underclass can only be slowed, let alone reversed, by radical reforms in education and in welfare. Such reforms, by reinstating conceptions of meritocratic selection and of the dependency of rights of public assistance on obligations to participate in reskilling programmes, may prove indigestible to many British social democrats.[25]

Any workable reform of welfare must begin from the fact that the Beveridge settlement has been destroyed not only by neo-liberal policy but also by the vast changes in family life and in the labour market that have occurred over the past half century. The changed economic situation of women in particular makes any attempt at reconstituting Beveridge undesirable as well as unfeasible. Whatever their structure, welfare institutions in future must be minimally paternalist, and friendly to diversity in forms of family life. A fundamental mistake will be made if communitarians follow the social engineers of the Right – or of the Left[26] – in viewing welfare policy as a device for the preservation or revival of 'the traditional family'. Its primary role in a liberal society is not to promote or protect any particular form of family life but instead to enhance individual competences – the control over their time and working conditions people need if they are to form families of any enduring kind – and so facilitate the formation of lasting personal relationships.

The view of welfare policy as an instrument for re-engineering forms of family life that have long broken down is mistaken for another reason: it neglects the fact that today's Britain, unlike Beveridge's, harbours a considerable measure of cultural diversity, which policy must respect. Recent immigrant communities, in all their own diversity, do not necessarily elevate autonomy over all other human interests, or revere it as an ideal. A welfare and social policy which aims to enhance individual autonomy cannot in such a multicultural setting be a policy designed to secure the proliferation of liberal individuals. If it were, it would be a policy of liberal cultural imperialism, an assimilationist programme which seeks to impose on diverse communities the value of autonomy which liberal society – at least in its own estimation – conceives to be essential for individual well-being. Public policy in a pluralist state which respects these traditions and communities may rightly protect autonomous choice of exit from them. It cannot be a programme aiming to restore a seamless monoculture animated by the liberal ideal of autonomy.[27]

The welfare institutions and policies whose ruins we inherit from the Beveridge settlement need radical revision in the context of a public culture in which the paternalism and cultural consensus which it expressed are unworkable and unacceptable. It is not only that economic changes, encompassing a vast transformation of the economic fortunes of men and women, have rendered earlier family forms unsustainable and indeed redundant. More, the moral beliefs that the 'traditional family' expressed are vanishingly remote from the lives of the great majority of the population. They cannot be revived by any political project, whether traditionalist-conservative or ethical-socialist in content. Yet welfare reform cannot be value-neutral, a vain search for a technical fix for poverty. The principal causes of most modern poverty are cultural and are not removed by the provision of income.[28] Nor can public policy be indifferent to the ways in which families are formed and dissolved. It is wholly wrong to penalize or scapegoat single parents; but it cannot be irrelevant to policy that single parenthood is only rarely a chosen condition. Concern for individual well-being is not shown by policies which treat one-parent families as if they were always, or even typically, expressions of autonomous choices. In a liberal culture in which autonomy is for most people vital to well-being, neither familial fundamentalism nor liberal neutrality is an intelligent response to the fragility of families. The goal of policy should be to enhance individual competences, to ensure that the obligations of parenthood are understood and accepted, and to assist single parents to return – or, sometimes, to enter for the first time – the world of productive work, participation in which is, for us, the precondition of self-esteem and independence.

In all these areas of policy, the aim being pursued is that of containing the centripetal forces of market individualism so as to reconcile them with the renewal of common life. It seeks to achieve this end by linking the distribution of particular goods with shared understandings of need, merit and desert, as these are found in the common culture. It recognizes, and emphasizes, that resolving conflicts which arise from the various claims of local justice requires that collective choices be made. Such choices can only be political, informed by ethical considerations which track the complex and sometimes conflicting demands of fairness. They aim to reconcile these demands not by invoking any 'theory of justice' but by articulating a common understanding of the sort of society we wish to live in. In so doing they express the key insight of the communitarian liberal perspective – that human lives conducted within a public culture that is desolated and fractured are impoverished, no matter how many individual choices they contain.

What we can hope for

It is a presupposition of all that has been argued here that, for us, individualism is a historical fate, which we can hope to temper, but not to overcome. Against both the newer forms of the New Right project and conservative forms of communitarianism, I have argued that there is no going back to the old moral world we have lost – even if, implausibly, such a reversion were desirable. The unintended cultural consequence of neo-liberal policy was to accelerate all the tendencies, inherent in late modern cultures, which act to deplete the common moral culture. Wholly apart from the ephemeral episode of neo-liberalism, the relationship between the permanent revolution of the global market and inherited forms of family and social life is not that of easy coexistence or stable equilibrium. It is one of inherent tension and endemic instability.[29] More particularly, individualist market institutions of the sort we inherit in Britain work to detach individuals from localities and communities and to weaken commitments to families. They do this by imposing an imperative of unending mobility on people and by routinizing high levels of economic risk, so that all relationships come to be perceived as revocable and transitory. It is in virtue of this contradiction between the imperatives of individualist market institutions and inherited social forms that we can be confident that the New Right vision of reviving the vanished mores of the fifties or the thirties by the provision of universal laptops is an unrealizable dystopia.

The combination of an individualist economic culture with an individualist moral culture which is our historical inheritance will be defended by those – mostly unreflective economic liberals, or those for whom repressive communities are still living memories – who see it as promoting the values of individual autonomy. It has been my argument here, however, that an anomically individualist society such as ours has become does not act to strengthen autonomy. That depends on the existence of a strong public culture, rich in options, and embodied in common institutions. Moreover, I have argued that autonomy is only one human interest, one component in individual well-being, even in a society such as ours; the satisfaction of other needs, for belonging and for stable relationships and attachments, is equally essential to our flourishing as individuals. The question then posed is: How may the incorrigible individualism of a late liberal culture such as Britain's be moderated and contained by common institutions, so that other human needs, no less imperative than that for individual autonomy, can somehow be met?

The human needs to which traditional social forms may once have answered have not diminished in importance merely because conservatives no longer take much interest in them. Against rights-based liberalism and social democracy, I have argued that the extension of a culture of rights, necessary as it may be in some areas of policy, is no antidote to the asocial individualism that is our chief danger. The liberal conception of a state that is neutral on all issues to do with the good life is not realizable in practice. Or if it is, it can only be short-lived, and at the expense of the liberal culture it properly exists to renew. A state committed to renewing a liberal culture cannot be silent, or indifferent, as to the fate of institutions and forms of common life on which such a culture depends for its survival. Against the social democratic ideal of across-the-board equality, I have argued that, like neo-liberal ideas of unrestricted market freedom, it goes against the grain of deeply held popular sentiments of fairness, in which notions of merit, desert and need are central. Only by respecting these sentiments can public policy hope to be effective. In the wake of social democracy, what policy should aim at is local justice, and the balancing of irreconcilable claims within complex fairness.

The historical aspect of my argument entails that it is not reasonable to hope to put the social democratic project back on the road. It belonged within a historical niche that is gone beyond hope of recovery. Nor will there be any renaissance of collectivist sentiment arising from the failures of neo-liberal individualism.[30] To imagine that there might be such a recovery is entirely to misread the lessons of the eighties, which all point to the overwhelming power and urgency within our culture of the demand for individual autonomy. If we are humbler in our hopes, we will no more return to the collectivist dreams of the past than we will strive to resurrect the vanished folkways of earlier generations. We will seek ways to make our economic culture more friendly to the needs of the people it exists to serve. We will aim to contrive institutions and policies which moderate its risks for them, and which make it less difficult for them to reconcile in their lives the need for enduring relationships with the imperatives of economic survival. We can hope in this way to make our individualism less possessive and more convivial.

There is no single reform of policy that can work as a panacea for our economic culture. It is an implication of my argument that many of the ills of our society can be cured only slowly and in part, since they arise from sources in our culture which governments can certainly aggravate by their policies, but over which their leverage is otherwise strictly limited. Our economic life is only an aspect of our flawed and fractured late modern culture.[31] Yet unless they are reformed so as to make their workings more humanly tolerable, liberal market institutions will lose political legitimacy. This is no small point, since it is an implication of the communitarian liberal view I have developed that – at least for us, as inheritors of a late modern individualist culture – there is no sustainable alternative to the institutions of liberal capitalism, however reformed.

The first duty of political thought is to understand the present. The danger of the new social democratic consensus is that it tracks a world which many of us are old enough to have lived in but which has now disappeared irretrievably. Would it not be another of history's ironies if we were to rid ourselves of the errors of the eighties without perceiving that, in concert with the silent forces that shape events, they have transformed our world irreversibly?

3
RAWLS'S ANTI-POLITICAL LIBERALISM

Nothing has done more to shape political philosophy over the past generation than John Rawls's book *A Theory of Justice*. For many, its publication a quarter of a century ago marked the rebirth of the subject itself. By any standards, the book must be ranked among the classics of political philosophy in English, comparable in importance with J. S. Mill's *On Liberty*, even if the leaden and graceless academic idiom in which it is written forbids counting it with Mill's essay as a masterpiece of English style. Rawls's book contributed to the renewal of the virtual hegemony of liberal thought and discourse in British and American intellectual life, a phenomenon so nearly pervasive that it passes almost unnoticed in the English-speaking world. Like Mill's book, *A Theory of Justice* has set the agenda of academic political thought for decades.

There the comparisons between Mill and Rawls end. For Mill's political theory, as it was expressed in *On Liberty* and elsewhere, was an attempt to apply a comprehensive conception of the good life for our species. It encompassed a distinctive view of the human virtues that was itself grounded in a definite conception of human nature and a particular interpretation of history. In other words, Mill's liberalism was a comprehensive worldview – a version of the religion of humanity that he derived from the Enlightenment and that sought to supplant the traditional faiths of the inherited western religions. By contrast with that of Mill, Rawls's liberalism, especially as it is restated in *Political Liberalism*, is distinguished by its systematic modesty, by its repudiation of liberalism as a *Weltanschauung* or comprehensive understanding of the human good. It affirms liberalism as a strictly political ideal that may reasonably be endorsed by exponents of very different views of the world.

In part, no doubt, Rawls's abandonment of liberalism as a worldview reflects the collapse of confidence in secular humanism in our time. Aside from a handful of fundamentalist liberals such as Francis Fukuyama, there can be few who any longer take seriously the Enlightenment expectation of progress towards a universal rationalist civilization. Rawls's assertion of a purely political liberalism, one that prescribes principles of justice for the basic structure of society rather than an ideal life for individuals or communities, has another, if not wholly unrelated source. This is in the cultural diversity of modern societies, in which the ideals of comprehensive liberalism – the ideals of individuality and autonomy that are central in the liberalisms of Mill and Kant, for example – must compete with other ideals, such as those of religion, traditional morality and communal solidarity.

Rawls grasps an insight of profound importance when he argues that this deep pluralism in modern society is not just a brute historical fact but instead the result of the unfettered use of human powers in a context of freedom. According to him, our society harbours conceptions of the good that are not merely incompatible but also rationally incommensurable: there is no overarching standard in terms of which their conflicting claims can be arbitrated. The liberal problem is to formulate principles whereby practitioners of these divergent conceptions of the good can coexist peacefully. This has been the problem of western societies, at least since the Reformation showed that uniformity in religious belief could not be achieved in a modern context without the oppressive use of state power. There can be no doubt that Rawls has stated a truth of enduring significance in his argument that the pluralist character of modern western societies deprives the ideals of comprehensive liberalism of any special authority in government. And this has a consequence: a liberal state is not one that promotes the ideals of comprehensive liberalism, but one in which rival ideals can flourish. These are truths of the first importance.

They are not new. They were stated, with a clarity that has never been matched, by Thomas Hobbes. At the start of the modern period, Hobbes held in *Leviathan* that the task of government is to maintain a *modus vivendi* among people with conflicting beliefs and values. Its overriding responsibility is to secure a civil peace, always precarious and provisional, in which rival commitments and worldviews can coexist and the advantages of commodious living can be safely enjoyed. Insofar as they are concerned with the same problem of how people with conflicting values and fundamental beliefs can live together in peace, the liberalisms of Hobbes and Rawls have a common agenda. Hobbes's 'liberalism of fear' (as Judith Shklar called it) nevertheless differs from Rawls's liberalism in a number of crucial ways. It supports the form of government best suited to the task of maintaining a civil peace, without attempting to prescribe in advance what that form might be. Hobbes held – commonsensically, one would have thought – that what is the best form of government for the purpose of civil peace depends on circumstances. In some historical contexts monarchy may do best, in others a republic; no one political regime is the standard by which all others are to be judged. For Hobbes, the goal of political philosophy is not to come up with an apology for any particular political regime. It is instead to understand the universal and permanent human needs that political institutions of all sorts exist to meet. For this reason political philosophy is inseparable from theories of human nature, and its conclusions, though they do not support a universal political ideal, have universal relevance. Hobbes's liberalism of fear is a political doctrine that has something to say to men and women everywhere.

The contrast with Rawls's political liberalism could hardly be starker. Rawls takes as his point of departure, not a general theory of human nature, but what he calls 'the public culture of a democratic society' – roughly speaking the intuitions common among American East Coast liberal academics. The upshot of his theorizing is not a political conception of general human interest, but an apology for American institutions, as they are perceived from the politically marginal standpoint of American academic liberalism. Unlike the liberalism of Hobbes, or of J. S. Mill, Rawls's liberalism has nothing to say to our contemporaries in Ankara, in Delhi, in St Petersburg or in Shanghai. It is silent on the dilemmas confronting those peoples, the majority of humankind after all, who do not enjoy the blessings of American institutions, and who may not even take any western country as their model. It is silent, also, on the events that have transformed the global political scene over the past decade. A careful reader could finish *Political Liberalism* without realizing that the past decade had witnessed, in the Soviet collapse, a historical event comparable in significance to the fall of the Roman empire. Such a reader might also not suspect that many recent conflicts that have raged in recent years have turned on issues of cultural identity – ethnic, nationalist and religious – that are suppressed in the abstract schema of Rawlsian liberalism.

The most basic assumption of Rawlsian liberalism, which is that the task of political philosophy is to specify once for all a set of basic rights and liberties that are immune from the vagaries of political conflict, denies the deepest truth of modern pluralism. This is that, since we hold to a diversity of incommensurable conceptions of the good life, we have no alternative to the pursuit of a Hobbesian *modus vivendi*. Our liberties cannot be fixed once for all – least of all by the philosopher – precisely because the *political* task is to reach a practical agreement on them that is bound to shift with circumstances. It is at just this point that the liberalism of fear has the sharpest relevance. The complete political irrelevance of Rawls's political liberalism, even in the United States, is an exquisite irony of his work upon which it would be ungenerous to dwell.

Rawls's *Political Liberalism* has some of the intellectual virtues found in the writings of J. S. Mill: clarity, rigour and fair-mindedness. Where it falls short of the standards set for liberal thought by Mill – or, in our time, by Berlin – is in the narrowness of its perspective, the parochialism of its concerns, and its strange silence on the major political events and issues of the age. The most striking feature of Rawls's political liberalism is its utter political emptiness.

4
IRONIES OF LIBERAL POSTMODERNITY

What must be true for irony to be possible? The question is a natural one for any reader of Richard Rorty's writings. The recurring theme in Rorty's work is that liberal cultures whose relationship with their most central and fundamental practices is ironic will be better – from a liberal perspective in which cruelty is the worst evil, the reduction of avoidable suffering the overriding imperative – than liberal cultures which seek 'foundations' for themselves in 'universal principles'. Rorty's ironists have given up that search. They have accepted that liberal cultures are contingent all the way down, historical accidents that could easily have been otherwise, for which no justification that is universally compelling can ever be given. They differ from traditional sceptics in not perceiving this absence of foundations to be in any sense a loss. Instead of seeking the identity of a liberal culture in the requirements of reason they find it in the sentiment of solidarity. They find it in sympathetic identification with a form of life whose local and contingent character they freely acknowledge. They think of different ways of describing the world not as more or less accurate representations of reality but as more or less felicitous ways of serving human purposes. Neither science nor ethics is a mirror of nature. In helping to rid us of the outworn metaphors that sustain both ethical and scientific realism, ironists make possible – Rorty imagines – a liberal culture that is an improvement on any that has gone before. They enable us to see the descriptions and redescriptions we give of things as expressions of our freedom and imagination. Here irony is the negation of the spirit of seriousness, a playful engagement in world-making that is not haunted by nostalgia for the 'one true' world that has been lost.

In Rorty's account, the relationship of liberal ironists with their culture expresses a kind of pathos of distance. They remain steadfast partisans of its values while regarding the universal claims that are integral to its public culture and to its self-image, which are laboriously defended by contemporary apologists for Enlightenment projects of various sorts, with detachment. The narrower question that Rorty's account naturally suggests is whether a liberal culture could renew itself, and even – as Rorty claims – improve itself if its self-understanding became ironic. The larger question is what difference internalizing a Rortyish 'postmodern' sensibility into the public culture of modern western societies would make to them.

A significant part of Rorty's work is a sustained polemic against a certain conception of philosophy – the conception, roughly, that Wittgenstein attributed to F. P. Ramsay and condemned as 'bourgeois'. In this bourgeois understanding, philosophers aim to secure foundations for the practices of particular communities. Rorty repudiates philosophizing of this kind, partly because he sees no need for the foundations that it seeks, and partly because he has a different conception of the subject, in which it is more closely allied to literature and the humanities than it is to any of the sciences. In this other understanding of philosophy, it does for us what a good novel does – it enriches our human understanding by exercising the imagination. Rorty's own writings – such as the marvellous essays on Proust, Nabokov and Orwell, collected in his *Contingency, Irony and Solidarity*, his writings on Heidegger, Wittgenstein and Davidson, and his book *Philosophy and the Mirror of Nature* – are themselves, perhaps, the most compelling current exemplars of this style of philosophizing.

Among philosophers Rorty's conception of the subject has been resisted for a number of reasons, some more compelling than others. His across-the-board dismissal of traditional ideals of truth has been found unpersuasive by those – and there are many – who wish to reject realism in ethics but hold onto it in the philosophy of science. Others, whose model for philosophy is the practice of the cognitive sciences, are reluctant to relinquish a conception of the subject in which it yields insights but produces nothing akin to cumulative knowledge. Insofar as these are merely debates within philosophy – about the proper purposes of the subject, or the varieties of realism – they are of little general interest. They concern a discipline that has long been, and seems likely to remain, culturally marginal to the last degree. They are, of course, a good deal more than that. All contemporary western societies are afflicted in varying degrees by a pervasive cultural self-doubt to which Rorty's conception of liberal irony is peculiarly relevant. The historic sources of the cultural confidence of western societies, in Christianity and in variations on the Enlightenment project, are fast depleting everywhere. What Christianity and the dwindling cultural legacy of the Enlightenment did was to confer on the local practices of western societies the imprimatur of universal authority. It should not surprise anyone that Rorty's spirited and resourceful attacks on the central foundationalist and realist traditions of western philosophy, together with his subtle and provocative defence of an ironic postmodern liberalism, have evoked the hostility at once of American neo-conservative culture-warriors and latter-day partisans of the Enlightenment project. Both fear that if Rorty's seeming insouciant relativism is accepted then anything goes. Though these critics may be political opponents, they are at one in their stalwart defence of the central western intellectual traditions that Rorty incessantly, and on the whole tellingly, attacks.

In Norman Geras's *Solidarity in the Conversation of Humankind: The Ungroundable Liberalism of Richard Rorty*, we have something we cannot expect from Rorty's neo-conservative critics – a critique of Rorty's postmodern liberalism that is consistently challenging and morally serious. Geras's argument against Rorty has four distinct strands, which are developed separately in the book's four chapters. A major strand that recurs throughout the book is Geras's argument that Rorty's account of the behaviour of rescuers of Jews during the Holocaust – as being motivated by sympathy for the fate of 'other Milanese' or 'fellow Jutlanders' rather than by universalistic concern for other human beings – goes against the evidence and the testimony of the rescuers themselves. A second argument aims to disentangle the different claims that are being made when Rorty tries to dispense with any idea of a common human nature. A third strand of reasoning attacks Rorty's claim that concern for the lot of the weak and oppressed has, and needs, no other basis than the traditions of specific (liberal) communities, and maintains that this radically particularistic communitarian interpretation of morality is incompatible with Rorty's assertion (in his 1993 Oxford Amnesty lecture) that 'the culture of human rights' is 'morally superior to other cultures'. A fourth line of criticism aims to confront head-on the moral and political implications of Rorty's anti-realism, and argues that if there is no truth there is no justice – and, perhaps more importantly, no injustice either. A recurrent theme in Geras's book is an immanent criticism of Rorty's postmodern stance, which suggests that it coheres awkwardly, if at all, with the liberal political causes to which he – like Geras – is committed. This political subtext of the book is, in fact, its real message. It is the claim that Rorty's postmodern view that there is no truth of the matter in ethics necessarily undermines the liberal universalist political moralities that the Enlightenment spawned.

How these four lines of criticism are meant to support one another is not very clear. Consider Geras's criticism of Rorty's account of rescuers' reasons during the Holocaust. It may be true that Rorty's (admittedly impressionistic) account does not square with much of the available evidence and testimony; but the heroic behaviour of the rescuers tells against Rorty's account of morality only if the universalist beliefs which apparently inspired them are not them-selves interpreted – as well they might be by Rorty – as expressing moral sentiments instilled by particular cultures or traditions. Geras is on stronger ground in his criticism of Rorty's attempt to do without any conception of a common human nature. It is hyperbolic to maintain, as Rorty sometimes does, that human beings are so completely malleable by socialization that there is no sense in talk of their having a nature in common. Perhaps talk of human nature might legitimately be dropped, as being lumbered with too much essentialist baggage; but that there are enduring human needs that are species-wide and largely resistant to socialization will not be disputed by anyone who accepts a Darwinian account of our origins and kinship with other animal species. There is a tension in Rorty's thought, at just this point, between the thoroughgoing naturalism he shares with Dewey and the Idealist conception of human beings as being constituted by their beliefs about themselves which he adapts from the later Wittgenstein. It is an implication of any coherent naturalist view, and a central insight of Freud's, that human beings have needs and desires which demand expression and satisfaction regardless of the beliefs about themselves that socialization has instilled.

What Geras's defence of a common human nature cannot do is to ground any universal political morality. It is an oddity of Geras's book that he seems to take the political morality of Enlightenment humanism so much for granted that he can write as if an argument *against* unrestricted cultural relativism were somehow an argument *for* the Enlightenment project of universal human emancipation. And there is no doubt that the justice he thinks Rorty's particularistic account of morality renders impossible is liberal justice, if rendered in a somewhat Marxian idiom. But of course history abounds with universalist moralities that are in no sense liberal. And, as we all know, the content of liberal universalism can itself vary abruptly and radically: affirmative action is defended, and attacked, as being demanded, or prohibited, by universal principles of liberal justice. It is a funny sort of justice whose limits are marked by different meetings of the American Philosophical Association – true at the Boston meeting, false in Los Angeles.

The inexorable implication of Rorty's work is that liberal cultures are only one sort of human culture among many; they can claim no privileged rational authority for themselves. Rorty cannot take a full-bloodedly particularist and historicist view of liberal cultures and at the same time make the standard liberal imperialist claim that western 'cultures of rights' are superior to all others. His affirmation of the contingency and irreducible diversity of the forms of moral life must surely be as tolerant of the extraordinary experiment underway in Singapore as it is of the liberal utopia he favours himself. Rorty's candid ethnocentrism is an advance on the dominant American school of Kantian liberal political philosophers, whose tacit agenda seems to be to come up with a transcendental deduction of *themselves*; but it shares with that school an unironic acceptance of the claims of western liberal cultures to moral superiority over all others.

In its most universal sense, an ironic consciousness is one which perceives that what is most essential in each of us is what is most accidental. Our parents, the first languages we speak, our memories – these are not only unchosen by us, they create the very selves that do all our later choosings. The central western traditions which, following Nietzsche, Rorty so bracingly chastises – the traditions not only of Christianity and the Enlightenment but also of Socratic inquiry – are deeply uncomfortable with the acceptance of final contingency which this ironic consciousness betokens. Much philosophy done in these traditions is best understood as a project of exorcizing the perception of contingency which irony expresses and transmits. In its more historically particular sense, irony is the recognition that practices and institutions that claim a universal authority in reason have no such justification. By contrast, this – the sense in which Rorty speaks of liberal ironists – is a highly specific cultural phenomenon, distinctive of and perhaps peculiar to contemporary western liberal societies. This kind of irony presupposes a public culture whose self-image incorporates universalist principles – with us, an Enlightenment culture. Can we reasonably expect western liberal institutions to survive unchanged a cultural mutation in which their universal claims are abandoned?

It may well be that Rorty's postmodern liberalism, like other varieties of liberal theory, expresses one of the illusions of the age – in which the future of liberal institutions is underwritten by the imperatives of modernity. That, after all, is the gist of all Enlightenment liberalisms – the expectation that, unless it is derailed by war or fundamentalism, modernization is bound to carry liberal culture in its wake. What else can account for Rorty's confidence that liberal societies will emerge stronger from the spread of an ironic consciousness? If the recent history of East Asia is any guide, however, the expectation that modernization entails the global spread of western liberal institutions is groundless, a deceptive shadow cast by a few centuries of European hegemony. For those who will not renounce the claim of western liberal cultures to moral superiority, the dependency of Rorty's postmodern liberalism on an illusion of modernity must seem darkly ironic. For those who can achieve a post-ironic view of liberal culture as merely one form of life among others, it will be an opportunity to go further along the path that Rorty has opened up, and think afresh about the conditions for a *modus vivendi* in a world in which diverse communities, cultures and regimes can coexist in peace.

5
SOCIALISM WITH A
PROFESSORIAL FACE

The clearest and most concise statement of John Roemer's project occurs at the end of his *A Future for Socialism*. In its concluding chapter he summarizes his argument as pivoting on two 'crucial ideas' – the idea that 'socialism is best thought of as a kind of egalitarianism, not the implementation of a particular property relation', and the idea that 'modern capitalism provides us with many fertile possibilities for designing the next wave of socialist experiments' (pp. 124–5). Associated with these ideas are two other claims – that 'the failure of the Soviet experiment is ascribable not to the egalitarian goals of communism but to the abrogation of markets' and that 'Modern capitalism does not . . . owe its success specifically to the embrace of the right to unlimited accumulation of private property' (p. 125).

Roemer's project appears to express two, mutually supportive interests – the political interest he has in developing a reformulation of the socialist project in a form that is feasible and defensible in the historical context arising from the Soviet collapse; and his intellectual interest in the ways in which the recent history of capitalism has shown the connections between market institutions and property relations to be far less determinate, and far more variable, than is allowed for in either standard economic theory or neo-liberal ideology. The upshot of both interests is a political and theoretical displacement and subordination of property relations. Within socialism, they are to be regarded in wholly instrumental fashion, their assessment and reform being governed by their contribution to the achievement of the egalitarian objectives in terms of which the socialist project is best understood. Within capitalism, property relations are recognized to be extremely complex and variable, embodied in diverse legal practices and cultures which create environments in which market competition can occur.

Roemer's two-pronged argument is that, since market institutions are far more significant in generating the competitive efficiencies and productivity of capitalism than are private property relations, socialism should not be conceived as the project of suppressing market institutions, or that of abolishing private property relations, but instead as the project of harnessing market institutions, of embedding them in a variety of property relations, with the aim of promoting important equalities. In Roemer's account, well-designed, or intelligently reformed, market institutions are functionally indispensable both to successful capitalism and to feasible socialism. The distributional goals which define the socialist project are compatible with a variety of property regimes, including 'social-republican' institutions – in which private property is constrained in its uses by requirements having to do with active participatory membership and the limitation of inequality – of the sorts found in some capitalist societies. More particularly, Roemer argues for a modified version of market socialism as most likely to achieve socialist distributional goals while maintaining, or enhancing, the efficiencies deriving from market competition. In Roemer's market socialism, though the capitalist corporation is in its current forms no longer the dominant form of productive enterprise, firms continue to be run on a competitive, profit-maximizing basis without intervention by political authorities. Further, there is no presumption as to any particular pattern of ownership rights for firms in a market socialist economy, with Roemer canvassing a range of possible regimes that encompasses an economy of labour-managed firms to one in which *de jure* property rights are unchanged but bargaining powers have been transformed. Roemer's pluralistic and radically revisionist model of market socialism is one in which market institutions may be conjoined with any among a large variety of property relations, provided socialist goals of equality are thereby advanced. In proposing this model Roemer sees himself as building on the results of the historic debate between Oskar Lange and Friedrich Hayek, by revising the original market socialist model in response to Hayek's and later criticisms (such as those of Janos Kornai). It may well seem that in modifying the market socialist conception so comprehensively Roemer has removed from it all features that are peculiarly, or even recognizably, socialist. Certainly, in Roemer's conception, socialism has ceased to signify any definite system of institutions; and it has no essential connection with the interests or needs of any social class. Yet his animating purpose is to give the socialist project another lease of life, in which it can survive the Soviet debacle and – as a corollary of acknowledging the failures of centralized economic planning institutions – be made compatible with the recognition of the functional indispensability of market institutions in modern economies. In this overriding project, however, Roemer signally – if perhaps also inevitably – fails.

Roemer's book is remarkable, and admirable, for its candour and rigour in argument; it is generous to a fault in its account of liberal critics of socialism, giving Hayek, in particular, all, indeed perhaps more than, the credit he is due; and it is further evidence, if any were needed, that the ephemeral political triumph of New Right ideology has in no sense resulted in a neo-liberal intellectual hegemony. Again, Roemer is undoubtedly right that successful market institutions come in many varieties, depend on a host of conditions not mentioned in the thin, neoclassical theory of market competition, and have no very determinate links with property institutions. In particular, contrary to neo-liberal orthodoxy, flourishing market institutions in no way presuppose the institutions of full liberal ownership characteristic of Anglo-American capitalism. Neo-liberal ideology has been pernicious, not only intellectually but also politically, in obscuring the diversity of forms of market institutions in the real world of human history, and occluding our understanding of the complexity of the conditions on which successful market institutions depend. Roemer's book performs a useful service in helping to dispel neo-liberal myths about the essential dependency of successful market systems on the institutions of Anglo-American capitalism.

At the same time, *A Future for Socialism* is testimony to the fact that liberal thought enjoys a hegemony that is now almost wholly unchallenged, at least in the English-speaking world, where liberalism has conquered or marginalized all its political and intellectual rivals. There are now few socialist (or, for that matter, conservative) theorists willing, or able, to state their views in terms that do not derive from liberal discourse. Roemer follows intellectual fashion, and conforms with the conventional wisdom of the American liberal academy, in that his revisionist market socialism is indistinguishable from the egalitarian liberalism long advocated by John Rawls,

Ronald Dworkin, Thomas Nagel and (latterly) G. A. Cohen. Roemer himself acknowledges that traditional socialists and Marxists may object that he is offering 'a liberal egalitarian creed' and responds with the argument that the ethical foundation of the Marxist critique of exploitation in capitalism is in a claim about unjust inequality in the distribution of ownership rights (p. 15). This hardly speaks to the objection that will be made by those who wish to preserve, and develop, a tradition of thought and practice that is distinctively socialist. For, even if we accept Roemer's interpretation of Marx's ethical objection to capitalism, it shows only an overlap, or a point of convergence, between the Marxian critique of capitalism and liberal egalitarianism. It fails utterly to show the presence of anything in Roemer's market socialism that is not also found in liberal theory.

The fact of the matter is that Roemer's attempted restatement of the socialist project incorporates all the worst features of contemporary Anglo-American liberal moral and political philosophy – such as its individualist and legalist preoccupation with justice and rights and its formalist and unhistorical methodology of 'concepts' and 'principles' – and eliminates the most valuable elements in socialist thought. The human subjects who figure in the model of a market socialist economy given in chapter 8 of his book are not bearers of specific histories, members of any particular culture or community; they are the ciphers of standard economic theory and of Rawlsian moral philosophy. The sense of human subjects as necessarily historical beings, which is prominent in classical Marxism, and the view of individual well-being as indissolubly linked with the flourishing of historic communities and solidarities, which figures in many traditions of ethical socialism, are absent from Roemer's account of market socialism. Yet more decisively, Roemer says nothing which links the conception of socialism he advances to the needs, or struggles, of oppressed people throughout the world. Tellingly, he writes that 'The most important work today concerning what the long-term proposal of socialists should be is that of political philosophers on egalitarian theories of justice' (p. 26). In this he acknowledges what is, in political terms, the most salient feature of the conception of socialism that he proposes: that it is not an articulation of the sense of injustice of any people, class or community, anywhere in the world, but rather a distillation of conventional liberal academic opinion. It is the voice of no broader social or political movement of any kind. Roemer's revised market socialism, if it is socialism at all, is socialism with a professorial face. For that reason alone, it is a version of the socialist project that has no place on any realistically plausible political or historical agenda.

It would be unfair, and indeed mistaken, to suggest that Roemer makes no effort to supplement his theoretical model of market socialism with attempts at a historical interpretation of the fate of socialism in the twentieth century; but these attempts are, almost without exception, ill-informed, conventional and naive to an extreme degree. Consider his account of the Soviet collapse. He tells us that 'the world may be vastly better off for the fact that it (the Soviet Union) existed' (p. 130), that its failure is 'ascribable not to the egalitarian goals of Communism but to the abrogation of markets' (p. 125) and, more specifically, that Soviet-style command economies failed because of 'the conjunction of three of their characteristics: 1) the allocation of most goods by an administrative apparatus under which producers were not forced to compete with each other, 2) direct control of firms by political units, and 3) noncompetitive, nondemocratic politics' (p. 37). This statement of Roemer's, which could as well have been made by Francis Fukuyama, Jeffrey Sachs or any among a vast number of neo-liberal publicists, certainly expresses a conventional western perspective; it amounts to the claim that the Soviet system failed because it was not a western capitalist democracy. It enunciates certain general truths about Soviet-style institutions, but neglects the particular historical and cultural conditions which produced the collapse of Soviet institutions in Russia: the demoralization and loss of the will to rule of Soviet elites that was an unintended consequence of Gorbachev's *glasnost*, the irresistible force of nationalist and secessionist movements within the Soviet Union, and the complete destruction within every Soviet institution of all allegiance to Marxist ideology. (It was the evident presence of these conditions in the Soviet Union in the summer of 1989 which enabled me to perceive, and to state in September 1989, that – contrary to all shades of western opinion – the Soviet Union was at that time in an objectively pre-revolutionary condition, such that Gorbachev's reformist project was by then doomed.)[1]

In fact, like most western commentators, Roemer offers no historical explanation of any kind as to why the Soviet system collapsed *when it did*: the three features he notes as characteristic of Soviet institutions were present from their beginning, and over a period of seventy years did not result in their collapse. In regard to the Soviet collapse, as in many other respects, Roemer fails to take to heart his own wise remark that history is 'an infinitely richer source than human imagination' (p. 126) – especially when imagination is impoverished by a form of theorizing in which history is barely acknowledged. His comments on the political prospects of market socialism, and on social democracy, further exemplify the vast distance between his theorizing and historical realities. He tells us that 'the opportunity costs of adopting market socialism' are the least 'in formerly Soviet states', where he admits 'the ideological ambience . . . is unfavourable' but nevertheless insists that 'introducing the kind of market socialism advocated here in some of these states will perhaps be possible in a few years' (p. 127). By contrast, while bearing in mind Roemer's own caveat that 'recent history has shown we tread on thin ice when trying to predict the future' (p. 126), I would maintain that one of the scenarios we can be sure the future does *not* contain for any of the post-Soviet states is the adoption of market socialism. Rather, in the wake of the failures of western-inspired neo-liberal policies of shock therapy to deliver economic results that can be politically legitimated, we will see in the post-communist states the emergence of a variety of hybrid regimes and economic systems, as the political elites of these states, often dominated by reform communist parties, struggle to improvise policies and institutions that yield a tolerable combination of the dynamic efficiency of markets with the popular demand for economic security, particularly against unemployment. In China, perhaps, TVEs – town and village enterprises having some features in common with some of the variants of market socialism discussed by Roemer, and discussed by him on pp. 127–8 of his book – may survive the marketization process that is currently underway in all sections of the Chinese economy; but, if they do, it will be on the margins of other market institutions, like social-republican institutions in western capitalist states, not as the germ of a distinct economic system.[2] In my judgement, the belief that any post-communist state will adopt market socialism will prove as baseless as the neo-liberal expectation that post-communist states will import the institutions of western capitalism – an expectation confounded everywhere apart from the Czech Republic. (Whether the Czech Republic continues to be an exceptional case, bucking the trends of other post-communist countires, remains to be seen, but I incline to doubt it.)

Roemer's treatment of what he calls 'the social and economic success of the Nordic social democracies', which he cites as evidence for the feasibility of his model of market socialism, is similarly uninformed and anachronistic. Roemer registers his – surely well-founded – 'scepticism with regard to the applicability of the Nordic social-democratic model to the world as a whole' (p. 119); but, characteristically, he fails to notice its disappearance in the Nordic countries themselves. He is aware that 'very special conditions are necessary' for the success of this model, and that these conditions no longer exist in Sweden (p. 54); but he nonetheless declares that 'We can say that the Scandinavian countries have remained social-democratic despite occasional victories of the oppositional parties' (pp. 109–10). The collapse of the Swedish version of the social democratic model, which became definitive with the referendum in December 1994, in which Sweden committed itself to full integration with European Union institutions increasingly dominated by neo-liberal policies, was evident several years previously, in the breakdown of Sweden's active labour policy, and the resulting increase in unemployment from around 2 or 3 per cent to about an eighth of the workforce. Except in Norway, where special conditions indeed prevail (including prodigal oil revenues, wisely deployed), a Nordic model of social democracy, on any reasonable understanding of what that once meant, no longer exists. It is true, and important, that market institutions in Germany and Austria, for example, and in Japan, remain in many respects profoundly different from those of American capitalism; but the belief that there exists in any major western country a distinct social democratic model of market institutions is now merely an illusion.

Our present historical situation is that market institutions, in all their undoubted variety, now possess a global hegemony that is unconstrained by any rival economic system, and subject to an ever-decreasing degree of political control. The permanent removal of market institutions from political accountability is, in fact, the explicit objective of the GATT project of global free trade, which has so far overcome all obstacles to its ratification by participating states, and looks set to become binding throughout the world. The neo-liberal project of disembedding market institutions from their undergirding cultures, and removing them from any possibility of effective political control, continues to advance globally, even as it suffers political setbacks in western democratic polities, and encounters electoral resistance in many parts of the post-communist world. Throughout the developing countries, structural adjustment programmes replicate the central elements of the neo-liberal project, evoking in some countries revolutionary movements of popular resistance. In at least one instance – the case of the Chiapas rebellion – popular resistance may initiate a civil war which functions as a model for resistance to the neo-liberal project in other parts of the world. For those still attached to classical socialist concerns with solidarity and community and the subordination of market processes to the satisfaction of human needs, the central political project of the age must be that of subjecting market institutions to the authority of indigenous political practice, and thereby re-embedding market processes in the cultures whose well-being they exist to serve. The most fundamental criticism that must be made of Roemer's book is that its central conceptions and proposals contribute nothing to thought on this project.

6
GREEN THEORY
UNDONE?

According to a common view that looks set to become part of conventional wisdom, environmentalist movements emerge along with a post-materialist culture which expresses a sense of economic satiety. They are creatures of economic growth, conceived in urban environments in the wake of consumer affluence; we do not find anything resembling western concern with the integrity of the natural environment in peasant economies, or, for that matter, in the newly industrializing countries. Environmental concern is on this view akin to a positional good, dependent for its very existence on the prosperity generated by long periods of economic growth, and it cannot be expected in times of economic uncertainty or hardship. It is the ultimate luxury of rich societies. Western governments which attempt to impose environmental concern on developing countries only reveal its positional character. The effect of policies which inhibit economic growth in poor countries in the name of environmental concern will not be to improve the protection of their natural environments, since that depends on a level of wealth which such policies prevent ever being achieved. If they achieve anything, these policies will only succeed in sheltering the environments of rich countries that are the beneficiaries of generations of industrialism and economic growth. The implications for policy of this conventional view are clear. The enforcement of western environmental standards on developing countries expresses the self-indulgent romanticism of late modern consumer cultures. It is both self-deceiving and inequitable, in that, if it was implemented consistently, its effect would be to deprive developing countries indefinitely of the wealth that makes environmental concern possible. Developing countries cannot hope to protect their environments by curtailing economic growth. On the contrary, only further and faster growth can enable them to deal with the noxious environmental side-effects of the growth they have so far achieved. They – and perhaps we – need more growth, if only to cope with the ills inherited from previous growth.

This emerging conventional wisdom on the relations of economic growth and the environment is seriously flawed in many respects; but it has a specious plausibility which makes it dangerous. If it comes to prevail, it will be in part in virtue of the work of Anna Bramwell, who in *The Fading of the Greens*, and in her previous book, *Ecology in the Twentieth Century: A History*, has developed a critique of environmental thought and movements that is sometimes thoroughly perverse, but which brilliantly illuminates their contradictions and failures. Bramwell's earlier work was important and controversial in giving the first systematic historical account of the role of distinctively environmentalist ideas and values in political movements of the radical Right, and, most particularly, in Nazism. In *Ecology in the Twentieth Century*, Bramwell interpreted what she called 'ecologism' as a doctrine arising from the history of science in the late nineteenth century. Ecologism, the political expression of ecological theorizings which claimed the authority of science but which articulated a revulsion against the mechanistic worldview which science embodied, was a body of ideas which invoked the organic and holistic character both of ecosystems and of human societies in support of a critique of modern urban and industrial life. Bramwell was criticized for focusing on the political ambivalences of ecologism, and, in particular, on the presence of ecological themes in Fascism and Nazism, but her critics were often parochial in their responses, treating her historical interpretation as a calumny on contemporary Green parties. In fact, Bramwell's thesis was not that ecological ideas have any inherent affinity with right-wing movements of blood and soil, but rather that they are politically indeterminate, being appropriated by very different political movements under varying historical circumstances. This is a historical thesis which tells us nothing as to the merits or otherwise of ecological ideas.

In *The Fading of the Greens*, however, Bramwell advances an account of 'the end of the brief era of dedicated Green national politics' (p. 1) which cannot be read primarily as an exercise in historical explanation. It is, instead, a sharp polemic against Green parties and movements, developed through the medium of genealogical history. Bramwell deploys a wealth of knowledge of contemporary thought and political life to give the reader a fascinating *tour d'horizon* of ecological thought and practice, and a powerful and unconventional intelligence which plays pitilessly on the ironies and paradoxes of the Green movements. The result is an intriguing and absorbing book. It is, at the same time, a perverse and wrong-headed book, whose effect can only be to strengthen the emerging conventional wisdom on growth and development. With characteristic provocativeness, Bramwell concludes *The Fading of the Greens* with a rhetorical question:

> We should salute the integrity and courage of the Green activists this century . . . But if one could return to earth a hundred years from now, would the result of their efforts be an idyllic and conserved nature? Or would it be a West further impoverished by the demands to share burdens with the developing world? If the latter, then the environmentalist will have failed. Because only the maligned Western world has the money and the will to conserve its environment. (p. 208)

This is a profoundly misconceived statement of the historical alternatives open to both western and developing countries, belied even by historical exemplars Bramwell uses in her book. It treats environmental concern as a function of affluence, and endorses the conventional view, well entrenched among mainstream economists and in international development organizations, that rapid economic growth is the cure for the environmental degradation that growth has caused. Taken in the context of much else in the book, it suggests that Green movements are symptoms of the malaise of urban consumer cultures rather than responses to genuine and deep difficulties faced by modern industrial societies. It at once underestimates the political importance that Green movements and parties have sometimes possessed and exaggerates the stability of the affluent western societies. It is far from being true that Green movements have functioned everywhere as the political expression of urban nostalgism: as Bramwell herself notes, environmentalism was a focus of intellectual and popular dissent in the Soviet Union (p. 192), and environmentalist movements played a significant role in triggering the Soviet collapse. Again, popular movements of protest against dams and logging have been politically significant in several developing countries, including India, and in Mexico a new revolutionary movement has arisen in Chiapas in response to the social costs of neo-liberal structural adjustment policy. In Bulgaria, and in some other parts of the post-communist world, Green movements now exist which seek to repair the damage inflicted on the natural environment and on traditional cultural forms by industrial development during the Soviet period. These are all politically significant movements, animated by environmentalist ideas, and evoked by real and urgent social and economic problems. They are of potentially large significance, not only for the countries in which they have arisen, but also for the rich western societies. For they all express a rejection of the western model of economic development which is propagated by the major aid agencies and transnational financial institutions. These new movements harbour the suspicion that development on the western model often creates poverty where it did not exist before, and produces patterns of economic activity in which the independence and integrity of local cultures is compromised or lost. Moreover, the development of local economies according to western models often does not yield economic forms that are as sustainable as the indigenous ones they displace.

Bramwell's book does not address the arguments of Green thinkers that the pursuit of economic growth in rich western countries has not yielded the benefits which might warrant its adoption as a model for development throughout the world. It is as if she believes that, whereas the pursuit of economic growth in advanced western societies may have had some unfortunate environmental consequences, it has broadly achieved what was expected of it, and whatever social problems western societies may have come from other causes. It is difficult to see what supports this belief. The massive economic growth achieved throughout western Europe over the past several decades has not in recent times gone with full employment and shows few signs of doing so. On the contrary, long-term unemployment has risen steadily higher, and stands at around 12 per cent of the workforce across much of the European Union. Further, those fortunate enough to be in work presently experience a sense of job insecurity unknown in living memory. Along with many commentators – such as John Kenneth Galbraith, with his conception of a culture of contentment made up of an affluent majority and a submerged and abandoned underclass – Bramwell does not take adequate account of the new insecurity of the middle classes, which is already a potent factor in political life throughout Western Europe. Where, as in the United States, large-scale structural unemployment has been avoided by policies aiming at maximum flexibility in the labour market, it has been at the cost of declining incomes for many, and levels of community breakdown and endemic criminality that have no parallel in any other advanced country. The thought that the constant mobility demanded by unfettered market institutions might – through its tendency to dissolve local communities – be implicated in the growth of crime receives no consideration in Bramwell's book. The idea that, impracticable as they now appear, Green proposals for relocalizing a significant proportion of economic activity in advanced societies may over the longer run be the only way in which we can hope to assure livelihood and avoid long-term unemployment for many people in them, is not seriously discussed. In this Bramwell is faithful to the conventional wisdom of the mainstream parties in all western countries, for which globalization is an unavoidable necessity to which there are no realistic alternatives.

In recent years we have witnessed a re-emergence of biological and Darwinian themes in social thought, perhaps most notably in the vogue for sociobiology among elements of the American Right. This is something of a paradox, in that the preferred mode of explanation for American neo-liberalism has always been economic. It is difficult to see how the thesis of *The Bell Curve*, co-authored by Charles Murray with the late J. Hernstein, according to which some of the most significant inequalities in contemporary American society reflect the genetic distribution of intelligence, can be squared with that of Murray's earlier book, *Losing Ground*. The latter was an exercise in economic reductionism, which maintained that the underclass in America – and, no doubt, everywhere else – was an artefact of welfare institutions that created perverse incentives regarding work and family life. Whatever its crudities and oversights – including the rather large omission of evidence regarding European countries, such as Germany and Austria, which have long had highly developed welfare institutions without producing anything remotely like an American-style underclass – the economic approach adopted in Murray's earlier work at least had the merit that the local disorders of American society were not explained by general and unalterable features of human biology.

It is to the surprising, and perhaps ominous recrudescence of biologism in recent social theory that Andrew Ross devotes some of the most interesting chapters of his wide-ranging book, *The Chicago Gangster Theory of Life*. Ross makes some shrewd and witty criticisms of recent excursions by natural scientists into sociobology, such as Richard Dawkins's writings on the selfish gene, from which the comparison of gene selfishness with the behaviour of a successful Chicago gangster is derived. His book is marred, however, by its advocacy of the least compelling of all forms of ecological thought – the 'post-scarcity' tradition of anarchist social ecology most commonly associated with Murray Bookchin – and by his consequent neglect of the sources of major social conflicts in resource-scarcities that are not created by bad or unjust institutions. Along with Maoism, fundamentalist Islam and conservative Catholicism, the free market libertarianism of Herbert Spencer and F. A. Hayek and the technological optimism of Herman Kahn or Julian Simon, post-scarcity anarchism asserts that, given existing and prospective technologies, there are no insuperable natural limitations to the growth of human population, and no forms of resource-scarcity that cannot be overcome by scientific innovation and institutional change.

This Promethean conception of the human species's relations with the natural world is endorsed by Martin Lewis in his *Green Delusions*. While recognizing that natural scarcities constrain human social and political aspirations, and affirming that the control of human population is a necessary condition of any future that is sustainable and tolerable, Lewis defends a 'Promethean environmentalism' that is distinguished from Ross's only by its moderate and anti-utopian tone. In an argument that is throughout pragmatic, resourceful and empirical, Lewis nonetheless embraces the most radical doctrines of scientific humanism, including the idea that biological diversity and ecological stability are to be achieved, not – as a less hubristic perspective might suppose – by moderating human claims on the earth, but instead by 'active management of the planet'. Like most writers on environmental questions, Lewis has not accepted the humbling of human pretensions and hopes, which is the chief lesson of Green thought in its deepest and most challenging forms.

The principal threats to the human and natural environments that we face at present are addressed by none of these books. They arise, on the one hand, from the project of transforming the world's diverse societies and cultures into a single market that is expressed in the GATT accords on global free trade. For, by removing trade from any possibility of political control and social accountability, the GATT project effectively makes the survival of the world's local and regional cultures, insofar as they are embodied in distinctive livelihoods and forms of economic activity, contingent on the fortunes of a single global marketplace. This poses a threat to human cultural diversity which is perhaps greater, and also less well perceived, than any that has hitherto existed, since it exposes communities and cultures everywhere to the permanent revolution of unconstrained global market institutions. The threat to our natural and cultural environments arises, on the other hand, from the transformation of war by new technologies and by new forms of state fragmentation. In the past generation, war has been transformed by new technologies from a conflict between states into one between whole human populations, in the course of which entire environments may be destroyed. Further, these technologies are available in an increasingly anarchic world, in much of which states have been fractured or destroyed by ethnic and religious conflicts. It is this combination of uncontrolled global markets with state disintegration in many parts of the world that poses the greatest threat to the integrity of the environment. We had a glimpse of what may be in store for us in the Gulf War, with its computerized slaughter and ecological terrorism. The prospect we may face is that of wars, often occasioned by conflicts over scarce natural resources, assuming an unparalleled destructiveness, as burgeoning human populations lay waste the earth, and local cultures are desolated by the ceaseless movement of global market forces.

7
WHAT COMMUNITY
IS NOT

The neo-liberal hegemony in Britain is over. The manifest failure of
the economic policies which it inspired has largely destroyed the
credibility of neo-liberal theory. The limitations and errors of the
shallow and narrow system of ideas which inspired public policy
throughout the eighties and much of the nineties are widely and
clearly perceived across much of British public culture. Except in the
Conservative Party, where it seems set to drive out the remnants of
traditional Toryism and may achieve for a time a dominance more
complete than ever before, neo-liberalism is a dead ideology. It is
nevertheless a fundamental mistake to imagine that the intellectual
battle against the New Right has been won completely or irreversibly. As yet the decline of the neo-liberal consensus has not been
accompanied by the rise of any successor to it. We find ourselves in
an uneasy intellectual interregnum. The last thing we need in Britain
now is any replica on the Left of the closed neo-liberal ideology
which brought us to our present pass. Yet a period of ideological
drift has real political risks. The danger must be that the New Right
could still enjoy another lease on power in the wake of political or
economic failures by Labour in government. In such circumstances,
the risk is that communitarian discourse will be appropriated by the
Right as a device for legitimating a second wave of neo-liberal
economic policies. The example of Gingrichism in the United States,
in which doctrinal adherence to free markets has been wedded to
cultural fundamentalism, suggests that this danger is not merely
theoretical.

We need to be clear what community can, and cannot, mean for us in Britain today. There is no overarching value of community to which all political movements can reasonably pay lip-service. Conceptions of community, and public policies aiming to promote it, will vary radically according to the political projects they express. The Old Right project, which was to restore traditional hierarchies in social life, sponsored forms of community which negated individual autonomy. The project of the New Right, which is to legitimate the economic inequalities arising from unfettered market institutions, will defend only those forms of common life that in no way require for their renewal curbs on free markets. The conceptions of community which these projects express may be coherent and defensible in their own terms; but they are at the furthest possible remove from what human needs demand in a late modern pluralist society such as Britain harbours today. What we lack are common institutions, which meet enduring human needs for membership and security without smothering the cultural diversity that our society contains. Such institutions cannot be advanced by any project of the Right. Lack of clarity on this fundamental point leaves the discourse of community up for grabs.

The move to a communitarian way of thinking should be welcomed as a first step in the formation of a successor to neo-liberal ideology. Communitarian thought works as a useful corrective to the central errors of the New Right. It identifies three disabling illusions in neo-liberal ideology. The first concerned the nature of the human subject. In neo-liberal thought society was theorized as a precipitate of manifold exchanges among individuals. These individuals were taken to be primordial natural facts on which the life of society stands. Social institutions were understood as means to the achievement of the purposes of these individuals. Society itself was little more than a voluntary association of such individuals. Where government appeared at all in this neo-liberal ideology, it was principally as an obstacle to the freedoms of voluntary association amongst such individuals. Intermediary institutions, which in Britain and other European countries have for many centuries stood between individuals and the state, figured in this neo-liberal picture chiefly by their absence from it.

The second neo-liberal error was its misperception of markets. Neo-liberal thought privileged markets over all other social institutions because market exchange was seen as the purest embodiment of human freedom. Markets were the expression of unconstrained human choice. Any interference with them was an interference with human freedom. For all practical purposes market exchange *was* individual freedom. The overriding task of government was to preserve and extend the freedoms of individuals in markets, especially those they exercised as consumers. If there was ever such a thing as a neo-liberal political theory, it consisted in a conception of individual freedom as a species of consumer choice together with a theory of the state as a vehicle for the protection of citizens from producer interests. The implication – which neo-liberal public policy was not slow to act upon – was that state action enhanced freedom when, and perhaps only when, it extended market exchange throughout society. Insofar as state institutions promoted market exchange they advanced freedom – however authoritarian they might in other respects be. The familiar association of neo-liberal public policy with centralization in government cannot be said, even from the viewpoint of neo-liberals themselves, to be wholly accidental. It expressed their contempt for freedoms of voice and participation, and their belief that protecting the freedoms of exit exercised by consumers in markets was the overriding responsibility of the state.

The third mistake of neo-liberal thought was its neglect of reciprocity and fairness as conditions of social cohesion. The productivity of free markets was supposed to be enough to assure stability in society. Concern about fairness was condemned as a fetter on market efficiency. Social justice was a dangerous mirage. Our duties to one another were minimal and almost entirely negative. The ethical life of society was embodied in the mutual recognition of rights, rather than in a reciprocal acceptance of duties and rights. In effect – and this states what is perhaps the chief illusion of neo-liberalism – the freedoms of market exchange were conceived to be self-justifying. Where neo-liberal thought engaged with the issue of how the free market was to maintain popular legitimacy in democracies, it produced only the claim that legitimacy would be secured for the institutions of the free market by their (supposed) superior productivity. The problematic aspects of attempting to secure popular acceptance of the free market where its workings are inimical to social cohesion were not considered.

Scattered throughout communitarian thought there can be found an incisive critique of these neo-liberal *canards* and illusions.[1] Following a long line of critics of individualism such as Hegel and Herder, and New Liberals such as Hobhouse, Bosanquet, and T. H. Green, communitarian thinkers reject the view that the life of society can be understood as an artefact of individual choices. Humans are *au fond* social beings. We are born into unchosen families. Our identities are shaped by the histories of the families into which we are born and by the languages we learn to speak. Whether we wish it or not we are born with a patrimony of historical memory. The core conception of neo-liberal theory, which is the idea of the free-standing individual chooser, is a fiction. There is no such thing as 'the individual' (or, for that matter, 'the market'). The reality is flesh-and-blood men and women, whose identities and choices are only possible because they articulate (and thereby often alter) common forms of social life. Social institutions are not mere means to ends chosen by individuals. They are expressions of continuity in society, in the absence of which the lives of individuals lose meaning and become impoverished.[2]

Communitarians also reject the neo-liberal view of markets. 'The market' is an immensely complicated cultural and legal institution, whose forms vary from society to society. Markets may serve human freedom but they can just as easily deny it. By itself market exchange makes no contribution to human autonomy. In a liberal understanding, at any rate, market exchange promotes individual freedom only insofar as people come to it equipped with the capacities, resources and options needed for an autonomous life.[3] This presupposes not only the individual capacity for effective choice but also a reasonable span of worthwhile options. If market exchange is to serve the autonomy of persons it must be embedded in institutions that are perceived to be fair and surrounded by the options assured by a rich public culture. In the absence of these conditions – as, perhaps, in post-communist Russia – market exchange is an instrument of unfreedom and exploitation. The economic system which licenses market exchange in such circumstances will not for long be popularly accepted as politically legitimate.

It is this recognition that 'the market' is not a free-standing institution that leads communitarian thinkers to fasten on the acceptance of reciprocal duties as the precondition of freedom in society. A culture of possessive individualism is too slight and shallow a form of ethical life to sustain the institutions of the free market for long. Free markets will be politically legitimate only insofar as their workings meet common standards of fairness. In the longer run, economic efficiency, perceived fairness and social cohesion are not real alternatives. (This is, perhaps, the true lesson of the East Asian tigers.) They are not conflicting values between which we are compelled to choose, but instead mutually supportive goods. Where economic efficiency and social cohesion do pull in opposite directions, that conflict is an inheritance of unintelligent public policy. In the neo-liberal period, such policy was modelled on the illusion that people could pursue their economic self-interest at the expense of their interests as social beings – as parents, friends, lovers or neighbours. This picture of human beings, and individual freedom, was fundamentally mistaken. Individual freedom is not a species of consumer choice. It is a public good which expresses a common form of ethical life.[4]

These communitarian insights are valuable correctives against the chief errors of neo-liberal thought. They suggest to me that current communitarian thought is best understood as a reform of liberal theory. Of course, communitarian thought has distinguished precursors, or exemplars, among ethical socialists such as R. H. Tawney. It exemplifies an intellectual and political tradition of criticism of abstract individualism that is far older and deeper than recent critiques of Rawls. In the context of the past two decades or so, however, communitarian thinking is a response to the conception of the sovereign individual chooser that has been advanced, or presupposed, in recent liberal thought both of the Left and the Right. Communitarian thinking aims to free liberalism not only from the mistakes of the New Right but also, and equally, from the legalism and abstract individualism of much recent left-liberal egalitarian thinking, particularly that of the dominant American Rawlsian school. If communitarian thinking contains a powerful critique of the poverty of the libertarian understanding of individual freedom as a sort of all-purpose consumer choice, it also encompasses a criticism of the left-liberal project of theorizing intuitions about fairness in terms of an overarching 'theory of justice'. As I understand it, communitarian thought conceives fairness not as the application of general principles derived from any theory of justice but as the distribution of social goods in accordance with the common understanding we have of them. It accepts that these common understandings vary, from one domain or context to another in any society, and, perhaps more radically, from one society to another. The project of a universal theory of justice, which animates much recent liberal theory, is rejected in this communitarian perspective. Such a project is, in truth, little more than another residue of abstract individualism. A communitarian way of thinking will therefore be as far removed from egalitarian liberalism as it will be from libertarian neo-liberalism. It encompasses a revision of liberal thought that is pretty far-reaching, and – in my judgement – long overdue.

Yet communitarian thought will be fruitless or harmful if it engages in any project of propping up traditional forms of social life or recovering any past cultural consensus. In its applications to a late modern society such as that of contemporary Britain, communitarian thinking must accept deep diversity in styles of life as a necessary precondition of the cultivation of a richer common culture. Recent communitarian thought, especially that which is heavily influenced by American conditions and concerns, often operates with an idea of community which is unworkable and dangerous in our historical conditions. For us, community cannot be a recipe for returning to a vanished face-to-face society, for recovering lost forms of 'organic' social unity, or for waging a cultural war against a perceived danger of imminent social breakdown. It cannot be a call for moral regeneration which passes over the ways in which, in the absence of intelligent public policy, free markets can weaken social cohesion. That is what community *is not*, and cannot be, for us. Among us, community means the cultivation of common institutions, within which people of different traditions and practices can coexist in peace. It means reforming the central institutions of the free market so that they are friendlier to vital human needs for security and autonomy. It means preventing social exclusion by enabling all to participate in the productive economy. It means developing institutions, countervailing or complementary to those of the market, which foster common life where the workings of markets risk furthering exclusion. It is concerned with contriving such a common framework of institutions within which diverse communities can live, not with any ideal of a single, all-embracing community.

The interest in autonomy – in being the part-author of one's life, by having a span of worthwhile options amongst which one chooses oneself – is pervasive and urgent in late modern Britain. It is expressed in the need for the control of economic risk that is addressed in much current discourse about insecurity. It this same interest in autonomy, which is now working through traditional institutions of all sorts, that will overthrow any communitarian policy that seeks a return to earlier modes of social or family life. Late modern individuals – such as most of us are – will not freely accept the hierarchies and forms of subordination, together with the modes of exclusion and closure of options, which sustained traditional institutions and social forms. No such *project of return* to the social forms of the past – whether its provenance be traditionalist-conservative or ethical-socialist – has any chance of prevailing against the ubiquitous late modern demand for individual autonomy. More specifically, any 'back-to-basics' communitarian project risks a political fate as ignominious and farcical as that which befell the experiment in familial and cultural fundamentalism with which the Major government toyed, briefly and disastrously, in 1993. Such a fundamentalist communitarianism has nothing to say about how enduring human needs for common forms of life are to be met in a cultural context marked by profound differences in worldviews and lifestyles and by the pervasive demand for individual autonomy. It does not confront the question of how diversity of cultural traditions can be accommodated within common institutions. Yet this must surely rank as one of the dilemmas of the age.

A key default of much recent communitarian thinking has been its neglect of the impact of economic change on the moral fabric of society. Particularly in America, communitarian thought has been weakened by an underestimation of the ways in which the workings of free markets can thwart human needs for enduring relationships and attachments. This can happen through the imperative to unencumbered mobility exerted on individuals and families in deregulated labour markets. Now I take it to be a datum of our historical circumstances that Old Left ideals of workplace community have been subverted by technological innovations and new modes of lean production. Any form of workplace community that is modelled on mass production, or which presupposes anything akin to 'jobs for life', is unsustainable in current and foreseeable circumstances. At the same time, communitarian thought suggests that businesses will not be productive over the longer run if companies cease to function as social institutions and become no more than disposable vehicles for shareholder profits. The idea that companies are no more than baskets of individual contracts is just another unfortunate inheritance of the neo-liberal period. Intelligent public policy will not seek, for the sake of shoring up job security, to stem the flood of technological innovation, or to revert to older forms of industrial production. What it will seek are terms of engagement within work which reconcile, better than has been managed so far in Britain or anywhere else, the needs of employees for enough control of economic risk in their lives to be able to plan them autonomously, and for a working environment informed by a culture of trust, with the need of management to achieve international competitiveness through enhanced productivity. Neither the deformed version of the Anglo-Saxon model of business enterprise which we inherit from the Thatcherite period, nor any of the varieties of the continental European model has achieved this reconciliation.

Communitarian thought must engage with economic policy, as it affects the needs of people at work as well as those of the growing population that is excluded from work. In my view, this cannot mean any reversion to the conceptions of community preserved in classical socialism or social democracy. That would be a Left version of the communitarian project of return. Late modern and early postmodern societies are too suffused by the individualist demand for greater autonomy for such conceptions to be any longer workable, or desirable. What it does mean is reforming the liberal capitalist institutions we inherit to make them friendlier to vital human needs. The institution of job-holding with which we are familiar may not be the best organization of individual economic activity in an age in which, owing to new information technologies, the division of labour has become more changeable than ever before. It is not just a job for life that has gone but also – and more importantly, perhaps – a vocation for life. In future people will need to be willing to reskill themselves, maybe more than once in a working lifetime, not just to keep pace with change in one occupation but also to replace it when technology has destroyed it. But it is idle to suppose that most of us can evolve from being job-holders into portfolio persons without the assistance of well-crafted public policy. Here is a task for the institutions of the state, in collaboration with business, that can only grow in importance in the future which we can foresee.

The institutions of the free market are potent destroyers. They wipe out not only defunct industries but also obsolete moralities. The task of communitarian thought in the post-socialist period is to search out ways of reconciling the workings of free markets with the human needs – for greater control of our working lives, for example – which the socialist tradition sought to defend. Communitarian thinking should focus on cultivating common institutions that meet these needs. Its debts to the past must be light, or else it will be appropriated to serve the backward-looking agendas of the New Right or the Old Left.

8

BERLIN, OAKESHOTT AND ENLIGHTENMENT

It is difficult to think of two more manifestly different writers than Michael Oakeshott and Isaiah Berlin. Oakeshott's chiselled, poetic, almost hermetic style, in which his debts to other thinkers are scrupulously effaced and a laconic abstention from any account of the historical context of his thought further occludes the reader's understanding of the author's personality and intentions, contrasts sharply with Berlin's coruscating and discursive prose, with its abundance of historical references and its captivating conversational verve. Nor are the clear and real differences between the two writers only, or even mainly, ones of style. They take different paths on nearly all matters of political and philosophical substance. If Berlin remains always a man of the Enlightenment, a follower of Hume and Condorcet in his commitment to rational inquiry, however qualified or indeed ambiguous his endorsement of their projects and hopes, Oakeshott belongs to that sceptical and sometimes fideist tradition, to which in their different ways both Montaigne and Pascal belong, and which in Kierkegaard finds full expression as a criticism of Hegelian system-building, which set itself against any Enlightenment project of refounding practical life – including religious and moral life – on reason. And, of course, while Berlin has always been a man of the liberal Left, Oakeshott never concealed that his sympathies were with the Right – even if it is far from easy to specify what kind of thinker of the Right he was in the end.

Such differences between the two thinkers are neither illusory nor superficial; they are genuine and profound. It is no part of my argument here, nor do I believe, that at some deep level Oakeshott and Berlin are in agreement. Nevertheless, the two writers do share common positions on a range of philosophical questions, which set them apart from the orthodoxies of their place and time. They both reject the positivistic belief that one mode of discourse – that of science, say – can act as a criterion of adequacy for all others; they are both pluralists, insisting on an irreducible diversity of forms of thought and practice. Further, they have common philosophical commitments – most particularly, a common commitment to 'philosophy' itself – which situate and limit their thought, and at the same time weaken the force of the criticism which each of them mounts of the central western intellectual tradition. Indeed, we can learn as much from these common limitations of their writings as from the insights they share.

It is noteworthy that the limitations that are peculiar to each thinker are not ones which those whose familiarity with their writings is slight and passing would expect. A central weakness of Oakeshott's thought is its formalistic account of political authority – an account which, in neglecting the ways in which polities express and depend upon particular cultural identities and their histories, has all the blind spots of the most unhistorical and rationalistic forms of individualism and of liberalism, from Hobbes and Kant onwards. In contrast, we find in Berlin's work – the work of a lifelong liberal – a far more incisive and subversive critique of the received forms of liberalism than anything that can be gleaned from Oakeshott, the avowed critic of liberal theory. At the same time, perhaps reflecting the unacknowledged influence on him of the later thought of Wittgenstein and of Heidegger, there is in Oakeshott – the defender of tradition – a more comprehensive (if in crucial respects still an incomplete) departure from the central, Hellenistic intellectual tradition of 'the West' than may be found explicitly in the main body of Berlin's writings. These unexpected contrasts are only a few of the instructive ironies and paradoxes which arise from a comparative assessment of the writings of this odd couple.

Both Oakeshott and Berlin are strong critics of 'rationalism'; but what they understand by rationalism is very different, and this difference is transmitted into their very different reasons for rejecting the Enlightenment project – 'the project', as Alasdair MacIntyre has put it, 'of an independent rational justification of morality'[1] – and for their common distance from central western intellectual traditions. Oakeshott's rejection of rationalism – the rationalism he finds already 'an intellectual fashion in the history of post-

Renaissance Europe',[2] articulated in the writings of Bacon and Descartes, but which he traces to far older sources, even extending as far back as Parmenides and Plato – is an application of his account of knowledge, in which theory is a sort of distillate of practice. If, for Oakeshott, all forms of knowledge are at bottom practical, the illusion of rationalism is in the supposition that techniques or rules can supplant the intimations of practical life: indeed, for Oakeshott, 'rationalism' *is* that illusion. It is this affirmation of the primacy of practice that supports his criticism of 'ideology', which is the treatment – in political life, for example – of incidents in practice as free-standing 'principles', having the authority to govern or to condemn the life of practice. Thus, 'principles' about 'liberty', 'consent', 'equality' or 'rights', principles of the sort that John Locke may have imagined himself to have been formulating in his political writings, are abridgements or distillations of a tradition of practical activity – the English tradition of politics which Locke, perhaps unwittingly, summarized. Similarly, for Oakeshott, any account of 'scientific method' can only be an abbreviation, necessarily incomplete and invariably somewhat distorted, of a particular idiom of practical activity. There cannot be a 'philosophy of science', of the sort projected by Popper, say, containing a 'theory' laying down a 'logic' of 'scientific discovery'.[3] If we may resort to a homely metaphor of the kind of which he was so fond, we may say that, for Oakeshott, theory is not the stern mother of practice, but instead its humble stepchild.

Oakeshott's account of the primacy of practice, whatever its particular incoherencies and its failure to acknowledge its affinities with other kindred accounts – in Heidegger, the later Wittgenstein, C. S. Peirce and others – is a valuable prophylactic against the illusion that practical life – moral and political life, for example – can be subjected to the authority of any theory or principle. Oakeshott's insight is that the content of all such principles invariably turns out to be a summation, inevitably impoverished by the process of abstraction that produced it, of passages in the miscellaneous life of practice. And the life of practice is not timeless; it is the creature of change and chance, and the practices that wax and wane in it are all of them historical achievements. Yet, most particularly perhaps in its applications to moral and political life, Oakeshott's account is not without difficulties, some of them fatal to it, which are of direct relevance to Berlin's wholly different criticism of rationalism. All of these difficulties may be summed up in Oakeshott's neglect of diversity and conflict among (and for that matter within) traditions of practical activity, especially moral and political traditions.

Oakeshott's deflationary analysis of political principles as summations of concrete historic practices is extremely powerful when applied destructively to the Kantian tradition of theorizing which is exemplified in much recent liberal political philosophy, in the writings of Rawls, Dworkin and others of that school. It is much less so if it is supposed to direct us to a source of unequivocal traditional knowledge in the pre-theoretical life of society. For the fact is that many societies do not possess a single, dominant or hegemonic tradition of political activity, but contain several, which contend for supremacy. It is true of France, of Spain, of Germany, of Italy, of Poland and of Hungary that they harbour not one but two or more traditions of political activity. (In France, political life is even now animated by conflicting attitudes to the Revolution, there are and have long been powerful anti-liberal parties, and the remnants of mass socialist movements exert a continuing political influence; in Hungary political practice in the post-communist period shows many continuities with its pre-communist history, with social democratic traditions in competition with nationalist ones; and so on.) Indeed this is true of pretty well every European country apart from Britain.

Oakeshott is able to write as if there could be recourse to a single underlying tradition of political practice of which theorizing presents mere distillates only because he is treating the British – or, to be more precise, the English – example as if it were a paradigm of political experience. In historical terms it looks much more like a singularity – a political culture dominated, at any rate from the seventeenth century onwards, by a whiggish tradition of political activity that has recurrently succeeded in marginalizing any rivals that may have appeared from time to time. The unfixedness and informality of the British constitution, its rule by convention and precedent, the ubiquity – at least until very recent times[4] – of tacit understandings as to the role of the state in social life – these are singularities of English political experience from which few, if any, general truths about political life can be derived. Yet Oakeshott's treatment of ideology in political life as a naivety produced by an erroneous theory of knowledge, where it is not mere pathology, depends upon the postulate of a single tradition of political activity which can provide the guidance that ideology or theory falsely promises. The reality – even in contemporary Britain, insofar as Thatcherism

imported ideological understandings of minimal government whose
historical matrix was American rather than European – is that of
several rival traditions or practices within political life, each of them
informed and animated (though – as Oakeshott rightly insists – not
governed) by ideas whose sources are often enough in 'theoretical'
discourse. The famously non-ideological character of political life in
England is far better described in terms of the hegemony of a single
– whiggish, Burkean or, later, liberal (including liberal-socialist,
Millian or Fabian) – political tradition, and its attendant political
ideas.

One way of stating the weakness of Oakeshott's account of
political life is to say that it is parochial; another is to say that it
neglects the porousness of the distinction between theory and
practical life, and the many ways in which novel theoretical dis-
courses can alter practice, and even spawn new practices. (Think of
the ways in which contemporary moral life has been altered by the
presence in it of ideas coming from the practice of psychoanalysis –
itself in part an artefact of a theory that modelled itself on the
authority of 'medical science'.) Probably the simplest way of stating
this weakness is to note the incongruity of the idea of pre-discursive
practical life in a culture, such as ours, which is reflexively discursive
'all the way down'. The disposition to theorize is not, among us,
confined to a small circle of speculative spirits; it is all but pervasive.
To think that a sceptical deflation of general ideas and principles,
which shows up their earthy origins in everyday practice, could
somehow curb this disposition is to disclose a sorry lack of historical
sense. It is a bit like Joseph de Maistre going to Russia in the hope
of finding a people that *philosophes* had not yet 'scribbled on', and
discovering one that spoke in the French idiom of Voltaire and
Diderot.

A different, and perhaps more radical way of marking the
weakness of Oakeshott's thought is to say that, when a society or a
polity harbours diverse traditions or forms of life, with their
associated worldviews, conceptions of the good and styles of
political activity, political reasoning cannot be internal to any one
tradition but must seek to identify human interests that are common
to practitioners of different forms of life. This was, after all,
Hobbes's project, when towards the beginning of the early modern
period he sought to theorize a form of political association that did
not depend upon divisive religious commitment. To be sure, Hobbes's
project expressed a characteristic illusion of the Enlightenment,

insofar as it aimed to give political (and moral) reasoning the demonstrative character of geometry; and it embodied a related Enlightenment illusion inasmuch as it had at its core a conception of individual rational choice which treated 'the individual' as a natural datum rather than a cultural and historical construction. Nonetheless, Hobbes was surely on the right track in perceiving that when a polity is sundered by warring traditions political reasoning must concern itself with human interests which the protagonists have in common, as well as with the interests they possess as subscribers to particular traditions of belief and activity.

It is odd that Oakeshott, who admired Hobbes inordinately, should not have grasped the salience in his own thought of this eminently Hobbist point. It is even odder that what Oakeshott should have taken from Hobbes is the formalistic account of political allegiance which is one of the points of commonality between Hobbes's thought and that of the rationalistic liberals who are Oakeshott's recurring targets of criticism. For Oakeshott is insistent in all his writings that political authority depends, not on serving human needs or protecting human interests, nor yet on any cultural identity or identities which its subjects may have in common, but instead only on its recognition of these subjects as characters of a certain type – persons, one might say, with their own ends and values, who make their own choices and who are unwilling to serve solely as means in respect of one another's purposes. This view, which has a point of origin in Hobbes's early proto-Enlightenment conception of individual rational choice but whose Kantian provenance in Oakeshott is beyond reasonable doubt, has all the weaknesses fatal to the dominant schools of liberal theory.[5] It refuses to recognize that, in political reasoning, nothing like a pure philosophy of right is possible; that claims about rights are not primordial or foundational but intermediary or conclusionary in political reasoning; that such claims turn on judgements about human interests, judgements that in turn reflect diverse conceptions of human well-being; so that no state can justify its authority to its subjects or citizens without engaging in a discourse about the good life which Oakeshott, with his formalistic conception of political authority, and the dominant schools of contemporary liberalism, with their incoherent conception of the neutrality of the liberal state, both reject as irrelevant to the authority of government. This fundamental truth – that the right cannot be prior to the good in political (or for that matter moral) thinking – has been argued for, demonstratively I believe, in Joseph Raz's immanent critique of recent liberalism.[6] Its upshot, in stark opposition to Oakeshott's formalistic account, is that the authority of any state must depend upon how it meets the needs of its subjects – which will themselves be determined, at any rate in part, by the conceptions of human well-being which citizens have as part of their cultural identities. And, in most modern states, the cultural identities of citizens or subjects will be plural and diverse, even in respect of many particular individuals, not singular and unequivocal. It is as if, relying on the illusion of a single tradition of political activity to give force to political allegiance, Oakeshott imagines that that illusion can be preserved by denying the relevance of cultural affinity and identity to political allegiance altogether.

It is, however, in its suppression of *conflict* that the cardinal weakness of Oakeshott's account of political life, and of practical knowledge, is to be found. Oakeshott's thought is an extended irony at the expense of theory as a guide to life; it does not appear to have occurred to him that similar ironies afflict the valorization of tradition. For Berlin, by contrast, there is no presumption whatever that traditions contain guidance which theoretical reason fails to supply; and the source of his critique of rationalism, and of the Enlightenment project, is precisely in Berlin's insistence on the reality of practical dilemmas which neither reason nor tradition can resolve. Indeed, for Berlin, 'rationalism' – at any rate in the sense in which he is critical of it – *means* monism, the (ultimately metaphysical) belief that all genuine values are compatible or even mutually constitutive. Berlin's most recurring theme is a pluralist denial of this reductive-monistic, 'rationalist' position. I have already noted that Berlin shares with Oakeshott the pluralist denial that any one mode of discourse can be authoritative for all. In his early philosophical papers he is as resistant to the positivist project of setting up an all-purpose criterion of meaningfulness as he is sceptical of the Austinian notion that philosophical questions can be settled, or even usefully clarified, by the examination of ordinary linguistic usage.[7] Where he diverges from Oakeshott is in his constant recurrence to the reality of conflict – conflict among goods that are uncombinable and may be incommensurable, among obligations whose stringency is undeniable, among evils none of which is avoidable, among traditions each of which exerts a genuine pull on our complex and plural selves.

It is the ultimate reality of irreducible diversity and conflict among and within forms of human life that grounds Berlin's rejection of all utopias, and of at least those versions of the Enlightenment project which presuppose human perfectibility or open-ended progress without concomitant cultural loss. What is distinctive in Berlin is not indeed any Augustinian affirmation of imperfection – a recurring Oakeshottean theme – but, much more radically, since it destroys the possibility of any kind of theodicy, his rejection of the very idea of perfection. It is Berlin's rejection of the coherence of the idea of the harmony of all genuine goods, as that is found in Plato, in Christianity and in many thinkers of the Enlightenment, that grounds his anti-utopianism and what I have called his *agonistic liberalism*.[8] The master-idea in Berlin is that of the incommensurability of some ultimate values – which is affirmed, not as a claim in moral theory, though doubtless it carries with it claims in moral epistemology, but as a deliverance of experience which moral theory from Socrates onwards has sought to repress. Berlin's agonistic liberalism is one which seeks to privilege the value of freedom on the choices among incommensurable values, and the part-authorship of one's life that freedom makes possible.

This agonistic perspective encompasses an insight subversive of all those forms of liberalism – the dominant forms in recent Anglo-American philosophy – which take their cue from Kant in advancing a theory of dovetailing basic liberties, or compossible rights. For, on Berlin's agonistic view, liberties no less than other human goods are irreducibly diverse, often conflicting and uncombinable, and sometimes incommensurably valuable. If this is so – as common experience strongly suggests – then the aspiration of theory to specify a set of basic liberties, or a structure of compossible rights, is hubristic. Indeed on Berlin's account – and here there is a parallelism with Oakeshott's view – there *cannot* be a theory of liberty which could resolve conflicts among liberties and between liberty and other goods. Even John Stuart Mill's theory – which remains far more plausible than subsequent theories of rights and contractarian doctrines of justice – breaks down on the incommensurability of the various components of happiness and of the many kinds of harm to which Mill's Principle of Liberty necessarily refers.[9] The task of theory must on Berlin's account be humbler than that of Mill's revised utilitarian theory, and far more so than recent theories of rights and justice; but this is not because theory is at best an abridgement of practice – which, on Oakeshott's account of the matter, could go on perfectly well without the attentions of theory – but because what theory illuminates and clarifies are conflicts and rational undecidabilities in practical life. There is here a fundamental divergence between Berlin's view of theorizing as a genuinely knowledge-yielding activity and Oakeshott's view, in which theory articulates knowledge which is entirely adequate in its original practical form. Here Berlin's position is akin to Max Weber's: it is a variant on the Enlightenment view, one in which what rational inquiry produces is not a unified, reconstructed morality but instead knowledge of the conflicts, sometimes rationally undecidable, that afflict the goods we cherish, whether or not in ordinary practical life we admit or even perceive these conflicts. On Berlin's view, then, though not on Oakeshott's, moral theory can alter and enhance our understanding of moral life; it can help us to see more clearly, and so – perhaps – to act more wisely. In doing so, however, it does not add anything to moral life. Like imaginative literature, it helps us to see better what is already there.

This difference is a clue to a much larger and deeper divergence between the two thinkers, which can be described as a difference about realism and human nature. Oakeshott's view of human beings was that of an Idealist, of one whose first love in philosophy had been Bradley, who had a lifelong admiration for Hegel and who qualified his admiration of Hume's scepticism only by regret at Hume's empiricism. I have to confess that I have never understood how Oakeshott was able to combine a self-understanding as a sceptic with an Idealist stance that in his later writings assumes an almost Wittgensteinian orientation.[10] A sceptical position, after all, requires the adoption of that 'false criterion of certainty'[11] – that foundationalist and representationalist standpoint – that Oakeshott finds in Descartes. Oakeshott's underlying position, however, is the Idealist one that human beings are what they think themselves to be: there is, at least in the human world, no thought-independent reality. This is a radically historicist account of human beings which contrasts sharply with Berlin's view, even when that is taken at its most historicist. For Berlin's consistent view is that, though human beings are unlike other animal species in that they have histories that cross the generations, identities that are expressed in cultures, and needs that are transformed by being satisfied, there is nevertheless a common human horizon of values that is, for all practical purposes, universal.[12] This horizon may be more easily expressible in terms of universal evils than of goods – the evils of torture, slavery and the myriad varieties of cruelty, for example – and, to be sure, Berlin does not suppose that we are in a position to draw up a definitive list of the items that frame this common moral horizon, or universal moral minimum, of the species. Nevertheless he is committed to the position – a commonsensical and correct position, in my view – that there are generic human evils, as well as perhaps goods, that – so to speak – go with the territory in which members of our species everywhere find themselves.

Humankind is for Berlin – as for Vico and Marx – a self-transforming species; but it is not on that account indefinitely self-transforming. Berlin's Vichian and Herderian affirmation of plurality and self-creation in human life,[13] his rejection of the Rousseauist belief in a constant, universal, generic humanity underlying the manifold differences of culture and history, is always qualified by his repeated assertion of a sort of minimum content of natural law. His account of this minimum differs decisively from traditional theories of natural law in that it recognizes conflict and incommensurability within the minimum content itself. Further, it has a distinctly modernist flavour in arguing that it is because these conflicts are real and unavoidable that choice has supreme value. Indeed, in some-what Kantian vein, Berlin seems to think that the permanent and universal reality of conflicts among incommensurable values is the necessary presupposition of the intrinsic value of choice, and allows what might be termed a transcendental deduction of the truth of liberalism – understood by him as the political morality which privileges individual freedom over other goods. This is, in effect, the normative content of Berlin's affirmation of the idea of human nature.

This Berlinian affirmation is not without its difficulties, some of them fatal to it. The core difficulty is not with the very idea of human nature, or with the departure from unrestricted cultural relativism that that idea entails. It seems to me a clear advantage of Berlin's view that it recognizes that there are human needs which cannot be altered merely by changing our conception of them. More generally, the claim that human beings are what they imagine themselves to be cannot adequately accommodate the reality of self-deception, indi-vidual and collective. Humankind is, as Hume observed, a very inventive species; but it does not invent its own biological endow-ment or mammalian ancestry, or the non-human environment in which it finds itself, and it is easily, and often, deluded about its own needs, possibilities and limitations. These divergences from unre-stricted cultural relativism – as we find it unmistakably in Oakeshott, and as many have found it in the later Wittgenstein – seem to me to tell in Berlin's favour, despite all the obvious and formidable difficulties we face in specifying the common horizon and making out its epistemic credentials. The difficulty for Berlin's conception of human nature, and for his view of a common moral horizon for the species, lies rather in the use he makes of it to ground liberal culture. It seems clear that his (or any other) version of the minimum content of natural law[14] cannot give a foundation for any particular form of life but only, and at best, support a prohibition on some forms of life as being particularly uncongenial to human well-being. It may rule out Nazism, say, but it will leave a vast range of regimes and cultures in the field, and it will afford no general privileges to liberal societies. More generally, the valorization of choice which is a feature of Berlin's liberalism is a moral standpoint for which no transcendental deduction is possible and whose culture-boundedness is patent.[15] And it is dubiously consistent with the value-pluralism which is Berlin's master-idea.

If Oakeshott's thought is to be faulted on account of its parochialism and the implausible Idealism which supports his historicist denial of anything that can properly be called human nature, the principal limitation of Berlin's thought lies in the opposite direction – in his attempt to deploy a conception of human nature to give a universal ground for adopting a particular (liberal) way of life. It may be that these diverging limitations of this odd pair have a common origin – in a shared reverence for 'philosophy' as a knowledge-yielding activity. Of course their conceptions of philosophy are very different. For Oakeshott, influenced by Bradley, Collingwood and Ryle, philosophy is a discipline capable of generating precise and definite results, which add up to a topography of experience, a sort of taxonomy of categories. No misunderstanding of Oakeshott's thought could be more complete than one which attributed to him the view that the practice of philosophy is to be assimilated to conversation; but such a misunderstanding would be natural enough, given Oakeshott's view – not especially original, since it was also held by Aristotle – that moral and political reasoning are closer to rhetoric than they are to demonstrative argument. In truth, Oakeshott attributed to 'philosophy' an authority, not indeed to ground specific forms of life but rather to establish correct descriptions of their constitutive or essential practices, which is thoroughly incongruous with the rest of his thought, which – like that of the later Wittgenstein – is (so to speak) methodologically nominalistic. There is a clear and irresolvable tension between

Oakeshott's late characterization of moralities as vernacular languages having no 'essence' in common (aside from a vaguely specified but still by Oakeshott misconceived 'non-instrumental' character) and his project of attempting to specify the 'essence' of law and history, which he also pursued in his later work.[16] It is difficult to see how Oakeshott could have maintained his anachronistic reverence for 'philosophy' if he had followed his nominalism through to the finish.

It is of considerable interest in this regard that, in what I take to be the canonical statement of his most considered overall view, 'The Voice of Poetry in the Conversation of Mankind',[17] 'philosophy', though characterized as a 'parasitic activity', is *not* ascribed the lack of finality that goes with conversation: it is 'the impulse to study the quality and style of each voice, and to reflect upon the relationship of one voice to another'.[18] Oakeshott's conception of philosophy as the construction of a final vocabulary in which the diverse modes of experience or practice are defined and their relations demarcated has a very long pedigree in western culture. It is a residue of Platonism in his thought. Oakeshott never thought to view 'philosophy' though the lens of radical historicism with which he looked at moral and political life. Had he done so, 'philosophy' might have suffered the transformation it underwent in the work of Foucault – a thought-experiment worth pondering.

Berlin's explicit conception of philosophy derives not from the idealism of Hegel, Bradley or Collingwood, but from Kant. His account of philosophical questions as neither logical nor empirical suggests that philosophy's object is the formulation of what used to be called synthetic a priori truths.[19] The difficulty for this conception is that Berlin recognizes that 'the structure of human thought' which in Kantian philosophy is supposed to yield these truths cannot be assumed to be invariant or immutable or to 'mirror' the way things are in the world. What we have in experience is not any set of unchanging, universal categories, but instead a miscellany of cultures with many commonalities, overlappings and family resemblances. Berlin's problem is, in a way, Wittgenstein's – that of finding a use for 'philosophy' when these Kantian, and foundationally western conceptions (or metaphors) are given up. It is a problem he has never solved – and whose reality he might indeed question. Yet it is difficult to see what role 'philosophy' has in Berlin's thought, other than as a cultural archaism. The authority for his central conception of value-incommensurability is not after all any sort of moral theory but rather common experience; it is as a deliverance of common human experience, reflected in the literatures of many cultures and periods, that the conception is justified. Perhaps 'philosophy' can clarify what is meant by incommensurability among goods and evils, relating and distinguishing such incommensurability of values from other varieties of incommensurability, in science and linguistics, for example; but otherwise moral theory or philosophy can do nothing to illuminate the experience of incommensurability that imaginative literature cannot do, and often do better. If, for Berlin, theorizing moral life can be a knowledge-yielding activity in a way it cannot be for Oakeshott, this is so by virtue of what moral theory shares with literature and the arts, not on account of any special powers of 'philosophy'. It is a pity that neither Oakeshott nor Berlin extends the critique of 'rational' to encompass a critique of philosophy itself. To do so, however, would be to follow the later thought of Wittgenstein and Heidegger and engage in an assault on central western intellectual traditions more comprehensive than either of them is willing to mount.[20]

The truth is that, despite their deep divergences, Oakeshott and Berlin remain committed to a conception of the authority of 'philosophy' whose origin is Socratic. Neither supposes that philosophy can govern practice; but each accepts the Socratic view that 'the practice of philosophy' can yield definite truths about human life that are unavailable by any other means. Neither holds to this belief with unwavering consistency, with Berlin ascribing to the study of history (particularly cultural and intellectual history) and to literature, and Oakeshott to poetry, the power of adding to our understanding of human experience that each nominally attributes to 'philosophy'.[21] Yet their common adherence to this traditional view of philosophy, in which its affinities are with the theoretical sciences rather than with literature and the humanities, shows them to be committed to a project of foundational inquiry that is central to western traditions and to the modern project of enlightenment. The common implication of their – conflicting – criticisms of the central western intellectual tradition is that this project of foundational inquiry must be abandoned. As to what then becomes of 'philosophy', and indeed of 'enlightenment' – that, as they say, is another story.

9
THE TORY ENDGAME

Introductory remarks

Ideas have consequences; but they are rarely, if ever, those that were intended or expected. The Hayekian ideas that inspired New Right policies in Britain from 1979 onwards have as one of their central themes the insight that social developments arise not from human design but rather from the unintended consequences of human actions. It can have occurred to few neo-liberal thinkers that the development of New Right policies, and their effects on social institutions, would provide dramatic exemplification of the Hayekian thesis; but, predictably and almost inevitably, they did. The casualties of New Right policy in Britain encompassed not only municipal socialism but also the long-standing network of interests and affinities that composed Tory Britain. The electoral consequences of the New Right's capture of the Conservative Party are, as yet, uncertain; but if they include a long period of opposition for the Conservative Party, and perhaps even its fracturing into two or more factions, then these developments will have occurred, at least partly, as unintended consequences of Hayekian policy.

The twenty short articles collected in this chapter offer a narrative account of a series of moments in the transformation of British politics by the unintended consequences of New Right policy. The narrative begins with a diagnosis of the state of the Conservative Party in the autumn of 1993. It was already apparent that the toppling of Mrs Thatcher as leader had not produced any shift from the neo-liberal policies she had long sponsored. It was becoming evident, also, that the metamorphosis of the Conservative Party itself, which was predictable on almost purely theoretical grounds, was in fact well underway. It had always been likely that the large social and economic changes produced or accelerated in Britain by Thatcherite policies would rebound on the Conservative Party itself, with the effect of changing its social and ideological composition and character. How could matters be otherwise? The Conservative Party has always maintained itself intact and in power by reflecting, and orchestrating, the balance of social forces in Britain. Policies which produced a profound shift in that balance could not fail to evoke a corresponding response from within the Conservative Party. So much had been understood, and possibly intended, by the architects of Thatcherite policy. What they did not anticipate was the destruction of the old culture of loyalty in the party produced by Mrs Thatcher's assertive and ideological style of leadership. They could not have foreseen that this would make possible Mrs Thatcher's removal from power, or that it would make a Conservative Party balkanized into warring factions a likelihood for many years. Above all, they did not and probably could not have foreseen the swift unravelling of the British class culture of deference which Thatcherite policies wrought. These developments are chronicled and assessed in sections 4, 10, 13, 14 and 20, which develop two continuing themes – that the Thatcher project has proved to be self-undermining, and that the Conservative Party which Margaret Thatcher inherited has turned out to be Thatcherism's chief political casualty.

Among the unintended political consequences of Thatcherism those in the Conservative Party may not be the most significant. The transformation of the Labour Party may prove to be at least as profound and enduring. The modernizing policies introduced in the two years following the election of Blair as leader in 1994 have effected greater changes in the party than the sum of those that occurred in it over the previous eighty years. To be sure, these were not changes made in response only to the challenge posed by the continuing hegemony of New Right policies; they were also attempts to track vast shifts underway in the real world beyond Westminster and outside Britain. The nature of a Left party in a post-socialist world in which globalization has removed many of the policy levers on which social democratic governments in the past relied is, as yet, unclear. The large revisions in Left thinking and political practice demanded by the late modern conditions form a recurrent theme of sections 2–4, 6–9 and 18.

The broader ideological meltdown of the late modern period is the subject of most of the remaining sections. In several sections (7–9, 15, 17, 19) I deploy themes from Green thought and communitarian thinking to test the limits of the prevailing intellectual and political consensus. In others (5 and 16, for example) I consider critically the tendency of both Left and Right in Britain to track an agenda set by American opinion rather than by developments in other European countries. The political endgames of which a narrative interpretation is offered in this chapter must be seen in the historical context of the larger intellectual and cultural changes that it also seeks to chronicle.

1 Down and Out in Blackpool

If the task that faced John Major when he became Prime Minister was that of constructing a coherent agenda of public policy for post-Thatcherite Britain, then there can be no reasonable doubt that he has failed. His policies have proved to be not an alternative to Thatcherism but Thatcherism on autopilot. They differ from Thatcherism only in lacking the instinctive grasp of the workings of democratic public opinion in Britain which sustained Margaret Thatcher in office for more than a decade.

Thatcher showed she had lost this grip on the public mind when she allowed herself to be persuaded of the virtues of the poll tax by the free marketeers of the New Right. In one policy fiasco after another, her successor has shown an insensitivity to public opinion that matches or surpasses hers during her last years in office. Any one of a number of policies – rail privatization, VAT on heating oil, tax on invalidity benefit – may turn out to be Major's poll tax. The question is not now whether he will be brought down, but when, and by whom.

The deeper questions are whether he could have succeeded, and whether a change in leadership could enable the party to find a post-Thatcherite agenda for British Conservatism that addresses the needs and sensibilities of the nineties. None of the omens augurs well. The parliamentary party remains in a state of aftershock from the toppling of Thatcher, the most important long-term effect of which has been to weaken the culture of loyalty which in the past enabled the Tories to overcome their differences and present a united front to public opinion and the Opposition.

This erosion introduces an element of instability which will bedevil Major's successor. Managing conflict in a party used to sectional and fractional strife will demand the highest political skills. At the same time, however skilful he may be, Major's successor cannot return the party to the old hierarchies and deferences that Thatcher swept away.

If another leader were to replace John Major during the coming twelve months, he would face the unenviable task of forging an agenda of policy that is both electorally viable and acceptable to the major factions within the party. He would confront a twofold difficulty, political and intellectual. In political terms the party is exhausted, its behaviour often suggesting that it has lost the will to rule. It is hard to believe that it can renew itself by the simple expedient of changing leader yet again. Divisions over Europe will persist, even though the collapse of European federalism may render Thatcherite nationalism an irrelevance.

The intellectual reason goes deeper. The Conservatives have no coherent view of the functions and limits of market institutions. The fundamentalist position, which sees government as the problem and markets as the all-purpose solution, is an inheritance of late Thatcherism and underlies the spate of privatizations, which no one wants and which have no perceptible benefits to anyone. It is also the philosophy which animates the demands of the Thatcherite Right for the reduction of the welfare state to a minimal safety net against poverty. This doctrinaire view fails to address the real dangers of the post-socialist age, which are the desolation of communities by unfettered market forces and the spectre of jobless growth producing an ever larger, and increasingly estranged, underclass. The older philosophy of One Nation Toryism understood the dangers posed by unfettered market forces, but was discredited by association with stagnant corporatism in the seventies. As a result, British Conservatism today has nothing of substance to say about the political task of the age, which is reconciling the subversive dynamism of market institutions with the human need for local rootedness and strong and deep forms of common life. Either Conservatives indulge in a nostalgism that is dangerous or embarrassing – as when the Prime Minister spoke of old ladies bicycling to communion across the village green – or they claim there is no conflict between markets and communities. This was the claim made by Reaganism, with results that are seen in the pathology of American individualism – epidemic crime and urban desolation. It is not a vision that appeals to the British electorate.

The dilemma of the Conservatives is that they inherit a simplistic neo-liberal ideology utterly at odds with the spirit and needs of the nineties. Reviving traditions of concern with community and social stability will be enormously difficult, partly because they have been routed in the party itself, and partly because economic and social changes have made the old vision of Britain archaic and unreal. Efforts to buttress neo-liberal policies on the economy and welfare with a rhetoric of religion and family values, of the sort made by Michael Portillo, are not electorally credible. Perhaps the government believes that its lack of any credible vision that squares with the actual lives of voters does not matter so long as economic recovery is maintained. This is almost certainly an illusion, since the public perception of the economic competence of the government has been shattered by Britain's forced departure from the Exchange Rate Mechanism, and it will not get the credit even if recovery is sustained.

British voters are a sceptical bunch. They have no interest in American-style crusades for virtue. They care more about conserving institutions they know and that seem to them to work – Bart's Hospital, say – than they do about capturing an imaginary Victorian past. Least of all do they care for doctrinaire policies of economic liberalism which do not address the ordinary human need for security in everyday life. The fact is that the Tories are increasingly viewed as a party that does not know what it wants to conserve in Britain and which is prepared casually to throw away long-established institutions and practices for the sake of a dubious economic theory.

The prospect is of the political initiative being seized by the Opposition, appealing to the electorate's genuine conservative instincts, and the Tories themselves passing into opposition, perhaps for a generation.

Guardian, 4 October 1993

2 A challenge to the old order

The election of the next Labour leader looks set to be the most decisive turning point in British political life since Margaret Thatcher became leader of the Opposition in 1975.

Thatcher's succession to the Tory leadership inaugurated the long period of New Right hegemony in Britain, the consequences of which we see in every area of national life. A decade and a half of neo-liberal policies has left us with power centralized in unaccountable quangos and traditional institutions of all kinds comprehensively emptied of legitimacy. The core institution of any stable society, the family, has been subjected to all the stresses of unchannelled economic change, leaving it fractured and resourceless in communities themselves rendered fragile and impotent by a form of public policy in which social life is reduced to a series of exchanges.

One clear result of the hollowing out of communities and traditional social forms by market-driven individualism has been a level of crime unparalleled in Britain for generations. Equally clearly, there has been no overall improvement in Britain's economic performance. British business has had to make do in a context of an increasingly deskilled workforce, crumbling infrastructure and grotesquely incompetent macro-economic management by the government. The upshot of the long hegemony of market ideology has been an acceleration of Britain's economic decline even as market forces have laid communities to waste.

The slow-motion collapse of the New Right in Britain creates a historic political opportunity for Labour. Will it grasp it by completing the process of modernization begun over a decade ago?

The new leader of the Labour Party will face a situation, in Britain and the world, which is radically different from that faced by the Labour Party at any time in its history. The working population of Britain is experiencing a level of economic insecurity unknown in its history, extending far beyond the traditional working class and biting deep into the lives of people in white-collar and professional jobs. This new situation gives traditional Labour ideals a political relevance far beyond Labour's traditional constituencies. The fear of unemployment and of illness, and the need for strong public services and forms of common life, are virtually ubiquitous in Britain today. At the same time, the institutions of economic planning and of social provision which Labour built up during the postwar period are in many respects flawed as models for the future. The Beveridge inheritance, which secured a decent framework of social provision for a generation in Britain, was adapted to a pattern of family life that has long since ceased to exist. The present mishmash of means-tested benefits neither targets real need effectively nor serves to promote the sense of common citizenship.

Most importantly, the old postwar model of full employment is flawed as a guide to providing a fulfilling livelihood to the millions who lack it in Britain today. Entirely fresh thought is needed on the changed relationship between job-holding and basic incomes in an economy whose dynamism makes the very idea of job security an illusion. As a strategy the structure of the postwar welfare state is too conservative a stance for Labour to adopt, partly because much of that structure has been torn down by the Tories but also because it no longer meets the most urgent human needs in our time.

Modernizing Labour policy to meet the needs we have today is not a move to the Right. To be sure, Labour can rightly and properly affirm those decent conservative values of community and family which the Tories have abandoned in their conversion to unfettered liberal individualism. To a considerable extent, they were the values which animated ethical socialism in the period before collective action and the institutions of national government became synonymous. The ethical vision they express, often but not always Christian in its origins, is one which sees individual self-development and collective action not as competitors but as interlinked and mutually supportive.

The modernizing project in the Labour Party is the most powerful political threat to the continuation of the New Right's hegemony in Britain today. There is no political force more feared by the Tories than Labour's modernizers, for they give expression to the electorate's deepest wish for an economically competent government that cares for the well-being of ordinary people. If Labour is prepared to bring its modernizing project to completion in its choice of a new leader, it will shift the balance of political initiative decisively, and probably irreversibly, in its favour. Another term of Tory rule would mean the dismantlement of the last obstacles to the continued desolation of communities by unchannelled market forces. It is partly to prevent such a nemesis that Labour must win the next election. Indeed, much of the work a Labour government will face on coming to power will be a job of salvage and retrieval, as it repairs the havoc wrought on British institutions by neo-liberal policies. But it will also have to tackle the greatest problem of the age – reconciling the demands of an efficient and dynamic market economy with the human imperatives of fairness and security. If Labour is ready to think boldly and afresh about the policies needed to match these objectives then it has every prospect of inaugurating a new settlement in British politics which, unlike the hegemony of the New Right, is open, pluralistic and self-critical.

To respond to the new dilemmas we face, Labour must be willing to elect a leader who is uncompromising in his commitment to change. Will the Labour Party elect Tony Blair as its next leader, and in so doing bring the hegemony of the New Right to an end?

Guardian, 9 June 1994

3 Killing the Leviathan

If Labour is returned to power after the next general election, its chief inheritance from the Conservatives will be the radically unbalanced constitution created by nearly two decades of Tory centralism. In a series of measures encompassing the weakening of intermediary institutions of all kinds, the near-destruction of local government and the creation of the Quango State, successive Tory governments have dismantled the postwar constitutional settlement in Britain just as they have undone the social settlement that grew out of the Beveridge Report. The result of this two-pronged Tory strategy has been the most centralized British state in its peacetime history, with unfettered market institutions sheltered by the authoritarian apparatus of an unaccountable quasi-governmental apparatus. It is this Leviathan, constructed to serve Tory objectives and manned by a new class of Tory nomenclaturists, that an incoming Labour government will inherit. What will be Labour's strategy towards this political legacy of neo-liberal economic policy?

Constitutional conservatives in the Labour Party like to think of the British state as a neutral instrument of public policy which they can capture and turn to their own purposes. If this was ever true it is a serious mistake in present circumstances. The current centralist structure of the British state is an artefact of the New Right project, constructed expressly to make the shift of power from democratic to market institutions irreversible. Pursued under four consecutive Tory governments, this Tory project has swept away irretrievably the institutions in which the postwar settlement in Britain was embodied. In consequence, a return to the pre-1979 *status quo* – which is the only coherent goal of Labour's constitutional immobilists – is not a real historical option. In the forms which Labour will inherit, the institutions of governance in Britain are not only wholly at variance with the pluralist vision which animates the new Labour thinking; they will thwart at every step policies aiming to promote

Labour's traditional values of fairness and public service. At this historical juncture in Britain, accordingly, constitutional reform is not – as the Tory chattering classes would like to have us believe – a marginal issue, concerning only a handful of middle-class idealists. It is a vital precondition of policies which deliver lasting improvement in the lives of the vast majority of people.

Labour is committed to a range of policies which will go some distance towards redressing the balance of power in favour of the ordinary citizen, such as the incorporation into British law of the European Convention on Human Rights. Useful and indeed essential as such policies will be, they still fall far short of the massive devolution of the powers of central government that is needed if the authoritarian bureaucracies of the quangos are to be returned to democratic accountability and the devastation of local government in Britain repaired. It is critically important that Labour's plans for devolution envisage the transfer to new democratic institutions in Scotland, Wales and the regions of real power and responsibility, not only for taxing and spending, but for the forms of welfare institutions and policy regarding health and education. The commitment to institutional pluralism that is expressed in all areas of the new Labour approach to policy implies that the forms of public services will legitimately vary, according to the traditions and circumstances of the people they exist to serve.

The new welfare institutions we need, for example, which are inclusive, enabling and responsive to the choices and judgements of ordinary citizens, will not come about under the aegis of Britain's centralized political institutions, which deny openness and suppress diversity. But such new forms will not be created either by the transplantation into Britain of institutions and policies which embody the centralizing project in Europe. Indeed, further upward devolution of the powers of government to the institutions of the European Union is precisely the reverse of what is presently needed. The creation of new tiers of government and bureaucracy, on the model of existing European institutions, in which power is exercised without public accountability and in the service of policies of harmonization which ride roughshod over local and regional needs and cultures, is at odds with Labour's core project of institutional pluralism. We have now in Scotland separate and distinct educational and legal institutions, and in Northern Ireland electoral arrangements different from those prevailing in the rest of Britain. Why should not the forms of public services, and the electoral systems, of regional governments throughout Britain be similarly diverse?

Policies of radical constitutional reform of this sort cannot be implemented without a clear public mandate – a fact reflected in Labour's commitment to a referendum on Scottish devolution. Devolution in Wales, and even more in the English regions, will work only if it answers to a manifest public need. Moreover, promoting large-scale devolution will demand both courage and resourcefulness from Labour. Why should Labour take the large political risk of embarking on radical devolutionary policies which must curb the powers of Westminster and which may – because of the 'West Lothian' factor arising from the possible over-representation of Scottish MPs – reduce permanently its presence there? The answer lies in the much larger political risks of constitutional conservatism for Labour. The danger courted by a Labour government that leaves the apparatus of the Tory state intact is that, its larger purposes frustrated by the neo-corporatist structures the Tories have built up, it will be perceived as weak and ineffectual.

Its new economic approach in particular could in these circumstances be vulnerable to markets acting on the belief that the policy framework it embodies is hostage to the changing fortunes of a precarious parliamentary majority. This is in fact the scenario envisaged by an increasingly influential body of Tory opinion, which is ready to countenance a few years of Labour rule so as to be able to press on further with the neo-liberal project when the Conservative Party has been captured in opposition by even more doctrinaire factions. The point about this strategy of revolutionary defeatism is that it expresses *the Tory scenario for Labour*. In stark contrast, the Labour strategy must be to emancipate Britain's social democratic majority and marginalize forever the neo-liberal ideologues who have ruled Britain – and, in the process, bankrupted much of British industry – for a decade and a half. The risk of a Labour government that neglects constitutional reform for pragmatic and bread-and-butter issues of economic management is that of losing the confidence both of the voters and of the markets, and thereby falling in with this Tory scenario.

For all these reasons, it is crucially important that Labour's intentions and priorities on constitutional reform are not left on the shelf to be abruptly dusted off when they are forced onto the agenda by the imperatives of a hung parliament, or quietly reshelved in the event that Labour achieves a working majority. The objective of

combining a full-hearted commitment to dynamic market institutions with concern for an undivided and harmonious common life
cannot be achieved under the authoritarian institutions of Tory neo-
corporatism. A stable framework of economic policy, enduring over
a decade or a generation, is needed to repair the damage inflicted by
years of Tory hegemony. If Labour is to grasp the chance which
undoubtedly now exists of securing a period of stability in which its
pluralist vision can find enduring institutional embodiment, it
needs, as a matter of urgency, to turn its back on constitutional
immobilism, and initiate a national debate on the deformation of
the British state into a sleaze-ridden, wasteful and blundering
behemoth.

Guardian, 3 October 1994

4 Suicide of the Leviathan

The eighties have been a long time dying. They were dominated by
a single project, the Thatcher project of limiting government, freeing
up markets and creating an enterprise culture in Britain. This was the
project inherited by the Major government, which pursued it with
a mechanical consistency that accurately expressed its incapacity for
fresh thought about the problems of the nineties. The Thatcher
project has now been definitively abandoned, its passing marked by
the failure of Michael Heseltine's privatization plans for the Post
Office, and government policy has been left altogether rudderless.
The real meaning of the end of the Thatcher era in British politics,
however, is much deeper than its significance as the point at which
the Major government entered a phase of irreversible decline. In the
broader perspective of history, it will be seen as the moment at which
the Thatcher project self-destructed, swept away by economic and
social forces it had itself released. In particular, it will be seen as the
moment in which the supreme irony of Thatcherism became politically visible – the irony of a project that, aiming to forge in Britain
a limited government that stood at arm's length from the economy
and ended the collusive corporatist relationships of the seventies,
instead built up a Corporate State of its own, a network of new
institutions in which market forces were harnessed to personal and
party interests. In this broader perspective, the self-defeating effect
of the Thatcher project has been to centralize power in a Quango
State which is perceived as serving the interests of an unaccountable

and self-perpetuating oligarchy. The result in the nineties of the neo-liberal economic policy of the eighties has been a regime of private poverty and public sleaze.

This is the real import of the current debate about sleaze – that it taps a profound public suspicion that over the past fifteen years the institutions of the British state have been so deformed that no clear or reliable distinction can any longer be made between those that are meant to be politically impartial servants of the public interest and those which serve the interests of the Conservative Party and members of the Conservative government. It is its recognition of this widespread concern that has compelled the government to set up the Nolan Committee – an act that already shows signs of leading to large and unanticipated changes in Britain's constitutional arrangements. For the setting up of the Nolan committee, welcome as it is, will not shore up the present constitutional settlement in Britain. It marks rather a new phase in its decay, as the crisis of post-Thatcher conservatism not only denudes the Major government of authority but at the same time empties the new British state that was constructed to embody the neo-liberal Thatcherite project of its legitimacy.

The terminal decline of the Major government's authority has its roots in the paradoxical and contradictory inheritances of Thatcherism. It cannot be properly understood unless they are understood. Mrs Thatcher came to power on the back of technological and economic changes that marginalized the industrial working class in Britain and thereby fatally weakened Labour's traditional electoral base. Her political genius lay in grasping that a new economic constituency existed in Britain – a social group that no longer accepted its old working-class identity and whose aspirations were individualistic and oriented around consumer choice and private freedoms. Part of the present crisis of conservatism in Britain arises from the fact that the same forces that eroded the old working-class identity and culture are now inexorably undermining middle-class culture and identity. The Major government has furthered the erosion of the Conservatives' traditional electoral base by identifying itself with the market-driven changes that are breaking up the security of the old middle-class way of life. The old class cultures that underpinned political allegiance in Britain for generations are now melting away – and the next casualties of this transformation will almost certainly be the Conservatives, who have done so much to accelerate it.

The first signs of the self-destruction of Thatcherite conservatism probably emerged in the middle to late eighties. In that heyday of neo-liberal triumphalism, membership of the Conservative Party began its precipitate decline, and the seeds of its endemic financial difficulties were sown. The waxing of private associations which neo-liberal ideology and policy sponsored had as its shadow the waning of collective allegiances, particularly towards political parties. This suggests that it was at the time of its unchallenged political hegemony that the social base of Thatcherite conservatism began to be eaten away, and its funding problems became intractable. It is against this background that the present debate about sleaze in British political life must be understood – a fact tacitly acknowledged by Lord Nolan's statement that the remit of his committee on standards in public life must include reference to the funding of political parties in Britain. It is difficult to believe that the opacity which characterizes party funding in Britain today will survive the process of scrutiny that the Nolan Committee has initiated.

It is equally hard to imagine the present forms of the Quango State surviving intact over the coming years. It is not merely that they are corporatist institutions of precisely the sort that neo-liberal ideology itself condemns. They are also a standing reminder that anonymous power is liable to be corrupted. Even if the vast majority of quango appointees are people of considerable probity, the popular suspicion remains that the power and resources they command will sometimes be used for self-interested purposes. Nor is this public attitude accidental. Power exercised without public scrutiny cannot be legitimated in the cultural climate of the nineties, partly because the institutionalization of trust articulated in the 'good chaps' theory of government in Britain is no longer popularly credible or acceptable. Politicians and public servants today confront a modern, sceptical, streetwise public opinion, which will not rest content with assurances of probity that depend on a culture of trust in government. That culture was a casualty of the hollowing out of institutional ethos which may prove to be the most enduring legacy of the eighties.

In destroying the public culture of trust in government in Britain, the neo-liberal architects of the Tory Quango State may, in the end, have performed a perverse act of public service. They have rendered untenable the pre-modern constitution which the Tories inherited in 1979. They have made a new constitutional settlement an almost inevitable outcome of the next general election. It is surely not

credible that our present constitution, with its remnants of heredi-
tary privilege and its reliance on a discredited class-based culture of
deference to authority, will be renewed unreformed in a society
which has had modernity relentlessly thrust brutally on it by neo-
liberal policy. The vitality of the current debate on sleaze is not, as
the government would like to believe, a media confection. It is a
testimony to the doubting modernist sensibility which the neo-
liberal policy of the eighties has helped to form in the Britain of the
nineties. It will be one of history's choicer ironies if, in uprooting the
old class culture on which British conservatism depended, the neo-
liberal policies of the Tories have formed an electorate that will
consign to oblivion the Leviathan they have created.

Guardian, 7 November 1994

5 The great Atlantic rift

The decoupling of the United States and the nations of the European
Union is now unmistakably underway. This is the real significance
of conflicts over policy on Bosnia – one that goes far beyond the war
in former Yugoslavia, beyond even the prospect of NATO being
irreparably damaged as a consequence of continuing unilateralism
in American foreign policy. These events are symptoms of a divergence between the United States and Europe – in their economies,
their forms of social life and their public cultures – which is deep,
growing and very probably irreversible. Europe and America have
long followed different paths of development, guided by different
conceptions of society and the role of government. Their differences
were masked for a generation or more by the common interest they
had in defeating Nazism and responding to the perceived danger of
Soviet expansionism. In the post-communist period these differences are likely to be increasingly profound.

The end of the Cold War and the weakening of the authority of
the Clinton presidency in the recent mid-term elections have set in
motion powerful forces that illuminate sharply how radically the
cultures of Europe and America differ already. Over the coming
years, almost inexorably, the cultural distance between Europe and
the United States will widen, making co-operation between them
ever more difficult. Co-operation will not be any the less important,
given that America and Europe will have vital interests in common
for the foreseeable future. It is not helped by the shallow and dated

Atlanticist rhetoric of common values which continues to dominate British public discourse. What is needed in Britain is in fact a clear perception of the distinctively European values which we do not share with the Americans.

The decoupling that is now underway occurs in the context of conflicting diplomacies over a Balkan war, but its roots are in the increasing strength of an American ideology of exceptionalism that has come to animate every aspect of life in the United States. According to this American worldview, the United States is not – what it appears to be to the rest of the world – a country like any other, with its own mixture of strengths and weaknesses, but instead a unique experiment, which is the model for a universal civilization. All other countries and cultures are at best poor approximations to this American model, at worst standing threats to it. The chronic legalism and moralism of American foreign policy, which identifies American values with those of all mankind and – except in matters of trade – lacks any coherent conception of national interest as that has traditionally been understood in Europe, spring directly from this universalist ideology. So does the American disposition to view every conflict, anywhere in the world, through the clouded prism of its own own ethnic and cultural traumas.

To be sure, these features of American foreign policy are far from new. They were exemplified in Woodrow Wilson's project of making over the old states of continental Europe after the First World War according to American principles of national self-determination. What is new is the combination of an aggressive assertion of American moral superiority with a strategy left rudderless by the removal of its Soviet ideological enemy. It is this unstable compound that makes the foreign policy arising from the new American nationalism – the nationalism of demagogues such as Newt Gingrich – so dangerously unpredictable.

What is also new is the comprehensive collapse in America of trust in the institutions of government. The United States, through the initiative of a Congress dominated by the free-market and religious Right, is now engaged in an experiment which is indeed unparalleled in any other country – that of withdrawing government from any responsibility for the welfare of society or the protection of communities and confining its functions to a repressive core having to do with the maintenance of law and order and the inculcation of certain supposedly basic national values. The auguries for this American experiment in economic Darwinism and moral fundamentalism are poor. The Reaganite project of using the institutions of criminal justice in the United States as an instrument of social engineering has left America with an incarceration rate five times that of Britain and fourteen times that of Japan, and a level of criminal violence unknown in any other advanced country. American cities have ceased to be enduring human settlements and are approaching the condition of states of nature. Cultural consensus has broken down in every major American institution, and especially in education. The United States no longer possesses any recognizable common culture or a political class that could speak for such a culture. It is now so far gone in balkanization into conflicting interests and warring cultural and ethnic groups that the claim of any administration to speak or act on behalf of an American majority can only evoke incredulity or suspicion. Unavoidably, the chaos of American institutions mirrors the incoherence of American culture itself. In truth, the United States now lacks a government in the sense in which that is understood in European countries.

The fundamentalist project of renewing 'American civilization' is, in these circumstances, a recipe for cultural war and social breakdown. The renewed ascendancy of the New Right in American political life will only fracture further what is left there of communities and speed the United States towards ungovernability. Even if, as is more than likely, it falls far short of withdrawing welfare entitlements from the American middle classes, and fails to reinstate a conception of family life that bears no relation whatever to the way most American families now live, the political triumph of the new fundamentalist project of the American Right marks the end of that older tradition of liberalism in America whereby its political culture was linked with those of Britain and Europe.

Given the growing distance of American culture and society from that of any European country, the hopes harboured by the British Left for the Clinton project were always an exercise in illusion. The belief of those on the neo-liberal Right in Britain that the debacle of Clintonism is an augury for the fate of a Labour government in Britain will prove no less deluded. The ongoing implosion of the United States, its wild oscillations between cultural introversion and messianic intervention, and its likely slide in coming decades into a kind of Brazilianization, are significant for Europeans, if at all, as evidences of the decline of the American model of unfettered individualism.

These signs of American decline should be heeded as a warning against our throwing away European cultural achievements for the sake of the chimera of the wholly free market. They should strengthen our commitment to the European project of reconciling individual choice and dynamic market institutions with social harmony and enduring communities. And they should spur the development of a post-federalist project for European institutions, now that it is clear that an inclusive Europe cannot be built on a federal plan. Above all, however, the spectacle of American decline, and of America's slow, faltering but inexorable disengagement from Europe, should embolden opinion in all parties in Britain to make the choice it has always so far steadfastly avoided – that between our being an outpost of a fictitious Atlantic civilization and our real destiny as a European nation.

Guardian, 12 December 1994

6 Reinventing the NHS

The Tory managerial revolution rolls on. As it does it is transforming British institutions beyond recognition. In an exercise in policy-making by intellectual inertia, a terminally enfeebled government is pushing ahead with measures which extend the Thatcherite project of marketization to the core functions of the British state. Having transferred many of the responsibilities of local government to anonymous quangos, and remodelled our intermediary institutions according to a primitive and anachronistic conception of business management, the Tories are now contracting out core responsibilities of the state to new government agencies that are responsible to no one.

In this they are only taking to its next phase a policy which they have already given a trial run in the National Health Service – the policy of breaking up institutions that have long worked successfully on a basis of professional ethos and a sense of public service, and replacing them with new managerial structures, often animated by a nomenclatural culture of privilege and secrecy. The new institutions being built up by the Tories are not those of a dynamic market economy but of a Corporate State. In the NHS Tory policy has created a bureaucratic apparatus of internal markets that is costly and inefficient, diverts scarce resources from patient care and threatens the autonomy of the medical professions. On any reasonable measure this Tory experiment in imposing market forces on the

NHS through the agency of a managerial revolution from above has been a ruinous failure. Labour, which is rightly friendly to markets in many areas of policy, will be entirely justified if it commits itself to reversing Tory market reforms in the health service. Indeed, sweeping away the NHS's current managerialist structures, and returning power and initiative to doctors and their patients, may well prove to be a vital element in Labour's modernizing project.

The Tories' strategy of fragmenting the NHS, and reconstituting it in managerial structures far removed from any kind of democratic oversight or professional self-regulation, is all of a piece with Tory managerialism in many other areas of public policy. Among the many new institutions thrown up by the Tories are the Next Steps agencies – such as the Benefits Agency, the Prison Service and the Child Support Agency – which are subject to no form of effective parliamentary scrutiny or accountability, despite the fact that they will soon employ four out of five civil servants. These new agencies illustrate one of Thatcherism's more obvious ironies – that a political project for which 'de-quangification' was once a mantra should have issued in a quangocracy. But the irony of history that is at work in the ongoing debacle of neo-liberalism in Britain is a deeper, as well as a crueller one. If Thatcherism ever had any historical justification, it was as a response to the corrupt corporatist institutions of the seventies, in which a triangular coalition of government, employers and trade unions shared out among themselves the spoils of a stagnant and declining economy. Yet the upshot of a decade and a half of neo-liberal policy has been the construction in Britain of a novel form of the Corporate State – a species of *market corporatism*, in which a growing proportion of the nation's economic resources is pre-empted by an expanding managerial class charged with the task of overseeing internal markets. This managerial new class disposes of vast resources, and exercises immense powers over individual lives, without being subject to the disciplines of democracy or of real markets, and – even when it is made up, as often it is, of decent people struggling to do an impossible job – without the guidance of any established professional ethos.

Nowhere has Tory market corporatism been more destructive than in the National Health Service. It is worth reflecting on Tory policy on the NHS, if only as an object lesson in ideological folly. By any international standard the old, unreformed NHS was a considerable success story. It was far from being perfect, but in an imperfect world it succeeded in delivering good health care to the entire British population, at a price in terms of proportion of national income – well under half that of American medical care, from which tens of millions of Americans are excluded – that was low and highly cost-effective. Furthermore, and perhaps decisively, the NHS was understood and trusted by the British people. There is not, and has never been, any popular demand for its reform. In fact there is deep public disquiet about its dismemberment. Within the health service, the impact of Tory managerialism has been to promote what an editorial in the *British Medical Journal* has called 'the rise of Stalinism in the NHS', a culture of mistrust and intimidation in which doctors and others are constrained from speaking out – about subordinating their clinical judgement to the demands of statistically measured efficiency, for example – for fear of being accused of jeopardizing the competitive interest of the NHS trusts in which they work. There is here, and elsewhere in the new structures of the NHS, a clear conflict between the new imperatives of competition and the traditional ethos of the medical professions. In imposing on the tried and familiar institutions of the old NHS a grandiose scheme of marketizing reforms, whose ultimate outcome even they could scarcely guess at, the Tories proved once again that they have lost the concern for the continuity of institutions that is their only principled *raison d'être*.

There is, then, an overwhelming conservative case – to be sure, one which today's Tories cannot be expected even to understand – for restoring the old National Health Service, as the fundamental institution within which health care is provided in Britain. But there is an equally powerful radical argument for rolling back the apparatus of trust hospitals and GP fundholders which is fracturing and distorting the practice of medicine within the NHS. A national guarantee of good medical care, free and universal in nature, was correctly seen by the Labour government of 1945 as a precondition of the transformation of Britain from a society of class-based inequalities to one of common citizenship. The forms of inequality with which ordinary Britons must contend today are different in many respects from those that the postwar Labour government confronted, and are not best addressed by policies which increase the powers of state institutions. Today, we can see that robust and adaptable market institutions are an indispensable instrument for enhancing the well-being of the great majority, and should be strengthened throughout the economy, and in every area of public policy where they add to well-being. Yet where, as in the NHS, markets demonstrably fail to serve the human needs which the service exists to satisfy, the modernizing project is best advanced by abolishing them, and recreating a service which is governed by judgements of medical need.

As it now stands – or falls – the NHS is a hybrid institution. It retains some of the features that derive from its inception, but these are increasingly eroded by the managerial institutions and culture that have been forced on it by Tory market corporatism. Labour will do us an enormous service – one that will highlight the gulf between its policies and outlook and those of the Tories and, in so doing, reap for itself a substantial electoral dividend – if it commits itself unswervingly to sweeping away the market structures that have deformed the NHS, and thereby returns to us one of the most successful and legitimate institutions Britain has ever possessed.

Guardian, 3 January 1995

7 Hollowing out the core

The idea of community is a potent symbol of the cultural losses of the eighties. The policies of the New Right have left in their wake a trail of weakened institutions and shattered expectations. From Bart's Hospital to the civil service, institutions once animated by an ethos of professional commitment have been casually dismantled, or subjected to a callow culture of contract and managerialism. From being enduring human settlements that span the generations and evoke strong loyalties, cities have become intersections of transients, emptied at nightfall by the fear of crime. From pension provision to long-term care for the aged, expectations on which people built their lives have been abruptly overturned. People's working lives are dominated by mistrust of their employers and fear of losing job security forever. In virtually every area of life, trust in Britain's institutions has drained away. The legacy of New Right policy is not a nation at ease with itself but a culture of anxiety and suspicion.

Against this background of pervasive insecurity the idea of community has acquired a powerful resonance in public discourse. It rightly targets the market individualism of the eighties as a major source of the soiled and frayed Britain we see before us in the nineties. But what does the idea of community mean for public policy? A notable feature of the recent vogue for communitarianism has been its lack of concrete policy proposals, and its reliance on a moralistic and sometimes reactionary rhetoric of personal responsibility. There is little in communitarian literature that focuses on the economic sources of the decay of communities – that addresses the reality of endemic job insecurity or the poverty that now afflicts even many of those in work. Instead, much communitarian discourse in Britain echoes American anxieties about family breakdown, and – if it has any definite implications for policy – develops a fundamentalist agenda for the restoration of the 'traditional' family. Such an American agenda for policy is wholly out of place in Britain. Our families, like our lives in general, are more improvised and fragmented than they used to be; but – as research from the Joseph Rowntree Foundation has shown – only 7 per cent of children live with mothers who have never been married, and we are far from the comprehensive collapse of the family that has occurred in many parts of the United States.

Family breakdown is real enough in Britain. But the increased fragility of our families cannot be unconnected with the strains imposed on them by economic policies that put flexibility of labour above any social consideration. Is it accidental that Britain, which has the highest divorce rate in Europe, also has the greatest labour mobility? There is, on the contrary, a close – and unsurprising – correlation between economic individualism and family instability. How are marriages to be lasting, if they need two incomes to make ends meet, and both partners are subject to incessant demands for job mobility? In neglecting this vital connection, American communitarians – such as Amitai Etzioni, whose book *The Parental Deficit* has had some influence with sections of the Left in Britain – show their kinship with American libertarians, such as Charles Murray, who advocate removing welfare support from single-parent families. They are at one in bowing to the free market while bemoaning its inevitably corrosive effects on family life. This American diagnosis, which accepts market individualism without question or criticism while calling for the restoration of a form of family life that is irrecoverably gone, does not help to advance public discourse or policy in Britain.

Communitarian thought has so far done little to illuminate the real threats to communities. These now come principally from the globalization of economic life – from global free trade and from the global and practically instantaneous mobility of capital, which have made the livelihood of every community more dependent than ever before in history on the fluctuations of the world market. Political debate and public opinion have not yet grasped how far-reaching and profound are the effects of globalization on our lives. It has already shattered the settlement over the distribution of income achieved in Britain by generations of wage bargaining. The freedom of companies to move to countries where labour is cheap, and the ever greater openness of markets to imports from these countries, has effectively destroyed the bargaining power of labour across much of industry. The result has been a rapid growth in wage inequalities, with the incomes of unskilled workers being driven down to levels which make supporting a family beyond the means of growing numbers of people. At the same time, globalization has accelerated the pace at which new technologies are wiping out clerical and middle-management jobs. The middle classes will be among the losers in this global competition, as they are pressed down into new forms of insecurity and poverty. The winners will be the few who command capital which they invest globally for maximum return, or who possess exceptional skills whose scarcity carries a premium.

Globalization is bound to undermine communities and to endanger the cohesion of society as a whole. It fosters a small elite whose economic interests do not coincide and may indeed conflict with those of the rest of society. It disembeds markets from their underlying cultures, severs them from the livelihoods of any particular locality or region, and levels the distinctive ways of life in which human beings express their diverse identities. Globalization forces communities to adapt to market-driven changes as best they can – or else perish. Above all, it removes markets from any form of political control or popular accountability and thereby closes off from communities any possibility of protecting their livelihoods and ways of life from the shifting fortunes of the world market. To accept the globalization of the economy is, in effect, to make the survival of communities everywhere conditional on changes in a world market which cares nothing for the stability of the societies it exists to serve.

In Britain, the debate about community has been hampered by a free market orthodoxy that accepts globalization as an inexorable trend which it is pointless to try to resist, and treats proposals for limiting free trade as beyond the pale of respectable discourse. Yet the conventional wisdom on globalization is a relic of the eighties that is ill-adapted to cope with, or even to perceive, the new dilemmas of the nineties. Communitarian thought which shrinks from challenging this defunct worldview risks becoming marginal and soon irrelevant, as looming crises reveal ever more clearly the power of global market forces to overthrow and sweep away the communities in which human beings have throughout their history found meaning and identity.

Guardian, 8 March 1995

8 The sad side of cyberspace

The new technologies and globalized markets which in recent years have done so much to hollow out local communities are presently spawning communities of an entirely new sort – the virtual communities of the Internet. The Internet communities are unlike any that human beings have ever known before, and – if their visionary advocates are to be believed – they are a great improvement on them. People join the Internet's virtual communities by choice, not as a result of the accidents of birth or history. They are free to communicate with one another without revealing their accent, gender, ethnicity or religion. There is no discrimination in the benign anarchy of the Internet. Its hierarchies are functional, fluid and ephemeral, its communities intentional and consensual, and people can exit from them at any time. On the Internet, human interactions are no longer cluttered with the trivia of our local and bodily identities. Formed not on the worn and crowded terrain of the earth but in the bodiless ether of cyberspace, the virtual communities of the Internet satisfy human needs for communication and belonging without imposing any of the constraints, duties and responsibilities that traditional communities demand. Virtual community is community at zero cost.

The bible of the Internet, and the authentic voice of the Internet worldview, is the new magazine *Wired*. For anyone interested in the technology and culture of the Internet there is really no need to read anything else. The cover of *Wired*'s first British issue sports a quotation from the eighteenth-century radical thinker and activist, Tom Paine, which sums up the magazine's uncompromisingly upbeat estimate of the emancipatory potential of the new technologies: 'We have it in our power to begin the world over again.' It is tempting to dismiss this as sales hype, but it is a good deal more than that. The publishers of *Wired* are selling more than a magazine – they are selling a utopia. It is, if you like, a designer utopia, customized for people who believe in technical fixes and not in morality or politics, who think that technology can enable us to avoid the hard choices and the long haul we face in the struggle to protect our human and natural environments. There are a lot of these people around.

The appeal of the utopia of virtual community comes partly from the magical powers it ascribes to technology. But in the real world of human history, new technologies never create new societies, solve immemorial problems or conjure away existing scarcities. They simply change the terms in which social and political conflicts are played out. The uses to which new technologies are put depend on the distribution of power and access to resources, and on the level of cultural and moral development in society. We *know* that new technologies are not in themselves liberating. Does anyone need reminding that the repression in Tiananmen Square was filmed on video cameras? Or that the Gulf War could not have been fought without computer simulation and smart bombs? Are the techno-utopians of *Wired* magazine in fact so innocent of history that they are condemned to repeat it?

The danger of the new technologies is that, allied with a techo-utopian ideology, they will be used to distract us from increasing poverty and isolation in our everyday lives. Virtual communities are poor surrogates for the communities we are fast losing. In schools and neighbourhoods, in streets and workplaces, human exchanges have an unfathomable depth of meaning that no computer can simulate. The mirage of virtual community serves to reconcile us to the growing dereliction of the social institutions and public places in which these unprogrammed encounters occur. If cities are desolated and schools stalked by fear, if we shrink from strangers and children as threats to our safety, a retreat into the empty freedom of cyberspace may seem like a liberation. Yet living much of our lives in this space means giving up part of what makes us human.

We are who we are because of the places in which we grow up, the accents and friends we acquire by chance, the burdens we have not chosen but somehow learn to cope with. Real communities are local, places in which people have put down roots and are willing to put up with the burdens of living together. The fantasy of virtual community is that we can enjoy the benefits of community without its burdens – without the daily effort to keep delicate human connections intact. Real communities can bear these burdens because they are embedded in particular places and evoke enduring loyalties. In the cyberspace in which virtual communities are formed, however, there is nowhere a sense of place can grow, and no way in which the solidarities that sustain human beings through difficult times can be forged.

We should reject the offer of the Internet communities to deliver us from the unchosen constraints of local life. The vision of a global virtual community repeats the mistakes of the eighties in its hubristic neglect of the human need for enduring attachments and forms of common life. The new technologies will serve us best if we treat them as modest devices, tools whereby we protect what is important to us. They can help existing communities to renew themselves and make it easier for new ones – real, not virtual communities – to form. Harnessing the new technologies to the needs of real communities in this way will demand active collective choice. The Internet may be a functioning anarchy but it is not an accountable democracy. Public debate is needed which focuses on the costs and risks of information technologies – for example, the threats they pose to privacy. The worst outcome – also, alas, the most likely – will be one in which the uses of the new technologies are decided not by informed public deliberation but by the uncontrolled imperatives of the market.

The illusion of virtual community is in its suggestion that we can somehow escape from our endangered and fragile earthly environment, with its divided societies and intractable conflicts, into the weightless freedom of the ether. It will be another of history's ironies if we are lulled by the utopia of virtual community into accepting the destruction by market-driven new technologies of what is left of the communities people have always lived in. For we can already see the end of the road for that utopia in the reality of postmodern poverty – in the spectacle of solitary tele-workers huddled over their desk-tops, stranded in the ruins of deserted cities, consoling themselves that the trap in which they are landed is a new kind of global freedom.

Guardian, 10 April 1995

9 Casualties of the carousel

Rising unemployment in the advanced industrial countries is only a shadow cast by a deeper trend – the decline of the institution of the job itself. It has become a commonplace of the nineties that we are now, almost all of us, at risk of being 'de-jobbed' – removed from the workforce by 'downsizing' policies that strip out whole layers of employment from organizations, replacing them by new information technologies or by 'outsourcing' from contract workers.

Even if it is not yet conclusively supported by the conventional statistical measures of labour mobility, this common perception of increased job insecurity in the nineties has a solid base in our experience. What it captures is our well-founded fear that, when we have once lost job security, we will never regain it. Our fate may not be that of those condemned to long-term unemployment, whose lives are an experiment in patience. Yet, once we fall off the merry-go-round that carries the dwindling population of those who still have traditional jobs, we will be compelled to spend the rest of our working lives in part-time or contract employment, delivering specific services or executing particular projects. We will become part of an ever-growing Lump of casualized labour that is swallowing people from all occupations and classes. It is the erosion of job-holding in the working economy, more even than the threat of unemployment, that accounts for the pervasive sense of increased personal economic risk in the nineties. Yet the causes of this shift are poorly understood, and public debate about its implications – which augur a transformation in our entire culture of work with which we are ill equipped to cope – is only just beginning.

In a challenging and timely book, *The End of Work: The Decline of the Global Labour Force and the Dawn of the Post-Market Era*, Jeremy Rifkin argues that the explosive growth of new information technologies is driving the shift from a culture of work based on old-fashioned jobs to one based on a contingent, 'just-in-time' workforce. For today's employers, a permanent workforce is a costly item in their inventory that, in conditions of intense global competition, they can no longer afford. Whenever they can do so they will adopt technologies which displace labour and, where that is not yet feasible, they will do all they can to replace job-holders in their workforce by contract workers. By pursuing these policies, employers are, willy-nilly, bringing to an end the era of mass employment.

In the United States, as Rifkin shows, this process is well advanced. It has already resulted in the temp agency, Manpower, becoming the single biggest employer in the country, with well over half a million people on its books. The displacement of labour by technology is occurring at a rapid pace throughout the American economy. It is wiping out jobs not only in manufacturing but in middle management, in banks and libraries, and in farming. Such changes are not only a death-knell for the working class but also spell ruin for many in the professions. If Rifkin is right, we are facing a development unparalleled in economic history – the technological destruction of jobs across the entire range of economic activity.

Rifkin's analysis is sure to be rejected as apocalyptic by the conventional wisdom of all parties. It will invoke earlier periods of economic history to maintain that, over the long run, new technologies create as many jobs as they destroy. Moreover, even if these will not in our circumstances be jobs of the old-fashioned sort, the conventional wisdom will insist that the new flexi-life of casualized work can be fulfilling and even – in the managerial jargon of countless downsizings – 'empowering'. What these conventional responses miss is a new instability in the division of labour that has already wrought deep changes in the culture of work. The combination of information technology with the pressures of a deregulated and increasingly global market in skills has done more than make the prospect of a job for life a historical memory. It has destroyed the idea of a career or a vocation on which our inherited culture of work was founded. The reality we all face now is not only, or even primarily, that we will have to change jobs more often. It is that we will have to change our whole occupations, perhaps more than once, in the course of a working lifetime. These changes are bound to have a deep and far-reaching impact on our whole culture.

In all modern western societies jobs have long been experienced not merely as means of acquiring income but also as the principal source of our social identity. As a consequence of the flux in which the division of labour has been thrown by the new technologies, however, we can no longer define ourselves by reference to any single occupation. In an economic environment in which skills are constantly rendered quickly obsolete, the match between the development of a career and the phases of the human life-cycle breaks down. We are then unable to tell any coherent narrative about ourselves in which our working life tracks the cycle of biological ageing. Our lives become fractured, formless and permanently provisional.

If Rifkin is even half right, the challenge posed to public policy by the technology-driven changes in work we are witnessing is far greater than is presently recognized, or admitted, on any part of the political spectrum. Social democratic ideas of returning to full employment by recurrent reskilling are likely to be not much less delusive than neo-liberal schemes in which workers 'price themselves back into jobs' at ever lower wages. At best, neither will do more than dent rising technological unemployment. We need policies which enable people to lead meaningful and productive lives in an economic culture in which the institution of the job itself is increasingly obsolete. New technologies make flexi-life of some kind inevitable for most of us. It will be humanly tolerable and fulfilling, however, only if public policies are adapted to the new realities of jobless work. We might then approach the point at which our sense of personal identity and self-esteem depend as much upon our contribution to the larger informal economy of family and community as on the possession of a permanent job. Or will we persist in policies which condemn those without work to permanent unemployment by seeking to compel them to return to a world of jobs that is fast disappearing?

Guardian, 27 April 1995

10 The passing of Tory Britain

The ongoing decline of the Conservative Party represents more than a cyclical downturn in the electoral fortunes of the world's oldest political party. It is a moment in the slow death of Tory political culture. Through a pervasive and often almost invisible network of affinities and loyalties, and through the persistence of class divisions which perpetuated the perception of the Conservative Party as the political vehicle of a ruling elite, the Conservatives throughout their history have crafted a public culture of Toryism that has assured their tenure in power as the natural party of national government. It is this Tory culture that – as a result of the policies of the past fifteen years, and of Labour's bold and resourceful seizure of the historic opportunity they now possess to supplant the Conservatives as the party of government – is now unmistakably dying.

During the long and wearisome interregnum of the nineties we have become accustomed to the spectacle of a rudderless government, navigating on neo-liberal auto-pilot as its bankrupt policies are repudiated time and again by public opinion and by its own supporters. In retrospect, the hair's breadth Conservative victory of 1992 was only a brief interval in their drift towards electoral disaster. Today's Conservatives are the casualties of economic and social forces they themselves released in the eighties, forces which sustained them in power for over a decade but which are now set to engulf them, as they shuffle, battered and baffled, towards an electoral meltdown that a change of leader – if it comes about – cannot avert. Even the replacement of John Major by Michael Heseltine cannot transform catastrophe into mere defeat – which is the most that any Conservative strategist can now hope for.

The destruction of Tory political culture by Conservative policies has occurred, in the first place, in the Conservative Party itself. The ignorant and uncomprehending scorn of the Thatcher and Major governments for the identity and continuity of long-established institutions, and their casual squandering in crass managerialist reforms of the ethos and culture that animate them, which have nearly wrecked the Civil Service and the NHS, has wrought a similar devastation on the Conservatives' party organization and morale. It has done so through the systematic contempt which successive Conservative governments have visited on local authorities – institutional pillars of the civic conservatism and communitarian virtues they claim to support – by capping and by the creation of the Quango State. In building up the Quango State, the Conservatives have created a new class of nomenclaturists that rivals, or surpasses, in its size and the resources it controls, the entire body of elected local officials in Britain. In displaying in this way their disdain for local democracy, Conservative governments have at the same time exhibited their contempt for their own councillors. In their own party, as in the country as a whole, Conservative policies have acted to weaken or destroy trust between the British people and its institutions. The result is a party machine that not only has been defunded by many of its traditional supporters in industry but which is being deserted by its workers on the ground throughout the country.

In its relations with the larger Tory culture of conservative voters, the Major government has committed the classic error of nomenclaturas everywhere, which is to mistake the familiarity conferred by power for stability in the underlying society. The last general election encouraged the illusion that the beneficiaries of the policies of the eighties would tough out even a protracted period of economic hardship, provided they could be assured of rising real incomes. The experience of the past several years, however, is that voters are as much, or more, worried about the economic risks that they and their families face – risks of the loss of their jobs and thereby their homes – as they are concerned about their post-tax incomes. In a curious reversal of the process of 'bourgeoisification' theorized by psephologists in the eighties, increasing job insecurity and shrinking equity in their homes have pauperized sections of the middle classes – most notably many of those who benefited most from Thatcherite policies – into common cause with working-class people worried about the erosion of health and education services. Indeed, fifteen years of neo-liberal policies have produced not an era of bourgeois equilibrium but an estranged and radicalized middle class, active in campaigns against road-building and the transport of live animals, and haunted by fears about its economic future. Huddled in its bunker in Whitehall, the government cannot address these concerns for economic security and environmental quality, since they are not even recognized in its ruling neo-liberal ideology.

If the historic role of Thatcherism was to be an agent of modernization of Britain's *ancien régime*, then it has – in a brutal, unintended and paradoxical way – fulfilled its function. The upshot of fifteen years of free market radicalism has been to sweep away the class deferences and to delegitimate the traditional institutions which supported the old Tory political culture. The pretensions of the Conservatives to any kind of expertise in government have become risible, and, if there is still anywhere a Tory claim to speak on behalf of a cultural elite, it is received by a streetwise popular culture as an exercise in camp.

That they can no longer claim to speak for the national culture seems to be recognized dimly even by Tories themselves. It is symptomatic that, when they inveigh against the long-overdue prohibition of the abhorrent sport of fox hunting, Tories commonly no longer use the old language of tradition but instead deploy the despised liberal rhetoric of minority cultural rights. In defending the indefensible as an element in the way of life of country folk, Tories are tacitly admitting that, on this and perhaps many other issues, they no longer voice the shared culture of most Britons. We are probably not far from the emergence of a sort of Tory multiculturalism, in which practices and privileges which public opinion condemns are represented as attributes of a threatened minority culture. The illusionless hard men of the Tory Right, once tight-lipped in their great-coats, have become just one more vocal pressure group. In the normal fortunes of political life, the Conservative Party will probably somehow renew itself, even in the wake of disaster, in a shape we cannot presently guess; but Tory England is as good as dead.

The Conservative rout in the local elections is a dramatic vindication of Tony Blair's strategy of One Nation Labourism, in which the genuine conservative values abandoned by the Conservatives are married to traditional Labour concerns for fairness and community. The self-destruction of Toryism has put in place several of the necessary conditions for a prolonged period of Labour rule, upon which Blair is systematically building. Yet the Conservative legacy to a Blair government will be a disillusioned, volatile and assertive middle class. It will be the demands of its new voters, rather than the remote prospect of resurgent union power, that will most likely test the mettle of an incoming Labour administration. In the longer and larger perspective, the principal task of a Labour government will be that of fashioning institutions in which the fractured and plural society that is the real Tory inheritance can find enough in common to be able to live with itself in peace.

Guardian, 15 May 1995

11 Fig leaf Victorians

Victorian values are back in fashion – again. They were introduced into British political discourse in 1983 by Margaret Thatcher, in an attempt to give the experiment in unfettered markets which was then underway a respectable historical pedigree. Now that that experiment is over, they have returned, this time as part of another political enterprise – that of telling a story which accounts for the ignominious failure of the free market project in Britain. How are today's Conservatives to explain the fact that a decade and a half of neo-liberal policies has not only failed to deliver the goods in the form of economic renewal but has coincided with a steep and steady rise in crime and family breakdown? For the authors of these policies, the answer cannot be that they were misconceived in the first place. The fault must lie with British society itself – with our liberal national culture, against which radical conservatism, equipped with all the resources of the most centralized democratic state in the world, has struggled in vain. This is the subtext of Margaret Thatcher's latest pronouncement on Victorian values in the forthcoming second volume of her memoirs, in which she calls for a return to 'traditional Christian morality'. Her views echo those expressed by other Conservatives, such as Alan Duncan and John Patten, in their recent books. It as if, like the East German communists in Bertolt Brecht's gibe at the time of the suppression of the workers' rising in 1953, British conservatives were to announce that they had lost confidence in the people and proposed to elect another. The story that is now being told by Conservatives about the past sixteen years is scarcely less grotesquely absurd. It is that Conservative policies have been undone, not by the damage they have inflicted on Britain's social and institutional fabric, or by the repugnance they have evoked among voters attached to traditional British notions of fairness and tolerance, but by doctrinaire liberal values, as these have been propagated by the intelligentsia through the schools and the media.

This is the message of the most sophisticated defence of Victorian values on offer – *The De-moralization of Society* by the American neo-conservative historian Gertrude Himmelfarb. Himmelfarb's book contains a good deal about the history of Victorian times, some of it illuminating, but her enterprise is political, not scholarly. It is to pin the blame for contemporary social problems on liberalism – in particular, on doctrines of moral relativism which she accuses liberals of spreading since the sixties – and to advocate a return to a morality based on religion and tradition. In targeting liberalism as the cause of our ills her aim is often unsure, partly because she rarely confronts the enormous differences in history and culture which divide Britain and the United States. It is odd to invoke liberalism as the explanation for the failure of the policies of the eighties. For these policies were expressions of liberalism in its most primitive and uncompromisingly Victorian form – the *laissez-faire* liberalism of the Manchester School which since then has displaced traditional conservatism in Britain. Perhaps it is because conservatism in the European tradition to which the Tories once belonged never really took root in the United States that an American historian can ignore the contribution neo-liberal policies have made to the erosion of traditional institutions in Britain. Equally, it is strange that Himmelfarb should acknowledge (in a footnote) that in 1980 the homicide rate in the United States was almost ten times that in England, without pausing to ask what differences between the two cultures might account for this huge discrepancy. But if she had so paused, she would have had to account for the fact that the United States is not only the most violent by far among advanced societies, but also by a long way the most religious, whereas Britain is among the least prone to criminal violence as well as one of the least religious.

Such rudimentary facts should lead us to reject any general claims about the relationship between the decline of religious belief and rising crime. More, they point to the Monty Pythonish aspect of the notion that anything as recondite as moral relativism could have the effects on society today's Conservatives claim. If moral relativism means anything, it is that our values derive from our culture. This is a position which tends to strengthen social convention and to weaken the claims of individuals – as is shown by the example of the East Asian cultures, in which 'absolutist' morality of the Christian variety is not greatly respected. It is, in fact, thoroughly frivolous for cultural conservatives to claim that the social changes they rush to condemn result from the influence of liberal intellectuals. Such changes – above all, changes in the form of the family, which are the chief source of moral panic among conservatives – arise from time-honoured beliefs and long-standing trends in modern western societies. The growth of divorce is fuelled by the ingrained bourgeois conviction that marriage and the family are vehicles for self-realization and romantic love, along with an improvement in women's economic opportunities which goes back at least to the First World War – aspects of our condition that no cultural conservative can reasonably seek to alter. And, if the family has become more fragile in recent years, it is disingenuous to pass over the impact on its stability of Conservative policies which have promoted mobility and individual choice over every other social value.

The story that is being told by Conservatives about the failure of the neo-liberal experiment neglects one very large and, for them, very awkward fact, evident after an evening's television viewing of soap operas and talk shows – that 'traditional Christian morality' is for most people in Britain today not even a historical memory. At the same time, it is a travesty of our condition to suggest that moral life itself is weak among us. The truth is that we have the makings of a strong and deep common moral culture in Britain today, but its content is rejected by cultural conservatives. This common culture is liberal about sexuality and marriage and is concerned about illegitimacy and one-parent families only where they are unchosen and harmful to the interests of children. It rejects religious beliefs about the value of human life and is favourably inclined to euthanasia. Increasingly, it departs not only from Christian values but also from humanism in its concern for the well-being of animals and the integrity of the natural environment, considered not as means to human purposes but as goods in themselves. It regards technology and economic growth with caution, as means not ends. This nascent common culture expresses itself in powerful new movements against road-building and the export of live animals – movements neglected by conservative politicians in all parties, but tapping resources of energy and commitment – not to speak of sheer effectiveness – that traditional political parties signally lack. It is this emerging consensus, as much as incompetence and sleaze in office, that has killed Thatcherism in Britain. The real lesson of 'Victorian values' is that any political project which ignores this reality risks becoming a piece of cultural kitsch.

Guardian, 30 May 1995

12 Addicts of Tory liberty

The attack on the state by the free market Right, which throughout the eighties targeted it as the chief enemy of human freedom and well-being, has recently moved into new territory in a campaign for the legalization of drugs. A growing number of Conservative thinkers and politicians have begun to advocate drug legalization as a remedy for rising levels of crime in which drug use is implicated. Among many of them, drug legalization is proposed as a further advance in the project of shrinking the state to an irreducible minimum which they have pursued for over a decade and a half in economic policy. It is difficult to think of a project that is more ill-fitted to the emerging dilemmas of the coming century. The libertarian suspicion of the state which such proposals express may have had some justification earlier this century, before the collapse of communism, when governments committed to central planning attempted to direct the lives of entire peoples. It is anachronistic and dangerous at the end of the twentieth century, when states are fractured or disintegrating in many parts of the world, and a new form of government by organized crime has arisen whose reach is worldwide.

Alan Duncan's and Dominic Hobson's book, *Saturn's Children: How the State Devours Liberty, Prosperity and Virtue*, is a notable example of the radical conservatism which inspires these new demands for drug legalization. The book is a serious engagement with fundamental issues, containing among other things a thoughtful and creative exploration of the possibilities of a Basic Income as an alternative to existing welfare institutions. It nevertheless exemplifies the backward-looking character of contemporary Conservative thought, which is so fixated on the danger of tyranny in a world of over-extended states – the danger of the world we lived in a generation ago – that it cannot perceive the threats to freedom and well-being posed by state disintegration and anarchy which endanger the world we live in now.

In our time, the state is a fragile and often impotent institution – an institution in retreat, not the devouring monster of Conservative demonology. This lag in thought and perception, which is far from being confined to Conservatives, allows the chief development in the history of the past decade – which is the weakness and fragmentation of states and the emergence of a new kind of criminalized anarcho-capitalism, in the post-communist countries and many parts of the Third World – to go uncomprehended. Yet we stand no chance of understanding the problems posed by illegal drugs if we do not understand how the collapse of states has brought into being an anarchic world in which globalized criminal organizations command many of the resources once under the control of governments.

The actual breakdown of states in many parts of the world has resulted in an increasing number of stateless nations, tribes and clans, who play a vital role in the criminal networks which control the world's supplies of illegal drugs. Chechens, Kosovan Albanians, Kurds, Tamils, Ibos from Nigeria – these and other dispossessed peoples have turned to the drug trade for a precarious living. Sometimes competing, more often colluding, the mafias operating among these peoples are often the most effective surrogates for political authority in territories – such as parts of former Yugoslavia – in which the state has been destroyed by war. In post-communist Russia, many of the assets once possessed by the Soviet state have passed into mafia control via the process of nomenclatura privatization. In Latin America, corruption and intimidation of officials by drug cartels has proved to be a decisive influence on policy. In each of these examples, power and resources have passed from sovereign states to criminal organizations, which either act as states where states no longer exist, or exercise leverage over them where they retain some degree of effective authority. The crucial truth yet to be grasped by advocates of drug legalization is that such a policy is meaningless when – as in many parts of the world where drugs are produced – states no longer exist, or have been captured by criminal mafias.

Conservative advocates of drug legalization point out that the need to finance drug habits is a major cause of crime, and that the price of drugs would fall dramatically if they were legalized. It is true that some forms of crime would probably decline in incidence under drug legalization, but many would not, and some might rise. The international mafias that are presently involved in drug production and distribution would not cease to be criminal organizations, employing violence in the pursuit of profit. Where drug use can itself act as a cause of anti-social behaviour – as with drugs, such as amphetamines and cocaine, which can produce aggression and paranoia in their users – their role in crime might be undiminished, or even – through the possibility of significantly increased consumption – enhanced.

There is an unanswerable argument for drug legalization where – as in the United States, which is the market that drug producers the world over exist to supply – drug abuse is an uncontrollable epidemic, which probably contributes to over half of the twenty thousand or so murders which are committed each year. In America, drug legalization is a well-founded counsel of despair, which only a public culture of moralizing optimism that denies the reality of its insoluble social problems prevents being acted upon. In Britain, where the drug problem is serious but not yet beyond containment, there is a powerful case for decriminalizing some drug use, and adopting a consistently therapeutic approach to users, while committing more resources to the detection of drug trafficking. But to create a free market for drugs in Britain, on the ground that the criminal mafias that currently produce and distribute them cannot be legally controlled, as advocated by Conservative libertarians, would amount to the British state's defaulting on one of its core responsibilities – the control of organized crime. It would be a further step toward a fragmented and divided society.

The anarchic new world order of stateless mafias and mafia-dominated states has emerged as an unintended consequence of policies which weakened the authority of sovereign states. Even the control of military force in many parts of the world no longer lies with anything recognizable as states, but is dispersed among political organizations, tribes and clans – a development which has transformed the nature of war. The anarcho-capitalist economies which have replaced central planning in many post-communist countries may well prove not to be a developmental phase on a path of convergence with western institutions but a stable system that endures for generations. For the foreseeable future much of the world will be anarchic. This is an ominous prospect at a time when inexorably increasing human populations are recreating in new forms many of the old Malthusian scarcities.

The evidence of the new mafias, which have pioneered an unexpected form of economic globalization in the wake of collapsing states, confirms what many have long suspected – that the libertarian condemnation of the state and celebration of the free market is a recipe for social breakdown and political instability. In Britain, despite its deformations, the state has been on balance a civilizing institution. To abandon the poor and the desperate to an unfettered market in drugs would be the final folly of radical individualism. The siren voices now calling for drug legalization should be resisted by all who seek to preserve what still remains of Britain's inheritance of social cohesion and civilized government.

Guardian, 19 June 1995

13 A radical departure

With John Redwood's announcement of his candidacy for the leadership the civil war within the Conservative Party moves into a new phase. His audacious challenge to John Major leaves no room for doubt that the party's Right now exercises the strategic initiative against an increasingly defensive and outmanoeuvred rump of traditional Tories. Redwood's role in the Conservative leadership contest signifies something yet more ominous – the impending rout within the Conservative Party of the remaining forces of One Nation Toryism. Whatever the outcome of Redwood's bid and of the leadership contest itself, one thing is clear. The victor's authority as Conservative leader will depend upon accepting terms dictated by the nationalist, free-market Right. The upshot of the contest can only be a decisive further radicalization of the party in the direction set by Margaret Thatcher in 1979.

Throughout John Major's premiership two incompatible philosophies have waged an intermittent and inconclusive conflict in the Conservative Party. The inheritors of Thatcherism have sought to defend, and extend, positions she adopted not only on Britain's relations with Europe but on law and order, social policy and public spending. The vision of Britain's national future which this New Right philosophy advances is that of British society reconstructed in economic terms on an American individualist model, but in its broader political dimensions it resembles more nearly the national-

ism of the Old Right in continental Europe. The result is an exotic
pot-pourri of Gingrich and Poujade that makes Thatcherism look
almost mainstream. True, the combination of minimalism about the
economic and welfare responsibilities of government with a commitment to the nation-state that is sometimes indistinguishable from
xenophobia is an authentic development of Thatcherite themes. But
the radicals of today's Tory Right take the implications for policy of
these themes further than Thatcher herself ever did when she was
still in office. In Britain's relations with Europe, the subtext of this
New Right agenda is a threat of withdrawal from the European
Union if a British attempt to renegotiate membership were to fail. In
domestic policy, it means following the lead of the American Right
and embracing the poisonous politics of family values – with which
Redwood flirted in 1993 in an attack on single mothers – and
populist tax cuts.

   This is an agenda for policy that turns its back on the concern for
social cohesion and institutional continuity that led liberal Tories –
Tories such as Butler, Boyle, Macleod, Macmillan and Heath – to
endorse the postwar settlement. It rejects entirely the European
project of a social market economy in favour of a form of British –
or, increasingly, though as yet *sotto voce*, English – exceptionalism.
It is, in effect, a Powellite agenda, whose dominance is likely to result
in a haemorrhage from the party akin to that of the Wets in the
eighties. Not only reformist liberal Toryism, but also the remnant of
the old patrician and paternalist Toryism – the traditional Conservatism of Whitelaw and Hurd – seem set to survive as an increasingly
marginal and impotent minority within the party. Leading Tories of
the centre and Left of the party, such as Kenneth Clarke and Michael
Heseltine, will find they have little alternative to accepting the terms
of the dominant free-market, nationalist tendency. The progressive
communitarian conservatism that survived as a tempering force
even in the Thatcherite eighties will be wiped out, as the examples
of Newt Gingrich's libertarian Contract for America and the resur-
gence from devastating electoral defeat of a Canadian Conservative
Party reconstructed on a Gingrichite model are deployed to support
an electoral strategy of right-wing radicalism.

   The political risks for the Conservative Party in adopting a radical
New Right policy agenda are, of course, colossal. Voter disillusion-
ment with the government in Britain has everything to do with
popular attachment to institutions such as the National Health
Service and with resentment at greed in the privatized utilities, and

nothing to do with rejection of the role of government itself. Again, fear of exclusion from the European Union will always be a far stronger electoral force than anger at the loss of sovereignty. If the Conservative Party emerges from the present leadership contest a party of the neo-liberal nationalist Right it will confirm that it has lost its grip on British political culture. The result could be a generation in opposition.

The strategic indecision of the Major years, in which the Conservative Party could not make up its collective mind whether it wanted to ditch the Thatcherite agenda or to deepen it, has been ended by a bold initiative from the Right. John Redwood's candidacy signifies more than a move in an internecine Tory power struggle. The endgame for One Nation Toryism – and, perhaps, for the Conservative Party as the party of government – has begun.

Guardian, 27 June 1995

14 Everyone a loser

Tomorrow's vote in the Tory leadership contest, in which a calculation of electoral self-interest will overwhelm every other consideration for nearly all Tory MPs, opens up Michael Heseltine's last chance of becoming Prime Minister. If the contest goes on to a second stage, it will be partly because enough of the small exclusionary electorate that decides this issue believes that Heseltine's political skills can still turn looming catastrophe for the Conservatives at the next general election into mere defeat. Heseltine's freedom from fixed political principles, his powers of rabble-rousing oratory and his mastery of the darker political arts are qualities that will attract Conservative MPs who are despairing of their party's prospects. It will not be Heseltine's position in the spectrum of Tory philosophy that moves them to such a gamble of desperation. It will be the conviction that he may well be their last chance to hold on to their seats.

Yet, even if a gamble on Heseltine were to pay off in terms of seats saved, a Heseltine premiership could not significantly weaken the Right's existing stranglehold on the government. It could do no more – at best – than stave off until after electoral defeat the next phase of conflict within the party, the upshot of which is likely to be its wholesale capture by the free-market nationalist Right.

Heseltine's singular political personality and career contain much that will commend him to those Conservative MPs who believe that a vote for John Major increases the risk to their seats, and more for the Right than is at first sight apparent. He can claim – and no doubt, if the opportunity arises, will claim – to have been a central figure in some of the most successful policies of early Thatcherism. His record during his time at the Ministry of the Environment of boosting the sale of council houses – and, for a while, the Conservative vote among their purchasers – can be invoked to show a commitment to the core Thatcherite ideal of a home-owning democracy. In present circumstances, that ideal could easily be translated into populist schemes for refloating the housing market, possibly on the back of an inflationary 'dash for growth' that would have the added appeal of wrecking the public finances of an incoming Labour government. Heseltine's relentless attacks on Labour unilateralism while at the Ministry of Defence exemplify a hard-headedness about national defence that is mainstream Tory. Indeed, he can maintain that he never belonged among the party's 'wet' liberal left – a claim that his more recent opposition to lowering the age of homosexual consent makes all too plausible. And, however bungled they may have been in practice, Heseltine's privatization initiatives on coal and the post office were calculated to win the approval of the Right.

The common Tory perception of Heseltine as a populist opportunist is, however, his greatest asset in the parliamentary party today. It has been strengthened by Friday's *Economist*/MORI poll which suggests that a Heseltine-led Tory party might lose over fifty fewer marginal seats than under any alternative leader. Yet Heseltine remains a high-risk option for the Tories. Does he not now have the public persona of a veteran of wars – about unilateralism, about industrial strategy – that most voters can barely remember? It is more than doubtful that Heseltine's incongruous combination of an antique and discredited Heathite corporatism with tactical concessions to the eighties privatization mania will inspire voters – especially despondent Tory voters – in the anxious nineties. And how could the intractable issue of Europe become any less disastrously divisive for the Tories under Heseltine's leadership? Even his formidable rhetorical skills cannot conceal the fact that closer European integration is one of the things Michael Heseltine has always believed in – and in his heart continues to support. Could Heseltine's value as an electoral asset survive the spectacle of yet worse Tory disunity on Europe?

It strains the imagination to envisage Heseltine having the capacity to end the parliamentary party's fratricidal divisions, when – however unfairly – many within it still hold him responsible for matricide. The political risk of Heseltine for the Conservative Party is that, more than perhaps any other senior Tory still in political life, he carries with him the burden of history. He is a perpetual reminder of the events to which the Tories' current divisions must all be traced.

The Conservatives' dilemma cannot be solved by Heseltine, since he is emblematic of the history by which they are imprisoned. In a delirium of panic and despair, Tory MPs may turn out John Major and opt for Heseltine as a last throw in political cynicism. They will not thereby cease to be a balkanized party whose warring factions already exhibit an oppositional culture and which – consciously or not – now yearns for the loss of power as a release from the responsibilities of government. It is only in opposition that the war declared by Thatcher and her followers on British conservatism's older and more moderate traditions – the One Nation Tories and the Christian Democrats – can be waged to a finish. Given the present balance of forces in the party, the likelihood then is of a transforma- tion of the Tory party into an anti-European party, but one whose closest affinities, ironically, are with the reactionary nationalist parties of continental Europe. In that event, however, the task of digging the party out of the electoral hole in which they will be buried by such a swing to the Right will fall to Conservatives of another generation. Whatever its upshot, the current leadership election will be remembered primarily as an episode in the Tories' ongoing disintegration as a party of government.

Guardian, 3 July 1995

15 Virtual democracy

In making its annual Congress accessible on-line and establishing a permanent presence on the Internet the TUC has set an example which other campaigning organizations, and all political parties, will be compelled to follow. One of the Internet's most pervasive spin-offs is the movement towards electronic forms of democracy. It is welcomed as a remedy for the alienation from traditional forms of political representation, and indeed from politicians, which has engendered powerful movements of protest and direct action on issues such as road-building and animal welfare. The decision by the

Labour Party to make its Brighton conference available on the Internet expresses the conviction – or hope – that embracing this new technology will enable it to tap into the youth culture that is at present dangerously estranged from all political institutions. It reflects another, more hard-headed belief – that the success in the United States of mavericks such as Newt Gingrich and Ross Perot, who have incorporated electronic democracy into the arsenal of populist political strategies, has lessons for political life in Britain.

The hope that electronic democracy will bridge the widening gulf between the political classes and an electorate which suspects that political elites are powerless in the issues that decide the quality of everyday life is a mirage. It is an example of a recurring illusion of our culture – that new technologies can transform our lives when political effort has failed. It expresses a misreading of the newer culture that is growing in Britain, which is as sceptical of technical fixes for social problems as it is of the efficacy, in current circumstances, of traditional sorts of political action. The political hopes now invested in the Internet suggest that its role in our culture is not that of a new technology – a spin-off from the combination of the personal computer and the telephone – so much as a new ideology.

The Internet ideology has its origins across the Atlantic, where conservatives are ranting missionaries for high technology, and it is left to a dwindling band of sceptical liberals to point out that the poor cannot eat laptops. In the United States, the Internet ideology is a familiar amalgam of techno-utopian futurism with libertarian anarchism which has deep roots in America's public culture of mistrust of government. Despite its distinctively American provenance, the Internet ideology has managed to find a niche in Britain, where it animates an intense subculture of users and enthusiasts. The recognizably American flavour of the Internet ideology may well account for the comparatively poor performance in Britain of its principal expression, the magazine *Wired*. It is impossible to avoid seeing the career of *Wired* so far as further evidence that the two cultures it straddles – British and American – are drifting apart. The Internet worldview to which *Wired* is dedicated is likely to remain highly marginal in Britain. This is not because of any superiority in scepticism or irony that the British like to claim for themselves, but because of an attachment we share with other European cultures to places and to earth-bound things – an attachment which the American-inspired Internet ideology rejects as repressive and atavistic.

The claims made by *Wired* for the Internet express hopes that are not dissimilar to those evoked by earlier advances in communications technology – such as television, the photocopier and the video recorder. These new technologies were imbued with the power to make tyranny unsustainable and democracy irresistible. Yet it is the unaccountability of the institutions that affect their daily lives, not the unavailability of video conferencing, that convinces people that traditional political parties no longer speak to them. Making these institutions answerable requires hard political work and a vigilant political culture – goods the Internet cannot supply.

The illusion that new communications technologies will work to renew democracy is not what is really distinctive in the Internet ideology. The freedoms that are central in the Internet worldview are not in fact political freedoms at all. They are freedoms from the constraints and limitations that go with living in delicate and endangered environments. Unlike the virtual communities of cyberspace, real human settlements are located in particular places, each with its own history and unique landscape. These local environments – for most of us, cities – are easily damaged or destroyed, and they are embedded in a global environment that human activity can now swiftly and irreversibly degrade. They are highly perishable structures which need constant repair if they are to be handed on intact to future generations.

The Internet ideology sees these local environments as restraints on our freedom. Its vision of a globalized culture is impatient with the civic and political duties incurred in sustaining local environments and communities. To be sure, there is no inherent reason why the new communications technologies cannot be harnessed to the service of environmental conservation. But the Internet worldview is inhospitable to the very idea that insuperable limits are imposed on human freedom by living in a fragile physical environment. It is even more resistant to the thought that we are defined by our histories and local attachments. The new virtual freedom offered by the Internet ideology is, in effect, freedom from these immemorial conditions of human life.

In Britain, the Internet culture seems likely to remain as marginal, and perhaps as ephemeral, as that which grew up around manned spaceflight. Already the sites of space missions evoke less interest than those of the Pyramids. Similarly, in much less than a generation, the Internet will provoke stifled yawns rather than passionate controversy. For all its aura of futuristic novelty, the Internet worldview harks back to a culture of technological optimism that – at least in Britain – is irretrievably dated.

The culture that is growing around us here, and which is expressed in new social movements of protest, is attuned to the beauty of mortal, earth-bound life. It is not hostile to technology but it is not tempted either by promises of yet another technological utopia. It prefers the hazards of making a home among mortal and imperilled things to the deathless safety of the ether. The vision of freedom from the world of everyday things conjured up in the Internet ideology is a sort of waking dream, in which constraints and obligations have melted away. This lucid dream of virtual freedom is at odds with the strongest current in the emerging public culture, which is a sense of the bonds which tie us to nature and each other.

The technologies of the Internet will be a permanent part of our lives from now on. No project could be more hopelessly utopian than a neo-Luddite attempt to stem their flow. Yet it is vital that our use of the new communications technologies should not be governed by the Internet ideology which presently surrounds them. We should reject the new freedoms that the missionaries of the Internet offer and commit ourselves instead to protecting the mundane freedoms we enjoy in our local environments. These freedoms – everyday freedoms to walk the streets without fear as well as democratic freedoms to challenge the increasingly anonymous institutions that rule our lives – are everywhere at risk.

Guardian, 15 September 1995

16 Culture of containment

The Conservatives have always represented themselves as guardians of law and order, but it is only in recent years that they have become the party of mass incarceration. In this, as in much else, they are following the example of the United States. A vast experiment is underway in America, as ambitious and as absurd as Prohibition. In the United States, incarceration is being used, on a scale unknown in any other democratic country, not as a last resort in the treatment of offenders but as virtually the only remaining institution which can stave off social breakdown. Through his speeches, his promised White Paper, and his studious excursions to view the American 'supermaximum' prisons, Michael Howard has made it clear beyond reasonable doubt that he regards the American model of incarceration as one which can and should be replicated in Britain.

In seeking to emulate the American experiment in mass incarceration the Conservatives are guided by a sure instinct. When social cohesion has been undermined by policies which promote free markets regardless of their impact on communities and families, the informal sanctions of public opinion cease to be effective restraints on criminal and anti-social behaviour, and only legal sanctions are left. Of these imprisonment, by excluding offenders from society altogether, is by far the most attractive to today's Conservatives. Since 1992 Britain's prison population has risen by nearly 30 per cent (with results for overcrowding and discipline about which prison officers have repeatedly complained). This expansion of Britain's prison population has occurred as a matter of policy, not as a result of an unexpected explosion in crime. When communities are derelict and families fractured, what remains that can hope to deter lawlessness aside from the threat of imprisonment? Here, as in the United States, the regime of unfettered markets is engendering a culture of incarceration as its primary defence against the disastrous consequences of the destruction of its core social institutions.

The American example is instructive as to what would be in store for us if Michael Howard's schemes were ever realized. At the end of 1994 just under five million Americans were under various forms of legal restraint, such as probation and parole. *A million and a half* of these were incarcerated in state, federal and local jails. In California prisoners already account for over 1 per cent of the population. A hugely disproportionate number of those imprisoned in every American state is made up of young black men. The number of Americans incarcerated is set to rise even further, as 'three strikes' laws are applied to habitual offenders, and new laws requiring inmates to serve the entirety of their sentences come into effect. By comparison, Britain's current prison population, even after its massive expansion since 1992, is around 52,400 – a figure that could rise by up to 20,000 if the Home Secretary's proposal to import American 'three strikes' laws were implemented. A curious and sad side-effect of America's experiment with imprisonment as a form of social engineering is the rapid ageing of the prison population, which – starting from a very low base of inmates over fifty years old – is generating an increasing number of penal geriatric wards, where lost and bewildered old people eke out the pitiful leavings of their lives. If these policies are replicated in Britain, can we look forward to the Tory Right arguing that expanding facilities for the aged and infirm in our prisons justifies further cuts in community care budgets?

To view America's Great Incarceration as primarily an error in penal policy would be a fundamental mistake. It is a logical response to the socially destabilizing consequences of revolutionary capitalism. The effect of the radical free market policies of the eighties was to break the frail bonds of community in urban America and abandon the people of the inner cities to their fates. The impact of Gingrichite policies in the nineties is to increase economic risk for virtually all Americans, while tearing away the welfare net which has afforded a measure of protection to the poorest and most vulnerable. 'Downsizing' or 'delayering' of corporations, in which whole strata of functions are stripped out, has increased job insecurity for millions at a time when the real hourly incomes of over two-thirds of Americans has been falling for nearly twenty years. In the current American economic climate, remaining in work requires tolerating a life of unceasing mobility and falling pay. At the same time, globalized competition is rendering a growing proportion of the American workforce economically superfluous even at poverty-level wages.

Crucially, Americans are exposed to this climate of chronic economic insecurity without the vital support provided, in Europe and in Asia, by functioning families and a fund of personal savings, which have been progressively eroded by the relentless demands of a 'flexible labour market'. The manifest effect of American revolutionary capitalism has been the 'delayering' of the core social institutions which undergird the economy – not the business corporation only, but increasingly also the city and, above all, the family. Where it has not been torn up, America's social and familial infrastructure has been allowed to rust and fall apart, as a burden which the unregulated market can no longer afford to carry.

In Britain, as in the United States, the delayering of social institutions by unrestrained markets and the emergence of a culture of incarceration go together. One result of New Right policies has been the exclusion from the productive economy of an ever larger proportion of families. In 1979 fewer than one in twelve British families had no working members, whereas today an astonishing one in five families is workless. Many of those in work earn too little to be able to found a family. Even when it does not create a workless underclass, revolutionary capitalism 'downsizes' families, by subjecting them to the pressures of declining incomes and incessant job mobility. This has happened in cities such as Swindon, where an American-style culture of mobility has emerged combining low levels of unemployment with very high levels of family breakdown. In such places we see New Right economic policies fostering a society of transients and strangers, in which every attachment and relationship is disposable, and enduring institutions, including the family, are unsustainable. We have here the central contradiction of New Right policy – between the destabilizing radicalism of market forces that have been emancipated from all political restraint and stable families and communities of any sort. It is because the regime of unfettered markets has broken up these core social institutions, on which the control of crime has always mainly depended, that it is now impelled to embark on the experiment in mass incarceration.

Locking up ever larger numbers of offenders is undoubtedly bad penal policy, and does little or nothing to control crime, but its significance extends far beyond our seething jails. It is a dark shadow cast by a dangerous utopia – the utopia of the free market. In Britain, new model prisons, built on an American design, duly privatized and administered by a Next Steps executive agency, are a fitting emblem of New Right policy in its final phase. When the Prime Minister talks of family values and old ladies bicycling across the village green, we will do well to remember America's waxing penal colonies, with their revamped chain-gangs and computer-monitored security systems, and their swelling population of superfluous souls.

Guardian, 20 November 1995

17 Close down the supermarket of nature

The conflict that is rending the League Against Cruel Sports signals what may prove to be an enduring shift in the conception of the relations of human beings with animals that animates our culture. Like the RSPCA and virtually every other animal welfare organization in Britain, the League Against Cruel Sports harbours rival groups, advancing policies and strategies which express divergent and conflicting philosophies. Increasingly, traditionalist campaigners for humane treatment of animals are being outflanked by more radical movements whose objectives encompass the liberation of animals from oppressive control by humans. This widening division within the animal welfare movement mirrors a larger and deeper cultural change, in which our inherited conviction of the privileged place of the human species in the scheme of things, which was a central element both in traditional religion and in Enlightenment humanism, is being abandoned, particularly by the young, and our impact on our fragile natural environment is beginning to condition the way we think about every other issue. A change of this magnitude is bound to have implications for political life which will be discomforting for cultural conservatives in all parties.

In this broader perspective the commotion in the League Against Cruel Sports is a small seismic shock, triggered by slow subterranean movements in British society. It is certainly not an issue merely to do with animal welfare. The League's most recent conflict was occasioned by remarks made by its Director, Jim Barrington, in *The Field*, the magazine catering for practitioners of blood sports, in which he appeared to soften the League's opposition to fox hunting. He maintained that banning fox hunting, rather than removing some of its cruellest practices, such as the use of terriers to dig out foxes, would create a disaffected class of country people, for whom the sport is a vehicle of their culture and tradition. This argument, which has a striking resemblance to many of the claims of the newly formed Countryside Movement, will persuade few in the current climate of British public debate. It exemplifies a sort of conservative multiculturalism, in which traditional practices that are abhorrent to the moral common sense of the great majority are defended as being integral to the way of life of a cultural minority. The political significance of a recourse by defenders of blood sports to a liberal rhetoric of minority rights which in the past they despised and ridiculed is that they perceive – correctly – that they can no longer hope for their pursuits to survive on the basis of any form of social deference. The vast economic changes of the Thatcher years have had, as one of their few benign unintended consequences, a transformation in the social composition of the Conservatives, such that even the Tory party can no longer be relied upon to stand up for traditions that are commonly identified with a defunct class culture. It is this change in the social make-up of the Conservative Party and in Britain as a whole, even more than the imminence of a Labour government, that dooms the defence of blood sports that Jim Barrington, the Countryside Movement and others have mounted. The advice given by his advisers to the Prince of Wales – if recent tabloid reports are to be believed – that he should consider giving up blood sports and definitely not be photographed initiating his son Harry into them, embodies a shrewd assessment of the risks of the monarchy's allying itself with a way of life that belongs in the past.

Fox hunting, like other blood sports, is a repellent practice that is no longer defensible. It should be banned. At the same time, blood sports are not by any measure our worst offence against the well-being of animals. They are only one aspect of our inherited relationship with other animal species against which Britain's emerging public culture has already decisively turned. We know from Gallup polls that 78 per cent of Britons are opposed to the transportation of animals in veal crates, and that over 50 per cent wish to see painful experimentation on animals prohibited. Moreover, public protests against the export of live animals have been among the most effective and successful forms of direct action for decades. These are not, as is often claimed, primarily manifestations of political estrangement, in which the blocked civic energy of people who can no longer identify themselves with the established political classes – the young, the excluded, and sections of angst-ridden Middle England – is directed at largely symbolic targets. They are signs of a real, and ongoing, redirection of public moral concern. We are witnessing a shift away from concern with other animal species and the natural environment as simply means to the satisfaction of human purposes to an appreciation of animals as creatures whose well-being matters independently of us, even though we are linked with them as interwoven strands in the web of life on earth.

Conventional thought of the sort that is still dominant in the major political parties views nature as a sort of supermarket, which it is prudent to keep well stocked. Policies of conservation, when they are considered at all, are understood as exercises in wise stewardship of an environment that exists to serve human ends. The well-being of animals, though it regularly swells the postbags of MPs, is seen as a humanitarian issue that is marginal to the main concerns of political life. This conventional and dated thinking is belied by the evidence of public opinion and by the conflicts and divisions that rack the leading animal welfare organizations. The fact is that it is the more radical groups within these organizations that are now more representative of public sentiment. This is not to say that the public supports the use of violence by extremist animal liberation movements, which plainly – and rightly – it does not. Nor does it mean that we are bound to accept theories of animal rights in which the straitjacket of contemporary legalism is stretched to embrace the lives of other species. What it does suggest is that the old anthropocentric view of the world which we inherit from Christianity and the Enlightenment, in which human interests have an automatic priority over those of all other living things, no longer animates the common ethical life in Britain. Instead, the public culture is informed increasingly by a concern for the renewal of the natural environment we share with other species, and by a fear that our collective impact on the earth may be degrading it irreversibly.

It is difficult to believe that these concerns will forever remain marginal to mainstream British politics. The passing of the inherited anthropocentric worldview, as a dominant element in our culture, inevitably affects the way we think about a host of other issues, from euthanasia and population policy to the control of new biotechnologies. Moving to policies that are more environment-friendly is rarely costless, and will sometimes call for hard choices. It is vital that these choices be the subject of informed political debate. As yet, however, in these issues, politicians lag far behind the public in both knowledge and concern. Unless our politicians learn to articulate our real public culture, in which concern for the environment and for the well-being of animals is a central concern, political life itself risks being ever more marginal for growing numbers of people.

Guardian, 19 December 1995

18　Labour in the wake of social democracy

The party that first formulates a post-Thatcherite project for Britain will set the political agenda for a generation. Yet it is only in the past year and a half that such a project has begun to acquire a definite shape. The profound changes in Britain's institutions and culture wrought by nearly two decades of Thatcherism have marginalized irreversibly the projects that contended with it in its heyday. The task facing Labour is not to salvage what it can from the wreckage. It is to shape an effective successor to Thatcherism, and forge a new political settlement in Britain. This cannot be done without bold policies which accept that the pre-Thatcher political settlement has gone for good.

The political fact of the age is the passing of social democracy. In concert with changes in the global economy and in technology, Thatcherite policies have wholly overthrown the social democratic policies in which Britain's postwar settlement was embodied. The experiences of Mitterrand's France in the early eighties and of Sweden in the early nineties suggest that any attempt to return to such policies would be interdicted by the international mobility of financial capital. British society has in any case changed far too deeply for such a reversion to be a real option. In practice – often no doubt unwittingly – Thatcherism was a modernizing project. Its effect has been to destroy the class culture of deference on which the British *ancien régime* rested. It is because this class culture exists no more in Britain that we can be sure that old-style One Nation Toryism – which in truth presupposes two nations, one practising *noblesse oblige* on the other – is now well into its endgame. These same changes have made the institutions of the paternalistic postwar welfare state, and the levels of taxation needed to support them, electorally unsustainable. The use of tax and welfare systems for purposes of egalitarian redistribution, which was a central strategy of social democratic governments in Britain and much of Europe, is now effectively precluded by voter resistance and by the global mobility of capital.

The facts and trends that rule out any return to pre-Thatcher 'normalcy' in Britain have undermined social democracy throughout Europe. The hope that social democracy can be revived at the level of European institutions is an illusion. The Rhine model of capitalism which was such a success in postwar Germany is buckling under the strain of unification and intensified global competition. This does not mean – as the New Right claims – that it must adopt the practices of American capitalism; it will doubtless renew itself in a changed form. What is true is that Britain cannot look for salvation from the extension of the Rhine model across Europe. It is not reasonable to expect the problems of the British economy to be solved by reshaping it – even if that were feasible – on a German model that is itself in flux and crisis. We have no option but to try to reform the variety of capitalism we inherit in Britain so as to make it more successful and friendlier to vital human needs.

The economic culture that will be inherited by a Labour government has been deformed by a neo-liberal policy of neglect. New Right policy was based on the idea that social cohesion was an automatic spin-off of economic success and fairness a dangerous delusion. The result of this policy has been a fractured and increasingly impoverished society. The lesson of Britain's ruinous experiment with New Right government is that there is in the long run no trade-off between economic efficiency and social cohesion.

Economic policies which neglect social cohesion do not work. Since 1979 the number of workless households in Britain, apart from pensioners, has risen from one in twelve to nearly one in five. This expanding 'underclass' of families excluded from the common life of society is substantially an artefact of New Right policies. These families are trapped in a neo-liberal dependency culture in which poverty and deskilling have been institutionalized. It would be a major error for Labour, inheriting such a legacy of neglect, to suppose that economic renewal can be achieved without deep reforms of the welfare state and education. The workings of a dynamic market economy will be accepted as fair by the public only if market exchange is curbed or excluded in many of our common institutions. The NHS should be rid of the fetish of market competition. It will not be trusted so long as its resources are allocated according to the accounting requirements of bureaucratic quasi-markets instead of judgements of medical needs.

In education, matching resources with common judgements of fairness has implications that will be deeply uncongenial for many social democrats. In a situation in which income inequalities have widened greatly, prohibiting or discouraging forms of meritocratic selection in state schools can only reproduce the two-nation education system which sets Britain apart from every other European country. The affluent minority will increasingly buy its children out of state schools, thereby reinforcing the symbiosis of a semi-defunct class culture with soft Left anti-elitism that has played such an unhealthy role in Britain's economic decline. Social democrats who reject meritocratic selection are colluding in a social distribution of skills and opportunities that is becoming unfairer by the day. They must recognize that there is a conflict of equalities – between their objective of greater equality of opportunity and their egalitarian opposition to selection in schools.

There is no *status quo ante* to which the welfare state can return. The result of New Right policy has been to make poverty more fearful and more hopeless, rather than to alleviate or prevent it. The long-term future for welfare institutions cannot be in shoring up the ruins of the Beveridge settlement. It must be in giving the principles of self-provision which Beveridge expressed a new embodiment. Though it has many features which cannot be replicated in Britain, the Central Provident Fund in Singapore is an instructive example of a scheme in which people make provision for their own needs through a common, state-administered institution in which they retain ownership of their individual contributions. Yet no such reform of the welfare state has a chance of working if it does not contain a credible successor to postwar full employment policies. Reintegrating the unemployed into the world of work will be the hardest test for any successor to Thatcherism and social democracy.

As it comes to a close, the New Right experiment in Britain has not left anything resembling a *status quo* that a Labour government could inherit. Instead it has destroyed the postwar settlement in both its economic and its constitutional dimensions – without putting anything in its place. The general election we are approaching is about more than a change of government. It is likely to signify a watershed in British politics deeper than that marked by Margaret Thatcher's victory in 1979. The difference is that the *ancien régime* that Thatcher inherited and appropriated then is now hollowed out and emptied of legitimacy. It is difficult to see how the legacy of neglect with which Labour will be confronted can be tackled successfully within the fragile structures of this half-demolished edifice. A key political condition of a stable post-Thatcher settlement is that the New Right be driven permanently to the margins of British politics. How can this be assured, so long as the Conservative Party remains a powerful national force, open to capture by its extremists in the wake of electoral defeat? A move from the present electoral arrangements to a more proportional system of representation would have as its most predictable result a decisive increase in the likelihood of a final split in the Conservative Party – thereby precluding, probably forever, the return of New Right government in Britain. The conclusion is inescapable. The precondition of an enduring post-Thatcherite political settlement is electoral reform.

Guardian, 29 January 1996

19 Nature bites back

The first crisis over the safety of British beef occurred within a month of the tenth anniversary of the explosions at Chernobyl. The two meltdowns that occurred on 26 April 1986, at the Chernobyl nuclear power station, seventy-two miles from the Ukrainian capital Kiev, created a mile-high plume of radioactive gas and particles whose fall-out was felt in countries as distant as Sweden and Greece. A large area around Chernobyl remains deserted and will be uninhabitable for several centuries. The long-term effects of this fall-out on human health and the natural environment are still not precisely calculable. They are undoubtedly highly significant. Official Soviet attempts to play down their seriousness were a key factor in fuelling the demands for *glasnost* (openness in government) and for Ukrainian independence which triggered the collapse of the Soviet Union itself.

The public health crisis that may result from links between BSE ('mad cow disease') and Creutzfeldt-Jakob Disease (CJD) in humans has repercussions and implications as profound as those of Chernobyl. It forces us to reconsider the culture of technological mastery of nature that we inherit from earlier ages. It compels us to question whether it is wise to go on treating nature – the earth, other species and even our human genetic inheritance – as merely a pool of resources to be exploited in the service of our present wants. Is it any longer acceptable that, whenever evidence surfaces of the riskiness of our interventions in natural processes, governments should consistently err on the side of technological optimism? Is there not now an overwhelming case for a genuinely conservative policy – one guided by prudence and respect for nature rather than groundless confidence in the powers of technology?

There can be little doubt that some of the responsibility for our current crisis falls on Thatcherite policies of deregulation which for much of the eighties allowed cattle to be fed meat rendered from sheep contaminated by scrapie. New Right policies rank long-term considerations of public health and the integrity of the environment a long way behind present risks to commercial profit. The immense power of the farming and food lobbies in Britain meant that neo-liberal policies in Britain in the eighties were bound to favour producer interests over public safety. In many ways the government's current predicament is a direct result of a fatal conflict between the power of these producer lobbies and an anti-government ideology committed to minimizing environmental risk. New Right thought scoffed at concern for the environment, denied the ecological responsibilities of government and aimed to privatize environmental risk by transferring responsibility to the market. In such a climate it was easy to confuse risks that are unquantifiable with risks that are insignificant. The risk to human health posed by the transmission of disease-bearing pathogens across animal species to the human species was not, and is not, exactly quantifiable; but, given the enormity of the danger posed by the possibility of an epidemic of CJD, it is not at all insignificant. During the Thatcherite period a policy of prudence, aiming to avoid or minimize such incalculable but catastrophic risks, never stood a chance of being adopted. The present threat to public health is probably only one of many malign inheritances of the eighties that we will have to cope with in the coming years.

It would nevertheless be a mistake to think that responsibility for the environmental dangers we are facing lies only with Thatcherism. A larger threat to human health arises from the hyper-industrialization of farming and from the technological hubris which pervades our entire culture. Farming today is an industry at the cutting edge of technological intervention in natural processes. It embodies, more even than much traditional manufacturing industry, the modern belief that the earth is made up of raw materials for human technological ingenuity to work on. Did it not occur to anyone that feeding animal protein to what nature has evolved to be a herbivorous species might be dangerous? Yet even such an act of folly is less hubristic than policies for the genetic engineering of animal species that are now on the scientific and commercial agenda. The industrialization of farming is only an incident in a much grander project of subduing nature to human designs. Is it altogether fanciful to see the threat of a major outbreak of CJD as a symptom of nature's rebellion against human hubris?

Much of our culture is still animated by the anthropocentric belief that the human species is independent of nature. This belief is at the root of some of the most admirable modern achievements. We have eradicated some infectious diseases and, in parts of the world, we have eliminated starvation and the worst forms of destitution. These successes have encouraged the expectation that the natural limits placed on us by scarcity and mortality can be progressively overcome. They support the conviction that there is no human problem that is not soluble by technological ingenuity. There are many signs that such hopes are hubristic. Tuberculosis and other infectious diseases are returning in forms that are highly resistant to antibiotics. Male fertility is declining, apparently as a consequence of changes we have made but not begun to understand in our everyday environment. The pursuit of intensive agriculture through the development of high-yielding crops has produced monocultures that are exceptionally vulnerable to disease. In these and other examples the modern project of constructing a technosphere in which the human species is freed from dependency upon the earth is coming up against limits imposed by nature. It is as if the earth itself were resisting our attempt to transform it into an adjunct of human purposes.

We cannot undo the technological progress of the past several centuries. Nor should we attempt to do so, since practically everything that is worthwhile in modern societies comes from their no longer living on the edge of subsistence – an achievement that only technological advance has made possible. The lesson to be drawn from the prospect of a CJD epidemic is not Luddism. It is that we must respect the natural world on which we depend more and invest fewer of our hopes in the project of transforming it by the use of technology. Farming practices which treat animals not as living creatures but as assemblages of manipulable genes and proteins must be reformed. Projects of genetic engineering that propose to alter species – including the human species – for the sake of commercial or even humanitarian benefit must be viewed with suspicion. The potential benefits of new technologies must always be weighed against their risks. We should be ready to err on the side of caution.

A genuinely conservative policy of this kind goes against the grain of much that is good in our culture. It is easily caricatured as unreasonably risk-averse. The evidence of recent history suggests that it is technological utopianism that is unreasonable. Unless we moderate our hopes of technology, the disasters of the past decade will be repeated, perhaps on a grander scale. It would be a sad commentary on the human capacity for learning from its mistakes if, ten years after Chernobyl, we were to fail to grasp the warning against human hubris that that disaster and the one that may be unfolding in Britain holds for us.

Guardian, 26 March 1996

20 Not with a bang

The Tory endgame has begun. The rejection by John Major, during Chancellor Kohl's visit to Britain in April 1996, of right-wing demands to rule out in advance Britain's joining a single European currency will be remembered as a defining moment in the undoing of Conservatism. The Prime Minister's remark that in a referendum on the subject a majority of the electorate would vote against joining is an admission that he is now hostage to his own party on this issue rather than an estimate of British public opinion. A leaked survey of members of the '92 Group' of Tory right-wingers disclosing that up to a hundred of them are preparing to fight the next general election on pledges to oppose a single European currency and institute a wide-ranging referendum on Britain's relations with the European Union suggests that the Conservative Party is nearing the brink of a historic split. John Major's strategy of bridging the divisions within his party on Europe has always been to hold to a policy of steadfast trimming and unalterable ambiguity. That strategy has already failed. The effect of Sir James Goldsmith's brilliantly executed political intervention can only be to accelerate a break-up of the Conservative coalition that is long overdue. Yet any split in the Tory party will be over much more than policy on Europe. It will be a parting of the ways between irreconcilably opposed kinds of right-wing thought and practice. It will signal unmistakably the end of anything resembling traditional Toryism. It will also mean the disintegration of the Tory political machine that has ruled Britain for most of the last 150 years.

Matters of political doctrine or history are far from the minds of Tory MPs at present. Electoral survival is the dominant concern, and sheer panic the prevailing emotion. Those who are proposing to campaign at the general election on a dissident Eurosceptic manifesto do so in a last effort to save their seats. Many hope by the threat of rebellion to force John Major and his Cabinet supporters to accept the terms of the Eurosceptic manifesto. This is a gamble of desperation based on the slenderest of calculations. There is probably no one who imagines that adopting a radically Eurosceptic agenda can now stave off defeat for the Conservatives. The objective of the right-wing rebels is to prevent a defeat they can no longer avert from becoming a full-scale catastrophe. They fear a cataclysmic wipe-out, followed by a decade or more in opposition, akin to that which engulfed the Tories in 1906 after Prime Minister Arthur Balfour failed to bridge their divisions over Tariff Reform. At the same time many right-wing rebels welcome defeat as a release from a party leadership which they despise and against which they have chafed since Mrs Thatcher was toppled in 1990. From that moment onwards the strategic interest of the Tory Right has favoured electoral defeat.

Since John Major's surprise victory in 1992, Conservative electoral defeat has actually been indispensable to the strategy of the Right, if only because another victory would make John Major unassailable. The risk of the Right's revolutionary defeatism is that it fosters in voters the perception that the Conservative Party has lost the will to rule and has itself become ungovernable. Once this belief is lodged in the public mind – as it was about Labour throughout the eighties – an electoral catastrophe is practically unavoidable.

The desperate calculations commonplace among Tory MPs today are not merely responses to the prospect of defeat. They are testimony to the collapse of the traditional Tory culture in which party loyalty was maintained for the sake of power. That has been supplanted by a culture of factionalism and ideological warfare. The Conservative coalition between One Nation Tories, whose overriding political goal is social stability, and neo-liberals, who elevate the free market above all other social institutions, has broken down. The intractable Conservative dispute over Europe is in part a symptom of this breakdown. But it is also an expression of the exhaustion of Conservative thought. None of the factions currently contending for control of the subsiding Tory wreck has serious answers to the questions that most trouble late modern Britain. How can the irreversible movement towards globalization be made friendlier to enduring human needs? How can the forces of creative destruction in the market economy be reconciled with social cohesion? Current Conservative thought has nothing useful to say about these dilemmas.

The Tory Right rejects the European Union as a fetter on the sovereign nation-state. It is also committed to a minimum government which does nothing to impede the workings of the unfettered global market. Right-wingers such as John Redwood have not yet perceived that national sovereignty means little when the economic policies of sovereign states can be vetoed by the free global movement of capital. Nor have they grasped that deregulated markets are potent solvents of traditional forms of social life. Last week's shabby manoeuvring over Lord Mackay's proposals to reform the law of divorce were partly early moves in the Tory succession struggle. They were also evidence that the Right has yet to understand that choice and change cannot be promoted throughout the economy but bottled up in family life. The remnants of the Tory Left are no less backward-looking. Their attachment to a Christian Democratic model of Europe contains no new thought on the problems facing European institutions. One Nation Tories have not yet engaged with the question of what the role of government should be in the wake of the demolition of the postwar settlement. They have not thought how to respond to effects of Thatcherism that are irreversible.

We should not expect that the Tories will split cleanly into two rival parties animated by clearly defined philosophies. A long period of bitter rivalries, internecine warfare and slow haemorrhaging of demoralized Conservatives MPs into other parties is a more plausible scenario. There will be an enduring shift of power within the main body of the Conservatives, as a result of which it becomes a thoroughly neo-liberal and nationalist party. Such a party is not electable in Britain – unless Labour too divides in the crucial area of its dealings with the European Union. The issue of EMU remains the most potentially unmanageable that has faced any British government since the Second World War. For that reason alone the Tory endgame is far from over. All we can be sure about is that it will not finish with a bang.

Guardian, 1 May 1996

10
BEGINNINGS

Tomorrow is easy, but today is uncharted.

John Ashberry, *Self-portrait in a Convex Mirror*

It is a commonplace that ours has become a culture of endings. We live amid the ruins of the projects of the modern age. They litter the landscape in which we must find our bearings. They stand in the way of any clear sight of the world as it is coming to be. The most unprecedented events of recent years are interpreted as stages on the way to worldwide modernity. We do not notice the obscure beginnings of a postmodern world, half-hidden in the shadows of modernity's failed projects. Understanding the present is made harder for us by unexamined inheritances from the past. We seek to comprehend the ambiguous interregnum between late modernity and the early postmodern period by invoking ways of thinking which belong to the modern world we are leaving. One such way of thinking is postmodernism. We will surely go astray if we take as our guide to the emerging postmodern world the *fin-de-siècle* poses of the postmodernists. They have nothing to teach us as to how we might learn to live in a world containing new limits on the hopes of progress that animated the modern age. We do better to risk thinking our way through the as yet unthought-of present.

I suspect that during the next few decades we will witness many surprising endings. We are ill prepared for a world that eludes the ways of thinking we inherit from the modern period. All the ruling schools of contemporary thinking expect modernization throughout the world to replicate the institutions and values of contemporary 'western' societies. They expect post-communist states to assimilate to western models that are already in flux and whose futures are themselves uncertain. They do not appear to have noticed the powerful anti-western movements that have arisen in long-established westernizing regimes such as those of Turkey and India. Or, if they have perceived these developments, they are explained as regressions or lapses from a historical tendency whose force remains inexorable. In these conventional expectations western thinking applies the Enlightenment philosophy of history that was held in common by Marx, Mill, Spencer and Hayek, in which western modernity was imagined to be the ultimate fate of all humankind. That philosophy does not help us to craft new institutions in which cultures that will remain fundamentally different can coexist in peace. It is, in effect, a programme for the universal adoption of semi-defunct modern institutions, such as the sovereign nation-state and the free market. It is an irony that the policies of western states should aim at integrating non-western societies into a modern world order at just the historical moment at which the dissolution of modernity's most distinctive beliefs and practices is unmistakably under way.

Consider the least expected historical transformation of our time – the Soviet collapse of 1989–91. In 'the West' (if 'the West' signifies anything now) the ruin of communist power has been interpreted as the triumph of 'democratic capitalism'.[1] Yet the disintegration of the Soviet Union was not – as triumphalist conservatives and neo-liberals sometimes appeared to believe – a success in western diplomacy or privatization policy. On the contrary, it was the spectacular failure in Russia and its dominions of a pre-eminently *western*, Enlightenment ideology. To think of the events that occurred in Russia during 1989–91 in the banal and deceptive terms of neo-conservative discourse, as the extension to Russia of 'western' values and institutions, is wholly to miss their radical novelty.[2] Those who do so fail to see both what has ended and what may be beginning in Russia. They do not see that, even as the Soviet collapse removed from the world one great western project for a universal civilization, it has also worked to speed a meltdown in western societies which derived whatever cultural identity they possessed from the perceived enmity of the Soviet Union. The result is that there is no stable world of western institutions or values into which post-communist societies could reasonably hope to be integrated. It is hard to think of a more delusive historical prospect than that of the Soviet collapse issuing, Fukuyama-fashion, in the universal adoption of 'western values'.

The beginnings of the world after the close of the modern age can already be discerned. We see them emerging from the shadows of modernity's failed projects. Yet these beginnings come to us obscured by traces from the past, one of which is postmodernism. The principal effect of postmodernist thinking has been to cloud our vision as we pass through the closure of the modern period. Most such thinking makes no real effort to theorize the present. It is animated by aspects of the central western intellectual tradition that are least useful, and indeed most dangerous, for us. One of these is universalism – the metaphysical faith that local western values are authoritative for all cultures and peoples. This western faith was expressed in the Socratic project of the examined life, in the Christian commitment to a redemption for all humankind, and in the Enlightenment project of progress towards a universal human civilization. It is foundational in the central intellectual tradition of 'western' societies – a tradition that is renewed in the postmodernist project of deconstructing cultures everywhere. In supposing that a postmodern condition is the historical fate of all societies, postmodernists cling to a westernizing narrative of modernity. The truth is that the fracturing of worldview that typifies late modern western societies presupposes a deep-seated cultural commitment to universal truth. In societies that have never harboured such a commitment, such as Japan, perspectivism is not a manifestation of cultural crisis. It is a natural way of looking at the world. Equally, it is only in decaying universalist regimes, such as the United States, that 'relativism' becomes an incurable local malady. Postmodernist thinking prevents us from seeing that modernity is an incident in one or a few histories, not in an illusive universal history.

Another inheritance from the central western tradition is humanism. Postmodernist thought consecrates, and thereby shelters from questioning, the peculiar hopes and illusions of humanism, which promises the domestication of nature by a single, universal civilization. Postmodernists understand the natural world as a cultural construction. Of course, postmodernists are entirely justified in rejecting the fundamentalist understanding of science, in which it is a mirror of nature. They are right to insist that there is not one way in which the world must be represented, and to deny that scientific inquiry is the supreme arbiter of all forms of human knowledge. But there are many ways the world cannot be represented, and human thought cannot alter these. Such limits on how the world can faithfully be captured by human thinking are denied by postmodernist representations of nature (including human nature) as altogether a cultural construction. The earth is then seen as an extension of human consciousness and activity, not an ultimate constraint on the life of humans and other animal species. Thus is replicated an ancient western humanist tradition that is now long outworn.

A humanist conception of the relations of humankind with the earth, and of humankind itself, is one in which humans are privileged over other animals in their place in the world as unique sites of truth, meaning and value. All major western faiths and ideologies – and, in this respect, Islam belongs with 'the West' – are varieties of humanism. All of them – Christianity, Marxism, the manifold kinds of liberalism, the positivist faith of scientific fundamentalists – think of humans as being not merely the currently dominant animal species. They all sanctify some human activity – be it that of religious worship, philosophy or scientific inquiry – as enabling humans to transcend the constraints of their animal ancestry. They all think of the earth as a resource in the service of the human enterprise – be it as an instrument for the achievement of human emancipation or as a site for the embodiment of distinctively personal values. This is an integral feature of 'western civilization', in its intermingled Graeco-Roman and Judaeo-Christian traditions, whether or not that civilization remains explicitly theistic.

A humanist self-understanding is primordial in the western intellectual tradition. It is peculiarly ill-suited to the realities and dilemmas of the emerging postmodern age. It has nothing in it of the sense of limits that is vital if we are to live in balance with the earth and in peace with one another. In the decisive area of our relations with our natural environment postmodernist thinking contains nothing which counteracts human hubris. Postmodernism is humanism in a late and radical form: it understands the natural world as an artefact of human thought. The limits that are imposed on our powers and hopes by the dependency on the earth of humans and other animal species are denied. The earth has no life of its own that might overthrow the hubris of its briefly dominant animal species. For postmodernists, the changing face of nature is a mirror-image of human thought and activity, not an independent reality. Nor, within postmodernism, is there such a thing as human nature.[3] We are what we imagine ourselves to be. Unlike any other animal species, we are free to deconstruct and reinvent ourselves, endlessly and without limit. We are not, as all other animals clearly are, ephemeral parasites lodged in the skin of our planetary host.

We are a self-creating species, whose links with the earth can be broken, and forged anew, by human will and the growth of scientific knowledge. We are in no sense unalterably bound by our evolutionary and our historical pasts. We can embody any cultural or political forms that we are able to envisage. The only limits imposed on human hopes are those arising from the poverty of human imagination. The natural limits of life on earth are acknowledged, if at all, only to be transcended, by new technologies which make of the earth an object of human will. Scarcity, contingency and mortality are not marks of finitude in ourselves and the earth. They are obstacles to be overcome. Our histories impose no insuperable limitations on human ambitions. By exercising our will and imagination, we can – in this postmodernist fantasy – rid ourselves of the burdens of the past.

Such a way of thinking cannot help us to coexist in peace despite our irresolvable differences. It cannot address the real need of the postmodern age, which is for common institutions within which different cultures, communities and ways of life can coexist in peace. Instead we are encouraged to hope for a world in which all our (conflicting) hopes can be satisfied. This is the humanist phantasmagoria that postmodernists renew. Its chief effect is to block our understanding of what is truly novel in the beginnings of the postmodern period. Humanist ideas continue to animate nearly all currents of contemporary thought, not only postmodernism. They undergird the failing political projects which narrow and darken the horizons of late modern societies throughout the world.[4] We will begin to understand our circumstances and prospects as we enter early postmodernity, and perhaps cope with them a little better, once we shed the projects that humanism has underpinned. In our historical context the political projects of modernity, whether of the Left or the Right, are irrelevant or inimical to our needs. To be sure, we cannot shed our histories, in which these projects have lately been central. We can learn to think of such projects as belonging to a past whose burdens we cannot be rid of but which we can perhaps hope to lighten.

The Left project of universal emancipation in a cosmopolitan civilization is at odds with an age when authority has drained away from Eurocentric Enlightenment ideologies and in which non-Occidental cultures are asserting their differences from us and each other. Moreover the emancipatory project of the Left is inimical to the limits set for human hopes by humankind's place in the natural world. At the same time the projects of the Right are all of them debris of modernity. The goal of making the world safe for 'democratic capitalism', which is the mission of the American Right and of the New Right everywhere,[5] is a survival from the early modern period. The New Right's objective of an unfettered global market is an anachronistic reinvention of the *laissez-faire* project of the mid-nineteenth century. Like the sovereign nation-state, the free market is one of the most prototypically modernist of political constructions, and a subverter of every kind of traditional community. Confronted with the dissolution of traditional communities by free markets, conservative thought in our time has become a rehearsal of nineteenth-century liberalism in its most primitive form. Along with other confections of the American ideology, globalized democratic capitalism is an atavistic hybrid of the Enlightenment with Pelagian Christianity. It is the late modern humanist consensus in its most banalized form. Ecologism, one of the strands of current thinking that imagines itself to be least in thrall to conventional thinking and the past, contains no alternative to this humanist consensus. In all its standard varieties, Green theory remains a pot-pourri of Enlightenment hopes and Romantic nostalgias. In political thought we are far from the time of endings and beginnings in which we live. We are ruled by defunct modern utopias.

There is little political thought today that struggles to understand the present. There seems to be no political project which acknowledges that the modern age, with its ruling illusions of the conquest of nature and progress towards a universal civilization, has truly come to an end. Postmodernism is not an effort to understand the present but a projection of Enlightenment hopes and fears that belong to the past. All contemporary political thinking is a variation on the Enlightenment project or on Romantic or fundamentalist reactions to it. What we most need, however, is to put the Enlightenment behind us, and view it, as we view the Renaissance or the Reformation, from a perspective of historical distance. Only then can we accept that all Enlightenment projects have by now become dead ends.

Nature, science and the ends of progress

Progress celebrates Pyrrhic victories over nature. Progress makes purses out of human skin.

Karl Kraus, *Half-truths and One-and-a-half-truths*

One aspect of our condition is given by the limits imposed on human activity by the earth itself. The expansion of human populations, together with the spread of industrial technologies the world over, is already altering the earth's climate in ways that threaten serious disruption to human economic and social life, and which endanger the well-being of many other species. The likelihood may already be that stability for the biosphere can now be reached only by a catastrophic reduction in human numbers. Yet, though it has often been given to apocalyptic speculation, standard Green thought consistently represses the possibility that contemporary conceptions of progress can come into ultimate conflict with the conditions of stability for the biosphere as a whole. Accepting that possibility subverts the humanist tenet that the progress of our species cannot threaten the integrity of the earth. It is time to question this humanist axiom.

There is no pre-established harmony between human well-being and the conservation of the earth. To utter this forbidden truth is to go against the mainstream of environmental and ecological thought. Conventional Green thinking affirms that there can be no ultimate conflict between the interests of the human species and the integrity of the natural environment. It is not difficult to see why mainstream ecological thinking should adopt this position. In all its standard varieties Green thought is a species of Enlightenment humanism. The project by which it is animated is universal human emancipation, not conservation of the natural environment which humans share with other species. The possibility that these two projects might not always coincide in their implications for practice is too threatening to be contemplated by most ecological thinkers. A conflict between them might easily create dilemmas that are insoluble. There is little utility for practical men and women in observing that the demands of human well-being may be at odds with those of other animal species. After all, public policy is formed and implemented by human beings. No measure that does not promise a benefit to humans is likely to gain a hearing.

If there can be an ultimate divergence between human interests and the protection of the earth, then the cause of the earth may well be already lost. Since humans now dominate the environment in which every other species must struggle to survive, their interests will inevitably displace those of these other species whenever there is a conflict. Of course this does not mean that human well-being will thereby be promoted. The extinction of countless other species by the growth of human populations may well presage the extinction of the human species. That is the conclusion of Richard Leakey, when he considers the effect that humans have had in bringing about a sixth vast extinction of species. The human species is already living on the borrowed time of 'extinction debt'. If – as seems entirely plausible – Leakey's argument is well founded, then we may have already reached the end of the human enterprise. The integrity of the earth may, perhaps, be preserved, but only at the cost of catastrophe for humans. In that case the End anticipated by apocalyptic thinkers among the Greens has already occurred; but almost no one has noticed.

These are, perhaps, rather desolate conclusions. Yet exploring the prospects they open up may not be a wholly useless exercise. If there is a divergence between human well-being and the integrity of the earth, it is at least imaginable that it could be narrowed by intelligent policy. For such policy to be even a remote possibility, however, the forbidden thought that human ambitions may conflict with the integrity of the environment must be pursued to the end. When we do this, we do not find much comfort in our reflections. But we do rid ourselves of humanist attachments that cloud clear thinking about our relations with other animals and with the earth. Such humanist attachments can do nothing to diminish the danger to the earth which humans, together with countless other species with which we share it, finally depend on for their survival and flourishing.

The dominant currents of contemporary thought about environmental matters have as their end-products utopian schemes in which human hopes of progress are met at the cost of subordinating the entire planet to human management. All such visions of planetary management are delusive. They presuppose institutions of global governance and sources of cultural wisdom that do not exist. As James Lovelock well puts it, 'From a Gaian perspective, all attempts to rationalize a subjugated biosphere with man in charge are as doomed to failure as the similar concept of benevolent colonialism. They all assume that man is the possessor of this planet, if not the owner, then the tenant.'[6] In practice, the management or stewardship of the earth's resources by global institutions would probably generate ecological devastation even worse than the random destruction of species, environments and human cultures that the earth presently suffers. Any divergence between the requirements of environmental stability and humanist aspirations would be settled, infallibly, in favour of the latter. That is the logic of planetary management. The earth becomes an instrument of human hopes. Nature can, and should be, unmade and remade by humans. We are not then far from the hideous project of humanizing nature which was central in classical Marxism and which functioned as the doctrinal inspiration of the Soviet ecocide.[7] This same project remains integral both to the liberal Enlightenment project, and to postmodernism.

If we shed humanist hopes we will not look to ideal social institutions, in which the earth is made an object of human will and hopes. We will instead think afresh on how the impact of human activity on other species and on the earth which we share with them can be moderated. This does not mean sacrificing human well-being whenever it conflicts with that of other life-forms. It means crafting policies and institutions whereby that conflict can be avoided or moderated. Many, though by no means all, modern hopes of progress are in principle achievable, *provided human numbers are reduced and there is a large-scale switch to low-impact technologies.* Consider agriculture – one of the greatest and most commonly neglected threats to the ecosphere.[8] We need to cultivate the earth to yield food for human populations. This entails, inexorably, the use for human purposes of some of the earth's soil, flora and fauna. It does not entail making the earth an object of a perilous biological experiment on whose outcome the human food supply then depends. It need not mean imposing on animals the untold suffering that accompanies a thoroughly unnatural lifestyle. It certainly need not encompass dangerous genetic interventions in plant and animal life, whose medium-term effect is to necessitate further interventions so as to maintain hyperproductivity and stave off new diseases, which is the trap in which the Green Revolution in farming has caught us.[9] The appeal of technical fixes such as the Green Revolution lay in their combination of scientific optimism with apparent cost-effectiveness. Yet we could feed human populations, more dependably and with a far lighter environmental impact, through modes of semi-organic farming that are less technology-intensive than our current hyper-industrialized agri-businesses. This is only one example of many that could be given, in which we can alleviate the human lot by the use of gentler and more earth-friendly technologies.

We can better the human lot by such means, however, only if we are readier to be proactive in controlling the growth of human populations. The greatest danger by far to the earth and to the non-human life-forms which it sustains comes from uncontrolled human population growth. Of course, nearly all contemporary thinking denies the reality of a human population problem. Or else, in line with Enlightenment humanism, it asserts that that problem is wholly soluble by reforms of unjust social institutions and practices. Thus, it is claimed that improvements in the economic circumstances of women, enhanced control by women of their own fertility, and a reduction in economic insecurity of families will together produce a benign 'demographic transition'. The background assumption of such claims is that the resulting level of human population will be indefinitely sustainable. It is assumed that the level of human population arising from family planning – the control by women of their fertility so as to limit their offspring in accordance with their and their partner's wishes – will coincide with the optimum number that is the goal of population policy. Nothing supports this assumption. It is merely the general humanist axiom that human welfare and the integrity of the earth cannot fundamentally diverge, applied in the crucial area of human numbers.

It is better to acknowledge candidly, with Garrett Hardin[10] and a handful of others, that family planning and population control are different enterprises. In many important contexts they will coincide or overlap. Policies enabling women to control their own fertility through unrestricted access to contraception and abortion, together with policies enabling people to exercise choice over the manner of their death by voluntary euthanasia, are mandated by concern for human well-being. They are also, in virtually all real-world contexts, policies that lessen the destructive impact of human numbers on other animal species and the earth. But they are highly unlikely to be sufficient to diminish human population growth so that the environmental impact of the species is indefinitely sustainable. (This is true, whatever the optimum human population turns out to be.) A concern for other species and for the biosphere as ends in themselves, and not merely as resources for human welfare, mandates policies for the control of human numbers. Such policies are justified, also, in that it is only a smaller human population than that which exists even now which can reasonably hope for a sustainably higher quality of life.

Policies for the control of population are opposed by religious fundamentalists of all stripes. They are also rejected by humanists – such as Karl Marx, Herbert Spencer, F. A. Hayek, and their many latter-day followers – who subscribe to the modern faith that human technological virtuosity will always outrun the depletion of natural resources. (John Stuart Mill is a magnificent exception among humanists in that he always recognized that his hopes of progress for the human species depended on control of its numbers. Moreover, with splendid disregard for his official utilitarian theory of value, he accorded intrinsic worth to wilderness.)[11] In their common anthropocentrism followers of the Enlightenment and religious fundamentalists are at one. At present it can reasonably be judged that no significant body of opinion exists anywhere which favours controlling human population for the sake of preserving the other forms of life with which we share the planet.

Nor, if scientific naturalism gives us a sound account of the human animal, should this be particularly surprising. Darwinian theory gives little support to the hope that human populations will act to control their numbers. The belief that humans will limit the growth of their populations in order to protect other species expresses a humanist rather than a Darwinian understanding of human possibilities. There is a sharp dissonance between the understanding of human behaviour given by Darwinian theory and the pre-Darwinian conception of humankind preserved in Enlightenment humanism. In its application to population policy, the clear implication of the Darwinian view is that the issue will be decided by classical Malthusian means. This is the view of Angus Martin, one of the few writers on ecological matters to have taken the Darwinian view of humankind to its end:

> Man is an animal. Perhaps we can now appreciate more fully the significance of that statement. Population growth in man stems from two factors. One (which he shares with all other animals) is that natural selection favours the individuals who rear the most offspring: those who achieve the greatest overproduction. The second, which is unique to him, is that his overproduction lives and reproduces because of his temporary control of mortality rates. The rest of the story is merely one of waiting for mortality to catch up.[12]

Yet, even working through Malthusian checks, a Gaian correction probably cannot prevent further irreparable damage to the earth by human activity.

The fate of science as a cultural institution in late modern societies seems to be to reinforce the instrumental understanding of humankind's relations with the earth. In pre-scientific, traditional cultures, a balanced relationship with the environment was sustained by animist practices in which the unity of humans with other animals and with the earth was affirmed. The impact of modern science, as of Christianity, has been to destroy such traditional beliefs and practices. Moreover, once gone, an animist relationship with nature cannot be recovered. The fatal gift of modern science is a disenchanted vision of the world. Such a vision carries with it an irretrievable cultural loss. It also removes, without replacing, pre-scientific cultural constraints on the human exploitation of nature. The impact of science as the sole remaining authoritative cultural institution in late modern societies is to reinforce the fusion of nihilism with humanism which is their real animating world-view.

To be sure, this is rarely a conscious project of scientific ideologues. Their understanding of science is primitive, and indeed pre-scientific. The conception of science favoured by an ideologue of science such as Richard Dawkins is patently pre-Darwinian. A Darwinian perspective would suggest that the growth of science is to be explained in terms of the increase in control of the environment it allows our species, rather than in the Platonistic, Christian and humanist terms of a search for truth. Scientific fundamentalists combine a formulaic adherence to neo-Darwinian orthodoxy with the Enlightenment faith that scientific knowledge can enable humankind to remake the jerry-built edifice of human society. Yet a consistent Darwinian naturalism undermines all such possibilities.

This is a dissonance that even the subtlest Darwinian thinkers have found irresolvable. Jacques Monod has written that if humankind accepts the message of science, 'man must at last awake out of his millenary dream and discover his total solitude, his fundamental isolation. He must realize that, like a gypsy, he lives on the boundary of an alien world; a world that is deaf to his music, and as indifferent to his hopes as it is to his suffering or his crimes.'[13] Yet Monod, too, writes as if humankind – perhaps exercising the freedom of will ascribed to it in religious worldviews which science has undermined – could *choose* to pursue truth. Correctly enough, he notes that 'The "liberal" societies of the West still pay lip-service to, and present as a basis for morality, a disgusting farrago of Judeo-Christian morality, scientific progressism, belief in the "natural" rights of man, and utilitarian pragmatism.' Yet Monod goes on to defend an 'ethic of knowledge' – a commitment to truth as revealed by science, which he connects, somewhat obscurely, with socialism. This is, in effect, humanism without foundations; at any event it is very dubiously consistent with the radically mechanistic and reductionist account of humankind that Monod derives from Darwinism, and which he himself devoutly defends.[14]

In a line argument similar to Monod's, E. O. Wilson has observed, no doubt correctly, that 'the final decisive edge enjoyed by scientific naturalism will come from its ability to explain traditional religion as a wholly material phenomenon.'[15] He does not consider how a rigorously naturalistic understanding of human activity would apply to science. It seems that his view of science, and thereby of humankind, is the humanist, metaphysical and ultimately religious one that scientific naturalism itself overthrows. Here Nietzsche's question is apt:

> the question, Why is there science? leads back to the moral problem: What in general is the purpose of morality, if life, nature and history are 'non-moral'? . . . it is always a metaphysical belief on which our belief in science rests . . . the godless and anti-metaphysical still take our fire from the conflagration kindled by a belief a millennium old, the Christian belief, which was also the belief of Plato, that God is truth, that the truth is divine.[16]

The view of scientific fundamentalists, that science enables uniquely privileged access to the truth about the world, belongs with this metaphysical and religious faith. It is difficult to reconcile with the results of scientific inquiry, such as Darwinism. In a consistently Darwinian perspective, science will seek truth only insofar as truth serves human interests – especially the interests in survival and pragmatic control of the environment. Like much else in Enlightenment humanism, the fundamentalist view of science is self-undermining. It is undermined by scientific inquiry itself.

Writing before the formulation of the Gaia hypothesis, the gambler and conservationist John Aspinall observed that perhaps only a Gaian correction in human numbers can preserve what is left of the non-human earth: 'Some of us are now driven to believe that a demo-catastrophe will be an eco-bonanza. In other words, a population readjustment on a planetary scale from 4,000 million to something in the nature of 200 million would be the only possible solution for the survival of our own species and the eco-system that nurtured us . . .' He sees that such a 'demo-catastrophe' might well carry with it much of the earth's non-human populations:

> The next great death might last a millennium but during it, and indeed before it, who knows how many genera of plant and bird and beast would be swept away? The followers of Gautama Buddha, the Judaeo-Christians, the disciples of Mohammed and Marx can all look forward to some distant chiliad, but not the earth-lovers. The question that faces them is eschatological. What will be left? The surviving world must be a diminished world; at its worst, in apocalyptic, irreversible decline; at its best, one savagely mutilated, even dismembered.

Aspinall concludes: 'Medical research should be funded into abortion, infanticide, euthanasia and birth control . . . The choice before us is a qualitative life for 200,000,000 humans in perpetuity in a partially restored paradise, or a quantitative countdown to Armageddon on a raped planet gutted of most of its resources. That we still have a choice or a chance may itself be an illusion.'[17]

The merit of Aspinall's view is that it understands a commitment to the earth to be a wager. Nothing in our scientific knowledge of humankind underwrites such a gamble. Policies which aim to protect the things of the earth as ends in themselves go against the grain of some of humankind's strongest biological imperatives. This does not mean that a commitment to the earth has no ground in the nature of humans. It may express the human need for contact with the non-human world which E. O. Wilson has called *biophilia*.[18] This is the need that is met by relationships with animals, by encounters with wilderness and by the attempts of many urban people to recreate a little countryside in their lives. It is, of course, only one human need, easily displaced from urgency by the insistent claims of other needs with a more direct connection with survival, and often dulled by long civilization. A post-humanist agenda for the conservation of the earth is, in effect, a wager on this human need.

Such a wager is more than likely a losing bet. The likelihood must be that the unmaking of nature by humans will not be prevented by human thought or activity but by nature itself. It will be averted, if at all, by a Gaian correction of the place of humankind among other forms of life on earth. The significance of the idea of Gaia in this connection is as a scientific-mythopoeic statement of humankind's utter dependency on the web of life on earth. As Lovelock has put it,

> Gaia, as I see her, is no doting mother tolerant of misdemeanours, nor is she some fragile and delicate damsel in danger from brutal mankind. She is stern and tough, always keeping the world warm and comfortable for those who obey the rules, but ruthless in her destruction of those who transgress. Her unconscious goal is a planet fit for life. If humans stand in the way of this, we shall be eliminated with as little pity as would be shown by the micro-brain of an intercontinental missile in full flight to its target.[19]

Lovelock's statement captures the central ethical content of the Gaian perspective. Gaia is not a replacement for theistic conceptions of providence but an alternative to them. Because Gaia concerns itself with the renewal of life on earth it can have no special concern for humankind.

It is important to note that the central conception of the Gaian perspective, which is that the biosphere can be understood as a single living planetary organism, can be stated in rigorously reductionist terms.[20] Gaia is a mythic image, to be sure; but that does not mean it is reducible to myth – it is also a scientific hypothesis. The Gaian perspective is the most potent antidote within late modern culture to the hubris of humanism. It derives its power, partly, from its origins within science. It opens up a perspective on life on earth, fully compatible with science and indeed derived from scientific inquiry, in which anthropocentrism is overcome. If it does not mark an end of humanism, the Gaian perspective at least establishes an alternative to humanist thinking in late modern cultures. Amongst us, humanism survives, not as a living tradition, but as a deadweight on new thought. Once the burdensome hopes of humanism are at last relinquished, what becomes of modern understandings of progress?

Post-humanism and the illusion of the End

> Do not expect too much of the end of the world.
> *Old Polish saying*

The goal of moderating the environmental impact of humans on the earth, while striving to render human life more tolerable to humans themselves, is the only project which truly overcomes anthropocentrism. It is a natural successor to humanism in all its manifestations, including standard Green thought. By anthropocentrism I understand the view that only the welfare of humans, and of other entities possessing human-like qualities of personality or consciousness, has ultimate or intrinsic value. Humanism is the ethical and political project that flows from this view. If anthropocentrism is defensible at all, it is only in the context of religious worldviews of a particular type. In Christian theism, persons are sites of intrinsic value because they partake of the nature of the divine, which is also a person and the source of all that has value in the world. All western religions, and some Graeco-Roman philosophies such as Stoicism, are anthropocentric in their conception of value. Non-Occidental religions depart from anthropocentrism in varying degrees. Buddhism affirms the value of all sentient life but ranks living things in a hierarchy in which liberation can be achieved only by humans. Hinduism, Bon and Shinto largely reject any such hierarchy. Only some kinds of Taoism appear to avoid anthropocentrism entirely and unequivocally, though there are many varieties of shamanism which it is difficult to assess.[21]

In western traditions, anthropocentrism has a point of origin in Greek logocentrism. From Parmenides and (perhaps) Heraclitus onwards, though not in the ancient pre-philosophical ways of thinking reflected in Homer, the central stream of Greek philosophy understood thinking and being, human reason and the order of things in the world, as mirrors of one another. Western anthropocentrism has another source in Hebraic traditions, in which the earth is given over to humans for dominion or stewardship. In both these traditions, the earth is valueless in the absence of human agents. In modern philosophy, the Kantian conception of persons as members of a kingdom of ends and as sources of what is of value in the world is scarcely intelligible outside its historical context in Christian humanism. Subjectivism in ethics is best understood as anthropocentrism in a modern, sceptical guise. A prime exemplar of modern anthropocentrism is Hobbes, for whom value is only human desiring. For Hobbes it is not that we respond to what has value in the world, but rather that by desiring we project value onto a worthless world.[22] In this subjectivist perspective, which is found in Hume and Nietzsche, value is an artefact of human agency. It is hard to see how such a subjectivist view could ever have arisen except in a cultural context, such as that of traditional Christendom, in which personal agents, divine and human, were privileged as sources of value.

The final metaphysical source of humanism in all its varieties is the anthropocentric belief that humans have unique value in that they alone among animal species partake of the nature of the divine. Modern secular humanisms, liberal or postmodernist, Millian, Marxian or Nietzschean, are only long shadows cast by the passing of Christianity. In Christian metaphysics, as in all forms of theism, it is only personality, agency or consciousness that confers value on a valueless world. The world has meaning only because it is suffused by personhood. A world without persons, human or divine, would be an empty world. It follows inexorably that everything other than persons has only instrumental value. The earth with its plenitude of life-forms is a site of value only insofar as it serves the purposes of personal agents. The earth serves the human enterprise, even as humankind serves divine providence. This anthropocentric religious worldview pervades all forms of humanism, including those – such as Marxism and the contemporary orthodoxies of scientific fundamentalism – which consider themselves to be radically secular. In late modern cultures it is only the Gaian perspective, within which it is life rather than agency or sentience which is the central criterion of value, that stands outside this anthropocentric and subjectivist tradition.

Green thinking is anthropocentric in all its standard varieties. It represses the possibility that human emancipation and the conservation of the earth may come into conflict with one another. The harmful effects of human activities on many other living things, and on the biosphere as a whole, cannot easily be denied; but within the dominant humanist current of Green thinking they are attributed solely to defects in human institutions. Remedies for these flaws in human social institutions will remove the causes of humankind's destructive impact on the earth. Once capitalism, social injustice, colonialism and the oppression of women have been removed, the relations of the human species with its natural environment will be harmonious. Nothing will then stand in the way of a human relationship with the earth that is indefinitely sustainable. The emancipation of humankind from these age-old evils solves most environmental problems, and renders the remainder eminently manageable. The emancipation of the human species from political and economic constraints will effectively guarantee the well-being of the other forms of life with which we share the earth. For this conventional wisdom within Green theory, Enlightenment hopes of emancipation and the conservation of the earth meet in a happy serendipity.

Such a coincidence is a mirage of western humanism. It is not a reality of any enduring kind. The truth of the matter is very nearly the opposite. A commitment to the earth entails a large deflation of human hopes. Accepting the limits on human activities implied by such a commitment demands radical revisions in modern conceptions of progress. To be sure, revising the modern understanding of progress need not, in and of itself, mean relinquishing the idea of progress itself. Yet, if we follow through the implications of a commitment to the earth, many hopes of progress will need to be given up altogether.

A post-humanist approach to environmental issues will not seek to contrive a utopia, or to recover an Arcadia, for the human species. Intelligent post-humanist policy will aim to mitigate humankind's destructive effects on the life of the earth, and to do so, wherever possible, in ways which render human life more tolerable to humans themselves. If such a policy is beyond our resources of thought and practical wisdom then the case of the earth, and thereby our case, is indeed hopeless. It is an open question whether such a deflation of human hopes is a live option for any modern western culture. Progress is the only real religion in every contemporary western society.

Though it may be distinctively modern, the belief in progress is not an aberration of the modern period without roots in the past. On the contrary, the understanding of human history which the idea of progress exemplifies has ancient roots in the Christian cultural traditions that inform nearly all contemporary thought. For us, rejecting the idea of progress means abandoning the comforting faith that human history is meaningful. Yet this historical faith is probably the only form in which an idea of salvation is accessible to late modern cultures. For such cultures, in which Christian providentialist hopes of human history have been repressed and reproduced in Enlightenment guises, giving up the idea of progress – the idea that the history of the human species can be told as a narrative of improvement or amelioration – implies relinquishing the conviction that human life itself is meaningful. It entails accepting a perspective on human life akin to that expressed in the *Iliad*, when the poet tells us that

> *Very like leaves*
> *upon this earth are the generations of men –*
> *old leaves, cast upon the ground by wind, young leaves*
> *the greening forest bears when spring comes in.*

*So mortals pass; one generation flowers
even as another dies away.*[23]

In this Homeric vision there is nothing akin to salvation. Humans are born, seek mates, forage for food, and die. That is all. In this ancient – and, perhaps, authentically postmodern – perspective, the human lot is no different from that of other animals. What is salvation to the tiger, or nirvana to the cockroach?

It is doubtful whether such a disenchanted vision can be tolerated by any culture that has been animated by humanist (Christian or Enlightenment) hubris. Yet such hubris has now reached the last corners of the earth. Humanism aims to transform all human societies into a monoculture modelled on western modernity. As John Livingstone has written of the 'exotic ideology' of humanism, 'Its stance is human chauvinist; its program is Baconian conquest; its means is Cartesian rationality; its instruments are science and technology. It is human imperialism in its most developed form. Originally a localized northern aberration, it is now world-dominant.'[24] The consequence of this dominance is that cultures whose traditions had enabled them to sustain a balanced relationship with the earth are being destroyed. In our historical context, the destruction of such traditional cultures typically occurs mostly by their forcible incorporation into the globalized economy, rather than by the spread of any westernizing ideology.

If Green thought had any distinctive contribution it should have been a critique of human hubris.[25] Instead, like other forms of Enlightenment humanism, it has indulged in the chiliastic hope that the failure of its most cherished projects of human emancipation will result in a cataclysmic collapse of human society. The options we face – so we are told – are utopia or oblivion. The true likelihood is infinitely more prosaic. A breakdown in the institutions of late modern societies, if it were to occur, would generate untold human suffering. In a longer historical perspective it would be a return to normalcy. The lot of humankind everywhere has always been to live under the harrow. War, anarchy and tyranny have been the condition of the species in nearly all societies of which history contains record. There is no reason why this normal human condition should not recur in a late modern context of high-tech weaponry and mass communications. Has it not already done so, in Lebanon, in parts of Russia and in former Yugoslavia? The belief that the failure of Enlightenment projects of human emancipation heralds the wholesale collapse of society is itself an Enlightenment superstition.

It may well be true, as Leakey and others have argued, that the human species is set already on a path to extinction by its present numbers and the scale of its environmental impact. The time-span for such an outcome, however, is probably that of evolutionary biology, not of human history. A comprehensive collapse of current institutions, with its attendant wars, famines and plagues, is doubtless a real possibility; but such a breakdown does not of itself entail either the extinction of the species or irreparable environmental damage. Even a thermonuclear war might inflict less harm on the biosphere than the continued growth in human numbers which further technological advances in food production may allow. Despite all its horrors, war in our historical context has made no significant or enduring impact on human population growth. Indeed, contrary to the Swiftian satirist who wrote the anonymous *Report from Iron Mountain*,[26] the institution of war has no redeeming ecological functions, at least in late modern times. Indeed, if the Gulf War is any guide, it seems likely that future wars will encompass ecological terrorism that is highly destructive of other species and their environments without having any significant medium-to-long-term effects on human numbers. The truth of the matter is that a collapse by civilized states into war, tyranny and anarchy would not be apocalyptic; it would be a return to a very familiar historical terrain.

Recent thought has been captivated by images of the End which delude us as to the real dangers which we face.[27] These are not dangers of Apocalypse, but of a reversal in which, newly equipped with technologies that are able to desolate our common environment without making it altogether uninhabitable, we return to a kind of historic normalcy. Political thought that seeks to respond intelligently to these present dangers will have to be ready to extinguish some of the hopes of progress and emancipation that were kindled by the Enlightenment. The task we face is that of moderating the hopes that are bequeathed to us by Christianity and the Enlightenment. The true measure of our entry into a postmodern condition is in the degree to which we are able to relinquish the idea of progress by which the modern age that is past was animated.

Political thinking after the illusion of the End

The certitude that there is no salvation is a form of salvation, in fact
it *is* salvation. Starting from here, we might organise our own life as
well as construct a philosophy of history: the insoluble as solution, as
the only way out . . .

E. M. Cioran, The Trouble with Being Born

The idea of progress which we inherit from Christianity and the
Enlightenment constitutes our greatest cultural impediment to the
alleviation of the human lot. It presupposes that betterment for the
species consists in approximation to a common civilization for all of
humankind. It denies that the rivalries among goods and the
dependency of goods upon evils which abound in our experience are
permanent features of the human condition. It resists as fatal to its
hopes for the species the truth that there is no common measure of
improvement for all societies. To be sure, the attachment of late
modern cultures to this idea of progress does not express any deep
faith in it. It testifies to the fear that, if this secular surrogate for
providence is given up, the meaning of human life is lost. Among us,
the modern conception of progress is not a living faith but a weak
antidote to nihilism. It is time this idea of progress was given up.

Relinquishing this idea of progress does not mean giving up all
attempts to ease the human lot. That result would follow only if
social betterment were impossible and all human problems insoluble. We know from the evidences of history and common experience
that any such view is absurd. De Quincey's observation that a
quarter of all human misery is toothache serves to remind us that the
contribution of anaesthetic dentistry to human well-being has been
significant and is not to be despised. Any diminution of avoidable
and meaningless suffering is an unmixed good. Among the unsolved
problems of late modern societies, some – such as the organization
of an affordable, convenient and environmentally friendly system of
transportation – are inherently wholly soluble. Nothing that is
intrinsically important or valuable would be lost if the private
automobile were consigned to a lesser place in the scheme of things.
Unlike population growth, say, transport is, in principle, a problem
amenable to a technical fix.

Yet we know, too – though this is repressed from consciousness
in late modern cultures – that such unmixed improvements are

rarely possible. Far commoner are gains that entail losses, goods that stand on evils, virtues that drive out other virtues and which support vices. Evils that are inherently entirely removable may in practice become irremediable because much that particular cultures have come to cherish stands on them. There are no, or very few, real technical fixes. It is the human experience of finitude, scarcity and mortality in all the things we value, expressed in this commonplace truth, that the modern idea of progress – as open-ended, across-the-board improvement in the human circumstance – seeks to exorcize from our consciousness.

In our historical context human needs are ill served by the modern faith in progress. The spirit that animates faith in progress resists the conception of humankind as an earth-bound species, which is distinguished from others of which we have knowledge only by its inventiveness and destructiveness. The inevitable implication of a perspective in which ours is only one amongst many animal species is that human nature is, for all practical purposes, a constant. Because it sets a limit to human hopes, any perspective affirming the constancy of our common nature is subversive of the modern idea of indefinite improvement, and irreconcilable with the postmodernist conceit that we are whatever we imagine ourselves to be. Equally, the view of humankind as an earth-bound species undercuts the postmodernist conviction that the natural world is a cultural construction, malleable by technology and by changes in our beliefs. Living in a postmodern culture means giving up these conceits.

It entails also shedding the modern notion of a universal civilization. The disposition to constitute for itself different cultures or ways of life appears to be universal and primordial in the human animal. Yet the idea of a universal human civilization, as we find it in Condorcet, J. S. Mill, Marx and Rorty, is compelled to treat cultural difference as transitory or epiphenomenal, a passing stage in the history of the species. Modern thinkers have been led accordingly to misconceive the telos of political life. The end of politics is not the construction of institutions that are universally rationally authoritative. It is the pursuit of a *modus vivendi* among cultures and communities. Because ways of life are always changing, the terms of peaceful coexistence among them are permanently unfixed. For that reason the end of politics is always unfinished.

The modern faith in progress is intolerant of the reality of limits. It cannot accept limits on the pursuit of what it regards as the noblest human ambitions. It rejects as misanthropy the observation that, in an overcrowded world, the attempt to alleviate poverty by conferring on all humankind the living standards briefly achieved for many in the industrialized countries risks harm to a fragile environment and to future human generations. The inordinate pursuit of human betterment means, also, certain loss for many other species. Our inherited idea of progress encourages us to regard as alterable impediments to our hopes the limits imposed by our natures, our histories and cultural differences, and by our place in nature. It supports the modern universalist project of subjugating the earth to the demands of a single civilization. It gives no support to the authentic postmodern project of crafting institutions in which we can live in a stable balance with other cultures, with other species and with the earth itself. In these and many other respects, the modern idea of progress by which we are still guided reproduces a humanist culture of hubris at a time when what we need most is an acceptance of limits.

Amending the modern inheritance so as to make it friendlier to the limits of progress will entail reforming radically some distinctive modern institutions. One of these is the sovereign nation-state. In modern thought the institution of the sovereign state has been an object of much hope and fear. Rarely has the possibility been allowed that the state might be powerless to control the most dangerous social forces. Yet the weakness of the state is a pervasive reality in late modern times. Overlooked or denied by those who remain transfixed by the totalitarian regimes that have wrought such destruction (environmental as much as human) in our century, the dwindling power of state institutions is a palpable fact of the age. Here I do not refer primarily to the reduction of the leverage of sovereign states over economic life that has been imposed by the emergence of a genuinely global market economy. That alteration has been much noted, and sometimes exaggerated, in recent thought.[28] It is true – as I note below – that the penetration of societies and communities nearly everywhere by global market forces has had profound and by no means unambiguously beneficial effects on human well-being. Yet it is not in this regard that the increased marginality of state institutions in late modern times is most striking, but in what has hitherto been their most centrally definitive function – the control of violence.

A defining feature of the period after the Second World War has been a metamorphosis in the nature of war. Organized violence has slipped from the control of states and passed into that of other institutions. Political organizations such as the Palestine Liberation Organization and the African National Congress, tribal, ethnic and clan militias in Rwanda, Chechnya and Bosnia, drug cartels and mafias in Colombia, Russia and Ireland – such diverse institutions have deprived sovereign states of their effective monopoly of violence. To a considerable degree war has become an activity waged by irregular armies which acknowledge no sovereign power. At the same time, most late modern states harbour post-military societies. The use of force as a tool of policy has dwindling legitimacy in such societies, and it is difficult to mobilize popular consent for any military engagement that threatens to be long or costly. The relations between such states do not rely chiefly on the threat of force in a balance of power but instead rest on mutual surveillance and openness. It is important to note, however, that late modern states of this sort must survive in a global environment containing many states which still regard war as a legitimate instrument of policy.

The evident weaknesses of the late modern state, shown in the metamorphosis of war, give urgency to the search for state institutions which do not embody sovereign nationhood. In much of the world today, it is the weakness of the nation-state in losing control of organized violence, rather than its role as the author of Clausewitzian war, that is its principal flaw. Yet the modern project of nation-building carries on with a vigour that the weakness of state institutions has not diminished. Throughout this century, the project of national self-determination has worked to overthrow empires – most recently the Soviet imperium.[29] It has at the same time worked to sunder peoples, in post-Clausewitzian wars of ethnic cleansing. In the wake of empires much of the world has reverted to a pre-modern condition of anarchy, in which state institutions of any kind are virtually absent. That is the condition of large parts of the post-communist Russian Federation, of much of Africa and probably of China. In only a few instances – Slovenia, Hungary, the Czech Republic, Poland – has the collapse of empire resulted in the construction of modern sovereign states having the appearance of legitimacy and stability. In western Europe – in Spain, Italy, Belgium, even the United Kingdom – national cultures created in the eighteenth or nineteenth centuries are fragmenting, with older regional identities reasserting themselves.

Throughout Europe the nation-state remains an important focus of democratic political life and a barrier to the homogenizing impact of global market forces. It expresses cultural identities to a declining extent, as these become more complex and plural and are devolved to localities and regions. At the same time, though it may retain centrality in democratic politics for a considerable period, the modern artefact of national cultures is evidently in the midst of unravelling. Indeed, even where it is a recent construction, the sovereign nation-state survives as a fading relic of modernity, with little leverage on the needs of the present. Above all, it contains no answers to the question of the age, which is how communities having different cultural traditions can coexist in common institutions.

A reflective observer has observed that 'what came to an end in 1989 was not just the Cold War, nor even in a formal sense the Second World War . . . What came to an end in Europe (but perhaps only there) were the political systems of three centuries: the balance of power and the imperial urge . . . the world no longer forms a single political system.'[30] The decline of Clausewitzian war, theorized in van Creveld's path-breaking study, *On Future War*, is only the most visible symptom of the redundancy of the modern European state which emerged from the Treaty of Westphalia in 1648.[31] The waning power in Europe of the modern nation-state, as an institution claiming a monopoly of force and exclusive jurisdiction over a definite territory, may from another perspective augur the emergence of a postmodern state. It may not be altogether fanciful to discern the beginnings of a postmodern state in the institutions of the European Union. Such a state contains many cultural traditions and communities, it is not unified by the modern artefacts of a national culture or a common ideology, and in it local and regional allegiances and surpranational institutions have to a significant extent displaced the exclusive loyalties of the sovereign nation-state. A postmodern state will be composed of post-military societies, but like any other state it must exist in a world in which the threat of military force remains a pervasive reality. Indeed this threat is harder to control now that Clausewitzian war is in decline. If a postmodern state does come into being in Europe it will have to survive in a world containing modern states and pre-modern anarchies, both equipped with late modern weapons technologies.

The postmodern state which may be developing from within European institutions is unfamiliar. Nothing guarantees its emergence. European institutions can develop into a postmodern state only if they cease to be instruments of cultural homogenization under the aegis of a neo-liberal ideology; but that condition may not be satisfied. Equally, insofar as the European project still, anachronistically, consists of constructing a modern sovereign state, albeit one that is transnational and federal in its structure and powers, it may well evoke a powerful countermovement in which national interests are reasserted and a politics of balance of power re-emerges. The unfamiliarity of postmodern European institutions, which in truth resemble those of pre-modern forms of empire more than they do any modern polity, may strengthen the forces – federalist as well as nationalist – which seek to shape them on modern models of statehood. A relapse into the politics of modernity is a permanent possibility in Europe.

If a postmodern state nevertheless emerges in Europe, it will be as a product of the singularities of European history. For that reason it cannot be easily replicated elsewhere in the world. The United States remains locked in the worldview and the institutions of the early modern world, in which sovereign statehood was central and liberal institutions were held to be universally authoritative. It is difficult to envisage any realistic scenario in which postmodern institutions can evolve within such a culture, still suffused by the universalist civil religion of early modern Europe. The fundamentalist liberal commitment to the universal authority of local American practices of rights is, by itself, an insuperable obstacle to the *modus vivendi* among different cultures which is the animating postmodern project. Those who imagine that postmodernity must drag in its wake a society such as the United States have been deceived by the modern idea of progress.

If postmodern institutions can take root anywhere it is, firstly, in the European cultures where modernity is oldest. But they may blossom too in those East Asian cultures – Singapore, Japan, Taiwan – that have managed to adopt the techniques of modernity without imbibing its illusions. Like modernity, from which it develops dialectically, the postmodern condition is far from being even in principle universal. Nothing suggests that postmodernity is bound to be the fate of all humankind. Indeed postmodern societies and states may not themselves survive for long in a world in which predatory modern states and pre-modern anarchies have easy access to late modern technologies of destruction. A precondition of the survival of postmodern states is that they develop effective strategies of response to the metamorphosis of war which is one of the most striking marks of the end of the modern period. They must be able to nurture sources of allegiance to their institutions as powerful as those by which they are likely to be threatened.

Amending the modern inheritance to enable a postmodern society to renew itself also means revising another distinctively modern institution – the free market. Like the nation-state, the free market is far from immemorial. Market exchange of various kinds may be universal and perennial, but the free market as a social institution is not much more than a century and a half old. As Karl Polanyi showed in his neglected classic, *The Great Transformation*, the free market is an artefact of statecraft that was constructed in England in the mid-nineteenth century. It is the unregulated individualist capitalism of nineteenth-century England – rather than, for example, French mercantilist capitalism or the corporatist capitalism of Germany and Austria – that was reinvented in the 1980s, and fused with American universalism to produce the vision of a global free market. That vision is only the modern, Enlightenment project of a universal civilization framed in economic terms.

The projecting of extending worldwide the singular institutions of Anglo-Saxon market capitalism is, in effect, the attempt to project individualist values into every other society. We can be sure that it will fail. It entails detaching the institutions of the free market from the cultural matrix of individualism through which they are reproduced and on which they remain wholly dependent. Like the Soviet project, the ongoing western – or, more precisely, American – project of installing individualist market institutions throughout the world will run aground on the realities of cultural difference and its own indifference to enduring human needs. A society in which the free market dominates every other social institution cannot satisfy human needs for belonging and membership, for security and continuity, which in the past were met by social institutions that were sheltered from the market. The hegemony of the free market leaves these human needs unmet. In societies whose traditions are not individualist the penetration of the free market means a major rupture in the transmission of the culture. A global free market, if it could be constructed, could be built only on the ruins of the world's diverse cultures. It would mean the universal triumph of western individualist values whose compatibility with any kind of social stability, even in their cultures of origin, is more than doubtful. The social backlash against the free market in its global form is likely to be as powerful as that against *laissez-faire* in late nineteenth-century England. The overwhelming likelihood is that the late modern project of a global market will fail as other modern utopian projects have failed.

Long before it fails, however, this late modern universalist project may inflict incalculable and irreparable damage on all other cultures. In a sort of Gresham's Law of economic systems, the competition between capitalisms which is the only form of systemic economic rivalry in the post-socialist era may yet result in a victory for the type of capitalism that is most socially destructive. The risk is that the form of capitalism that in the longer perspective of history has the worst prospects of survival may at this juncture succeed in displacing and destroying others with far better long-term prospects. An urgent necessity of the emerging postmodern condition is accordingly a reform of the free market which re-embeds it in the life of society. The autonomy of market forces must be moderated, cultural and political controls over markets re-asserted, and their links with human needs re-established. But it is difficult to exaggerate the difficulties confronting such a project in a historical context in which, because of the globalization of economic activity in many spheres, markets are more radically disembedded from social life, more removed from political and cultural constraint, than at any time in modern history.

It is no part of my purpose here to suggest how that re-embedding of economic activity in the life of society might in present circumstances be achieved. Preserving more humane varieties of capitalism from destruction by the free market may require the imposition of political limits on economic globalization. Restraints on global free trade, whether by classical protectionist policies or by other means, may be among such political limits on globalization. No one should imagine, however, that any such policies can by themselves do more than act at the margin to diminish the worst social effects of the global free market. Imposing political limits on economic globalization, necessary as it may be to do so, leaves unchecked the destructive autonomy of market forces that is indigenous in the western societies that launched the movement to a global market. Globalization itself is, after all, only a perverse and atavistic form of modernity – that, roughly, of nineteenth-century English and twentieth-century American economic individualism – projected worldwide. Perhaps it is our historical fate to endure the working out to the last consequence of this project of modernity. In that case any talk of a postmodern condition must be – at best – premature.

One reason why the re-embedding of market forces in social life may be unachievable by us is the weakness of our cultures themselves. We do not live in strong and deep communities which global market forces endanger. We live in shallow, fractured societies, in which all forms of common life have long been hollowed out by individualism. Unless market forces are subjected to the imperatives of communities, enduring human needs cannot be met. Yet it is an open question whether the forms of social life any longer exist amongst us that could subordinate the market to human needs. The fragmentation of communities and the scattering of their cultural resources is now so far gone in most western societies that the project of harnessing the energy of the free market for the enduring needs of their inhabitants may have become merely another late modern illusion. If we do not gain a measure of social control over the life of the market, however, even the greatest cultural achievements of modernity may be dispersed by its anarchic energy. An institution as subtle, complex and fragile as the modern city may easily be blown away by the gale of market forces. If the modern age is indeed coming to a close it is primarily the subversive and destructive force of the global free market that is consuming it. In the late modern phenomenon of the omnicompetent market, modernity may have become self-consuming.

The difficulties we face in any project of exerting social control over market forces are only an aspect of a much larger cultural debility. An imperative of late modern societies everywhere is to gain control of technology. Such societies are unsupervised laboratories for an enormous ongoing experiment in technological innovation.[32] They are, for all their inhabitants, sites of incalculable – indeed, often unknowable – risk. Common prudence dictates a precautionary policy towards new technologies, which is ready to restrain them if they carry any risk, however incalculably small, of catastrophic side-effects. Yet it must be doubted if late modern societies have the cultural resources to sustain such prudent risk-aversion. Their soil may have become too thin for technology to be securely earthed in any firm ground. This is a limitation, perhaps insuperable, of all political measures for the conservation of the environment in our time. Political action may stave off, or mitigate, the most immediate risks of new technologies to human societies and the earth on which they depend. Such action may sometimes be a vital necessity, if it reasonably promises to stave off disasters capable of inflicting the most irreversible damage to the earth. Action to render safe and then to dismantle the crumbling civilian nuclear power programme of the post-communist countries may be an important, and neglected, example of this kind. Similarly, aid to those few countries implementing serious population control policies, such as China and Egypt, is amply justified on grounds of human well-being as well as of the integrity of the environment. In a historical context in which even the most radical policies can alter humankind's impact on the earth only at the margin, it is no small thing to do good in minute particulars.

Political action to protect our common environment confronts dilemmas, some perhaps insoluble, arising from the scale of the threats it faces, the practical obstacles to coping with them put up by organized interests and anthropocentric ideologies, and the disorder and weakness of late modern cultures. It is unreasonable to be hopeful about population growth in a world in which an unprecedented proportion of the human population is young and fertile. It is foolish to imagine that even well-conceived restraints on dangerous new technologies will for long inhibit their dissemination when sovereign states can elude the jurisdiction of transnational authorities and much of the world lives in anarchic societies lacking effective state institutions of any kind. It is self-indulgent to dream of an ecological conversion that would conjure away these intractabilities. Even if, improbably, such a conversion were to occur, a culture that had been so transformed would still have to survive in an unregenerate and perilous world. Perhaps it is true that only a turning in our relations with the earth, in which it ceases to be a resource for the satisfaction of our needs and a ground for the play of the human will, can alter fundamentally our relations with technology. Of that turning, however, there are few signs. We must do what little we can without waiting on it.

It is a prototypical conceit of modern humanism to imagine that technology can be controlled simply by an exercise of will. In truth the relations of human beings with technology are never merely ones of ends to means. Our lives are profoundly conditioned by the technologies we develop whether or not we will it so. The notion that a Luddite act of refusal of technology by any community could bring it under human control is a characteristic humanist folly. The belief that we could by such an act of will capture technology for human purposes exemplifies an understanding of human beings, and of technology, that is itself technological. The belief of religious fundamentalists that a re-enchantment of the world can be effected by an act of commitment to a theistic worldview expresses an analogous faith in the human will. These expressions of revulsion against modernity embody, in effect, the same modern self-understanding that is expressed in the instrumentalist and humanist conception of our relations with the earth. No deep change in our way of life can proceed while these self-understandings hold sway. Science and technology will serve human needs only insofar as our societies contain cultures and communities whose self-understanding is rich enough and deep enough to contain science and technology – and sometimes to restrain them. Of which late modern society is this true?

'The sickness of a time is cured by an alteration in the life of human beings, and the sickness of philosophical problems could be cured only through a changed mode of thought and of life, not through a medicine invented by an individual.'[33] One of the principal conceits of the modern period has been an overvaluation of what taking thought can do for human life. In this errancy modern cultures are neither novel or original. They invoke an intellectualist or rationalist self-understanding that is as old as 'philosophy'. It was expressed in the Socratic project of the examined life, and unsurpassably exemplified in the life of Socrates himself. Rightly called the purest thinker of the West, Socrates embodied, if he did not originate, the understanding of humans as rational animals. By now it is very old news that such an understanding of ourselves is one of the many things that comes to an end with the modern age. Yet the idea of humans as thinking beings remains, perhaps, the chief obstacle to thinking in our age. It embodies what must first of all be given up if we are to begin to think, which is the certainty that we know already what we are and how we are to live. The present inquiry has been intended as no more than a prelude to thinking. The preparatory thinking that is most needed in our time is that which is ready to put our certainty in question.

NOTES

CHAPTER 1 THE STRANGE DEATH OF TORY ENGLAND

1 I have considered the decay of the postwar British settlement during the Callaghan Labour government in more detail in my monograph, *The Undoing of Conservatism* (1994), reprinted as ch. 7 of my book, *Enlightenment's Wake: Politics and Culture at the Close of the Modern Age* (1995). I examined the contradictions of neo-liberal ideology in the Introduction to my book, *Beyond the New Right: Markets, Government and the Common Environment* (1993).

2 An exception might be made for the thought of Michael Oakeshott, in which a criticism of the Enlightenment is obliquely pursued. However, though Oakeshott's thought was an object of reverence in the New Right think-tanks, particularly the Centre of Policy Studies, it was never an influence on policy – in the way that Hayek's was, say – and, no doubt wisely, he held himself aloof from quotidian politics. Analogously, Roger Scruton's *Salisbury Review* adopted a stance of Jacobitic or quixotic resistance to the spirit of the age, which sometimes encompassed opposition to aspects of economic liberalism; and its influence on practising Conservative politicians was correspondingly negligible.

3 I do not mean to imply that Popper's and Hayek's thought were at all points convergent, but only that neither of them belonged to a recognizable tradition of British or European *conservative* thought.

4 Not all British classical liberals were, or are, opposed to European federalism. Sir Samuel Brittan, the distinguished economic commentator, is perhaps the most noteworthy among several exceptions.

5 A significant part of this new insecurity among the middle classes in

Britain no doubt derives from the globalization of the economy and new technologies rather than from any impact of domestic policy. This does not mean that the neo-liberal policies of the past seventeen years have not worsened insecurity for the Tories' core supporters – and it certainly will not stop the Tories being held to electoral account for doing nothing to make the new job insecurity more humanly tolerable.

CHAPTER 2   AFTER SOCIAL DEMOCRACY

1 For political statements of conservative communitarianism, see Robin Harris, *The Conservative Community* (1992), and David Willets, *Civic Conservatism* (1993). For a Left version of conservative communitarianism, see Norman Dennis and A. H. Halsey, *English Ethical Socialism* (1988). The elements of a liberal communitarianism are, I believe, to be found in the writings of Isaiah Berlin and Joseph Raz. See my book, *Berlin* (1995); and Joseph Raz, *The Morality of Freedom* (1986).

2 I have defined and defended pluralism in *Enlightenment's Wake*, particularly in chs 10–12.

3 Compelling statements of this view are Antony Lester's 'Can We Achieve a New Constitutional Settlement?' in Colin Crouch and David Marquand (eds), *Reinventing Collective Action* (1995), Anthony Barnett, *The Defining Moment: Prospects for a New Britain under Labour* (1995) and Tony Wright and David Marquand, 'Come the Revolution', *Guardian*, 23 October 1995.

4 *The Times*, 20 July 1995.

5 In a later article, Rees-Mogg endorses a sort of cyberspace anarchy as an alternative to any kind of national government. See *The Times*, 31 August 1995. It is difficult to see how this wild dystopia can be described as any kind of conservative vision; but it is typical of a certain kind of right-wing thought today.

6 See my monograph, *The Post-communist Societies in Transition: A Social Market Perspective* (1993), republished as ch. 6 of my book, *Enlightenment's Wake*.

7 David Goodhart, *The Reshaping of the German Social Market* (1994), p. 37.

8 This does not mean that we cannot make useful borrowings and adaptations from other economic cultures, as Will Hutton has argued in his important and illuminating book, *The State We're In* (1995).

9 For a compelling statement of one such post-federalist European project, see Sir James Goldsmith, *The Trap* (1994) and *The Response* (1995).

10 This is true of the Borrie Report of the Commission on Social Justice,

of the Dahrendorf Report on Wealth Creation and Social Cohesion in a Free Society, and of Patricia Hewitt's notable T. H. Marshall Memorial Lecture, *Social Justice in a Global Economy?*

11 See my *Beyond the New Right*, ch. 3, pp. 76–92.

12 I remain indebted here to Joseph Raz's critique of libertarian, rights-based and egalitarian political moralities in his book, *The Morality of Freedom* (1986). However I think that context-specific principles of fairness are necessary in many areas – areas where human needs are not satiable but are yet basic, where they are satiable but cannot all be met, and – perhaps most fundamentally – where the criteria of satiability itself cannot avoid including norms of fairness.

13 By contrast, *The Economist* has argued ('The Myth of the Powerless State', 7 October 1995) that 'global integration has left government with about as many economic powers as they ever had.' This may be true; but – as *The Economist* recognizes elsewhere in the same article – the effect of global integration has been to alter the consequences of using these powers, and thereby to impose new constraints on their uses. It can be argued that the impact of economic globalization (in its various manifestations) on the macro-economic policies of sovereign states has been exaggerated; it is silly to suggest that the costs of certain policy options have not greatly increased as a consequence of globalization – increased so much, indeed, as to remove them from the political agenda.

14 I have learnt much from Michael Walzer's writings on these issues, in particular his book, *Spheres of Justice* (1983), and from Jon Elster's *Local Justice* (1992).

15 There are some interesting observations on these issues in Adrian Wooldridge's *Meritocracy and the Classless Society* (1995) and in Stephen Pollard's *Schools, Selection and the Left* (1995). It may be worth noting that support for meritocratic practices in educational contexts does not commit anyone to the view that society as a whole should be reordered according to a comprehensive meritocratic conception of justice – a conception destroyed by critics as different as Hayek and Michael Young. Nor, of course, does such support entail that meritocratic criteria are the only ones relevant in all educational contexts. It is obvious that special needs and disabilities may also be salient.

16 This does not imply any opposition on my part to the institutions of welfare rights. On the contrary, I support them – but as alterable artefacts of legislation, not as derivations from illusory 'theories of justice'. See my *Beyond the New Right*, pp. 99–110, for an elaboration of this point.

17 I am well aware that on available evidence the extent of the growth of job insecurity remains somewhat controversial. See on this *Income*

Data Services Focus Quarterly, 74 (March 1995), 'The Jobs Mythology'. What is less controversial is the expectation that job security will decline in future, and with it our inherited culture of work which presupposes job-holding as its central institution.

18 On this large and important topic, see Matthew D'Ancona's fascinating monograph, *The Ties that Bind Us* (1996).

19 Various schemes are discussed in the *Citizens' Income Bulletin*, particularly nos 18 (July 1994), 19 (February 1995) and 20 (July 1995).

20 A useful brief guide to Frank Field's thinking on these issues may be found in his Introduction to Peter Lilley's *Winning the Welfare Debate* (1995). A more comprehensive statement of Mr Field's proposals can be found in his *Making Welfare Work: Reconstructing Welfare for the Millennium* (1995).

21 Not all forms of targeting involve means-testing. Some involve categorization by other factors – age or disability, say – and do not necessarily carry the moral hazards of means-testing. A comprehensive welfare reform of the sort we undoubtedly need must recognize that different forms of allocation of benefits are appropriate, depending on the shared social understanding of the goods concerned, and on the consequences of their mode of allocation. Pluralism is unavoidable here too.

22 For a New Right defence of a basic income, see *Saturn's Children: How the State Devours Liberty, Prosperity and Virtue* (1995) by Alan Duncan and Dominic Hobson.

23 It may be that limited and conditional Basic Income schemes have an important role in any policy aiming to protect the human interests once promoted by full employment policy. I do not discuss this possibility, since I am concerned to assess Basic Income schemes in their most distinctive and radical form.

24 Of course, some welfare rights are properly recognized to be unconditional, or, more precisely, to be owed independently of contribution to society. The welfare rights created by some disabilities may fall into this category. There is no single ethical justification for all forms of legitimate welfare provision.

25 Obligations to accept reskilling were a key element in the immensely successful Swedish pro-active labour policy, which still repays study despite its collapse along with much else in the Swedish social democratic model.

26 For a nostalgist Left version of familial fundamentalism, whose implication for welfare policy is large-scale social engineering, see Norman Dennis and George Erdos (Foreword by A. H. Halsey), *Families without Fatherhood* (1993).

27 I am aware that this is a great simplification of complex issues. For a helpful critique of standard liberal views on multiculturalism, see Bhikhu Parekh, 'Superior People: The Narrowness of Liberalism from

Mill to Rawls' (1994). See also Joseph Raz, 'Multiculturalism: A Liberal Perspective', in his book, *Ethics in the Public Domain* (1994). I have addressed some contrasts between Raz's and my own view of multiculturalism, which has a pluralist rather than a liberal bias, in the Postscript to the second edition of my book, *Liberalism* (1995).

28 I argued this in my first published criticism of neo-liberal policy, which appeared in June 1989. See my *Limited Government: A Positive Agenda* reprinted as ch. 1 of my *Beyond the New Right*, pp. 33–4.

29 This is a point not sufficiently acknowledged in Francis Fukuyama's study, *Trust: The Social Virtues and the Creation of Prosperity* (1995).

30 This is the hope of several contributors to Colin Crouch and David Marquand (eds), *Reinventing Collective Action*.

31 I have examined some aspects of late modern culture in my *Enlightenment's Wake*.

CHAPTER 5 SOCIALISM WITH A PROFESSORIAL FACE

1 See my *Post-Communist Societies in Transition*, reprinted in *Enlightenment's Wake*, pp. 41–2.

2 On TVEs, see Paul Bowles and Xiao-yuan Dong, 'China's Reform Assessed' (1994) pp. 49–77.

CHAPTER 7 WHAT COMMUNITY IS NOT

1 The best philosophical statements of a communitarian perspective remain Alasdair MacIntyre's *After Virtue* (1980) and Michael Sandel's *Liberalism and the Limits of Justice* (1981). As far as I know, neither of these writers has any formal connections with communitarianism as a movement.

2 This was an insight preserved in conservative philosophy, before that was lost in the neo-liberal hegemony. For an interpretation of the disappearance of traditional conservative thought, see my *The Undoing of Conservatism*, reprinted as ch. 7 of my book *Enlightenment's Wake*.

3 I have tried to set out how markets both serve and deny individual autonomy in *The Moral Foundations of Market Institutions* (1992), republished in *Beyond the New Right*, ch. 3.

4 I have developed these communitarian criticisms of neo-liberalism more comprehensively and systematically in my pamphlet, *After Social Democracy* (1996), reprinted as ch. 2 of this book.

CHAPTER 8   BERLIN, OAKESHOTT AND ENLIGHTENMENT

1 MacIntyre, *After Virtue*, p. 38.
2 Michael Oakeshott, *Rationalism in Politics* (1977), p. 13.
3 The positivistic project of a 'logic of scientific method', applicable to the study of human society as much as to physics or chemistry, was one Popper never gave up. Conversations with Hayek and Popper, whose philosophical views are often bracketed together, suggest to me that their differences were far greater than either of them was ready to admit publicly. Hayek was much closer to Oakeshott in his rejection of any unitary 'method' for 'science'.
4 The significance of 'Thatcherism' may have been as an attempt to impose a new, American ideological style on political life in Britain. That it failed to do so, while yet having irreversible consequences for British political culture, is argued in 'The Strange Death of Tory England' (ch. 1 of this book).
5 I have criticized the Kantian dimension of Oakeshott's thought in my article, 'Oakeshott as a Liberal', in my book, *Post-Liberalism: Studies in Political Thought* (1993), ch. 4.
6 I refer to Joseph Raz's seminal book, *The Morality of Freedom*.
7 I have discussed Berlin's conception of philosophical method more systematically and comprehensively in my book, *Berlin* (1995), especially on pp. 12–13.
8 Ibid., ch. 6.
9 I have discussed Berlin's and other central criticisms of Mill's doctrine of liberty in my book, *Mill on Liberty: A Defence* (second edn, 1996).
10 I base my understanding of Oakeshott's views on my memory of many conversations I had with him about these questions. However, I believe that Oakeshott's published writings alone would support the interpretation I advance here of his thought. The Bradleian influence is clearest in Oakeshott's book, *Experience and Its Modes* (1933 and 1986); the influence of Wittgenstein can I believe be detected in several of the essays in *Rationalism in Politics*, and traces of Ryle's, Winch's and Heidegger's thought are to be found in *On Human Conduct* (1975).
11 This Wittgensteinian-sounding phrase comes from Oakeshott, *Rationalism in Politics*, p. 19. The question of Wittgenstein's possible influence on his Cambridge contemporary Oakeshott is discussed by J. C. Nyiri in his interesting contribution to Brian McGuiness (ed.), *Wittgenstein and His Times* (1982), pp. 61–4.
12 As with my intepretation of Oakeshott's views, I base this account of Berlin's position on many conversations I have had with him over the years. It does not have his authority, but I believe it corresponds with the position he adopts in his published writings.

13 These Vichian and Herderian aspects of Berlin's thought are most accessible to the reader in his study, *Vico and Herder: Two Studies in the History of Ideas* (1976).

14 The expression 'minimum content of natural law' is, of course, that of the late H. L. A. Hart. Conversations with Hart led me to think his inspiration for the thought which that expression embodies came from his reading of Hume. A similar thought animates many of the writings of Stuart Hampshire.

15 Berlin sometimes acknowledges this, as in his approving citation of an unnamed author – in fact Joseph Schumpeter – in *Four Essays on Liberty* (1969), p. 172: 'It may be that the ideal of freedom to choose ends without claiming eternal validity for them, and the pluralism of values connected with this, is only the late fruit of our declining capitalist civilisation ... "To realize the relative validity of one's convictions", said an admirable writer of our time, "and yet stand for them unflinchingly, is what distinguishes a civilised man from a barbarian."'

16 Oakeshott characterizes moralities as vernacular languages in his book, *On Human Conduct*, pp. 63ff; and he attempts a real definition of history and of law in his book *On History and Other Essays* (1983).

17 Some interpreters of Oakeshott have attempted to periodize his thought, and it may well be true that different accounts of philosophy and its place in relation to other forms of inquiry can be found at various points in his writings. (There is in Oakeshott's early writings an explicitly hierarchical account of modes of understanding, with philosophy at their apex, which is muted in later works.) I am still inclined to regard the doctrine of 'The Voice of Poetry in the Conversation of Mankind' in *Rationalism in Politics* as a statement of his philosophical outlook on which Oakeshott was never able to improve, and whose central claims he never retracted.

18 Oakeshott, 'The Voice of Poetry in the Conversation of Mankind', p. 200.

19 See Berlin's 'The Purpose of Philosophy' in his book, *Concepts and Categories* (1978), pp. 1–11.

20 I am influenced here by the writings of Richard Rorty, particularly on Wittgenstein; but I do not claim that my line of thinking follows his.

21 It may be significant that Berlin mentions Herzen, and not any philosopher of the conventional sort, as the principal influence on his thought; and that Oakeshott once spoke of Valéry as the writer from whom he had learnt most about the modern world.

CHAPTER 10 BEGINNINGS

1 For an interesting, if sometimes hyperbolic critique of 'westernization' and 'the West', see Serge Latouche, *The Westernization of the World: The Significance, Scope and Limits of the Drive towards Global Uniformity* (1996).

2 I attempted to theorize the novelty of the communist collapse in my paper, 'Totalitarianism, Reform and Civil Society'. See my *Post-Liberalism*, ch. 12.

3 Perhaps the most powerful recent statement of the postmodernist view of nature (including human nature) as a cultural construction is to be found in Richard Rorty's *Philosophy and the Mirror of Nature* (1980). For a critique of some aspects of Rorty's postmodernism, see my 'Enlightenment's Wake', in *Enlightenment's Wake*, pp. 169–78.

4 For a powerful critique of both Left and Right projects, see Anthony Giddens, *Beyond Left and Right: The Future of Radical Politics* (1994). It should be noticed that Giddens does not share my view that, notwithstanding the absurdities of postmodernist thinking, some contemporary societies and states show signs of an emerging postmodern condition; he believes such societies are approaching a condition of 'high modernity'. On this and related matters, see his *The Consequences of Modernity* (1990).

5 For a naive exposition of this project, represented as an exercise in philosophy of history, see Francis Fukuyama, *The End of History and the Last Man* (1992).

6 James Lovelock, *Gaia: A New Look at Life on Earth* (1979), p. 145. See also Lovelock's book, *The Ages of Gaia: A Biography of Our Living Earth* (1989).

7 See Murray Fesbach and Alfred Friendly, Jr, *Ecocide in the USSR: Health and Nature under Siege* (1992).

8 As Lovelock has wisely noted, 'The things we do to the planet are not offensive nor do they pose a geophysiological threat, unless we do them on a large enough scale. If there were only 500 million people on Earth, almost nothing that we are now doing to our environment would perturb Gaia. Unfortunately for our freedom of action, we are moving towards eight billion people with more than ten billion sheep and cattle, and six billion poultry . . . Bad farming is probably the greatest threat to Gaia's health' (*The Ages of Gaia*, pp. 178–9).

9 On this, see Goldsmith, *The Trap*, *The Response* and *Counter-culture*, vol. 6 (1996).

10 Garrett Hardin, *Living within Limits: Ecology, Economics and Population Taboos*, ch. 24, 'Birth Control versus Population Control', especially the section on 'Post-Darwinian policy: a step yet to come', p. 258. See also Hardin's books, *Stalking the Wild Taboo* (second edn,

1978); *Promethean Ethics: Living with Death, Competition and Triage* (1980); and, for an early canonical statement of Hardin's views, *Nature and Man's Fate* (1961).

11 I have discussed Mill's anticipations of contemporary ecological concerns in *Beyond the New Right*, pp. 140–2.

12 Angus Martin, *The Last Generation: The End of Survival?* (1975), p. 42.

13 Jacques Monod, *Chance and Necessity* (1974), p. 160.

14 Ibid., p. 159.

15 E. O. Wilson, *On Human Nature* (1979), p. 201.

16 F. Nietzsche, *Joyful Wisdom* (1960), book 5, no. 344, p. 279.

17 John Aspinall, *The Best of Friends* (1976), pp. 132–4, 139. See also John Aspinall, *Random Thoughts on the Human Animal* (1967). Aspinall's thinking is of considerable significance, not only for its uncompromisingly consistent repudiation of anthropocentrism, but also because it shows that a fundamental reorientation of our relations with animals need not mean incorporating them into modern legalist practices of rights.

18 See E. O. Wilson, *Biophilia* (1984) and his great book, *The Diversity of Life* (1992), especially pp. 348–51.

19 See Lovelock, *The Ages of Gaia*, p. 212.

20 Ibid., chs 2 and 3.

21 See, on Taoism, A. C. Graham, *Disputers of the Tao: Philosophical Argument in Ancient China* (1989); on shamanism, Mircea Eliade, *Shamanism: Archaic Techniques of Ecstasy* (1972).

22 For a strikingly favourable assessment of Hobbes's thought, see Elias Canetti, *The Human Province* (1986), pp. 115–17.

23 *The Iliad*, tr. Robert Fitzgerald (1974), p. 146.

24 John A. Livingstone, *Rogue Primate: An Exploration of Human Domestication* (1994), pp. 57 and 140.

25 The school of Deep Ecology is committed, in principle, to rejecting anthropocentric conceptions of value; but it has rarely explored the limits imposed on human hopes and ethical ambitions by an ecocentric perspective. The moral and political outlook of Deep Ecology is, for the most part, that of the most conventional forms of the liberal and socialist Enlightenment project. On Deep Ecology, see Arne Naess, 'The Shallow and the Deep, Long-Range Ecology Movement' (1973), pp. 95–100. For a useful consideration of the more formal philosophical aspects of Naess's attempt at an ecocentric theory of value, see I. Gullvag and J. Wetlesen (eds), *In Sceptical Wonder: Inquiries into the Philosophy of Arne Naess on the Occasion of his 70th Birthday* (1982), section V. An ecological-holistic interpretation of Spinoza's ethics has been advanced by a philosopher heavily influenced by Naess, Jon Wetlesen, in his *The Sage and the Way: Spinoza's Ethics of Freedom*

(1979). An environmental current which is clearly ecocentric in its orientation, and which appears to reject the liberal humanist attachments of most ecological movements, has emerged in the United States in the form of the groups loosely linked together as Earth First!; but its policies and strategies are marred by chiliastic thinking.

26 *Report from Iron Mountain on the Possibility and Desirability of Peace* (1967). The author was Leonard C. Lewin, who also wrote the dystopian fiction *Triage* (1972).

27 J. Baudrillard's *The Illusion of the End* (1992) is a witty critique of millennial tendencies in recent thinking.

28 A level-headed guide to controversy about globalization can be found in Paul Hirst and Grahame Thompson, *Globalization in Question* (1996).

29 I do not mean to imply, after the fashion of much shallow western discourse, that the Soviet Union was an empire just like the empires of nineteenth- and twentieth-century Europe. European states such as Britain and France possessed empires; the Soviet Union *was* an empire. Indeed Russia remains an imperial state, not a nation-state, even today.

30 Robert Cooper, *The Post-modern State and the World Order* (1996), p. 16.

31 On this, see David Held's excellent study, *Democracy and Global Order* (1994).

32 On this point, see Ulrich Beck, *Ecological Politics in an Age of Risk* (1995).

33 L. Wittgenstein, *Remarks on the Foundations of Mathematics* (1967), p. 57.

REFERENCES

Aspinall, John, *Random Thoughts on the Human Animal*, privately printed, 1967.

Aspinall, John, *The Best of Friends*, New York and San Francisco, Harper and Row, 1976.

Barnett, Anthony, *The Defining Moment: Prospects for a New Britain under Labour*, London, Charter 88, 1995.

Baudrillard, J., *The Illusion of the End*, Cambridge, Polity Press, 1992.

Beck, Ulrich, *Ecological Politics in an Age of Risk*, Cambridge, Polity Press, 1995.

Berlin, Isaiah, *Four Essays on Liberty*, Oxford and New York, Oxford University Press, 1969.

Berlin, Isaiah, *Vico and Herder: Two Studies in the History of Ideas*, London, Hogarth Press, 1976.

Berlin, Isaiah, *Concepts and Categories*, London, Hogarth Press, 1978.

Bowles, Paul and Xiao-yuan Dong, 'China's Reform Assessed', *New Left Review*, 208 (November–December 1994), pp. 49–77.

Bramwell, Anna, *Ecology in the Twentieth Century: A History*, Oxford, Oxford University Press, 1989.

Bramwell, Anna, *The Fading of the Greens: The Decline of Environmental Politics in the West*, New Haven and London, Yale University Press, 1994.

Canetti, Elias, *The Human Province*, London, Picador, 1986.

Cioran, E. M., *The Trouble with Being Born*, London, Quartet Books, 1993.

Cooper, Robert, *The Post-modern State and the World Order*, London, Demos, 1996.

Crouch, Colin and David Marquand (eds), *Reinventing Collective Action*, Oxford, Blackwell, 1995.

D'Ancona, Matthew, *The Ties that Bind Us*, London, Social Market Foundation, 1996.

Dawkins, Richard, *The Selfish Gene*, Oxford, Oxford University Press, 1976.

Dawkins, Richard, *The Blind Watchmaker*, Harlow, Longman Scientific and Technical, 1986.

Dennis, Norman and George Erdos, *Families without Fatherhood*, London, Institute for Economic Affairs, Health and Welfare Unit, Choice in Welfare Series, no. 12, 1993.

Dennis, Norman and A. H. Halsey, *English Ethical Socialism*, Oxford, Oxford University Press, 1988.

Duncan, Alan and Dominic Hobson, *Saturn's Children: How the State Devours Liberty, Prosperity and Virtue*, London, Macmillan, 1995.

Eliade, Mircea, *Shamanism: Archaic Techniques of Ecstasy*, Princeton, Bollingen, 1972.

Elster, Jon, *Local Justice*, Cambridge, Cambridge University Press, 1992.

Fesbach, Murray and Alfred Friendly, Jr, *Ecocide in the USSR: Health and Nature under Siege*, London, Aurum Press, 1992.

Field, Frank, *Making Welfare Work: Reconstructing Welfare for the Millennium*, London, Institute of Community Studies, 1995.

Fukuyama, Francis, *The End of History and the Last Man*, New York, Free Press, 1992.

Fukuyama, Francis, *Trust: The Social Virtues and the Creation of Prosperity*, London, Hamish Hamilton, 1995.

Geras, Norman, *Solidarity in the Conversation of Mankind: The Ungroundable Liberalism of Richard Rorty*, London, Verso, 1995.

Giddens, Anthony, *The Consequences of Modernity*, Cambridge, Polity Press, 1990.

Giddens, Anthony, *Beyond Left and Right: The Future of Radical Politics*, Cambridge, Polity Press, 1994.

Goldsmith, James, *The Trap*, London, Macmillan, 1994.

Goldsmith, James, *The Response*, London, Macmillan, 1995.

Goldsmith, James, *Counter-culture*, vol. 6, privately printed, 1996.

Goodhart, David, *The Reshaping of the German Social Market*, London, Institute for Policy Research, 1994.

Graham, A. C., *Disputers of the Tao: Philosophical Argument in Ancient China*, La Salle, Ill., Open Court, 1989.

Gray, John, *Liberalisms: Essays in Political Philosophy*, London, Routledge, 1989.

Gray, John, *Beyond the New Right: Markets, Governments and the Common Environment*, London, Routledge, 1993.

Gray, John, *Post-Liberalism: Studies in Political Thought*, London, Routledge, 1993.

Gray, John, *Berlin*, London, HarperCollins, 1995.

Gray, John, *Enlightenment's Wake: Politics and Culture at the Close of the Modern Age*, London, Routledge, 1995.

Gray, John, *Liberalism*, 2nd edn, Milton Keynes, Open University Press, 1995.

Gray, John, *Mill on Liberty: A Defence*, 2nd edn, London and New York, Routledge, 1996.

Gullvag, I. and J. Wetlesen (eds), *In Sceptical Wonder: Inquiries into the Philosophy of Arne Naess on the Occasion of His 70th Birthday*, Oslo, Bergen and Tromso, Universitetsforlaget, 1982.

Hardin, Garrett, *Nature and Man's Fate*, New York, Mentor, 1961.

Hardin, Garrett, *Stalking the Wild Taboo*, 2nd edn, Los Altos, Calif., William Kaufman, 1978.

Hardin, Garrett, *Promethean Ethics: Living with Death, Competition and Triage*, Seattle and London, University of Washington Press, 1980.

Hardin, Garrett, *Living within Limits: Ecology, Economics and Population Taboos*, New York, Oxford University Press, 1993.

Harris, Robin, *The Conservative Community*, London, Centre for Policy Studies, 1992.

Held, David, *Democracy and Global Order*, Cambridge, Polity Press, 1994.

Himmelfarb, Gertrude, *The De-moralization of Society*, London, Institute for Economic Affairs, 1995.

Hirst, Paul and Grahame Thompson, *Globalization in Question*, Cambridge, Polity Press, 1996.

Homer, *Iliad*, tr. Robert Fitzgerald, New York, Anchor Books, Doubleday, 1974.

Hutton, Will, *The State We're In*, London, Jonathan Cape, 1995.

Kraus, Karl, *Half-truths and One-and-a-half-truths*, ed. Harry Zohn, Montreal, Engendra Press, 1976.

Latouche, Serge, *The Westernization of the World: The Significance, Scope and Limits of the Drive towards Global Uniformity*, Cambridge, Polity Press, 1996.

Leakey, Richard, *The Sixth Extinction*, London, Macmillan, 1996.

Lewin, Leonard C., *Report from the Iron Mountain on the Possibility and Desirability of Peace*, Harmondsworth, Penguin Books, 1967.

Lewin, Leonard, C., *Triage*, New York, Dial Press, 1972.

Lewis, Martin W., *Green Delusions: An Environmental Critique of Radical Environmentalism*, Durham, NC and London, Duke University Press, 1994.

Lilley, Peter, *Winning the Welfare Debate*, London, Social Market Foundation, Occasional Paper 11, 1995.

Livingstone, John A., *Rogue Primate: An Exploration of Human Domestication*, Toronto, Key Porter Books, 1994.

Lovelock, James, *Gaia: A New Look at Life on Earth*, Oxford, Oxford University Press, 1979.

Lovelock, James, *The Ages of Gaia: A Biography of Our Living Earth*, Oxford, Oxford University Press, 1989.

McGuiness, Brian (ed.), *Wittgenstein and His Times*, Oxford, Blackwell, 1982.

MacIntyre, Alasdair, *After Virtue*, London, Duckworth, 1980.

Martin, Angus, *The Last Generation: The End of Survival?* London, Fontana/Collins, 1975.

Miliband, Ralph, *Socialism for a Sceptical Age*, Cambridge, Polity Press, 1995.

Monod, Jacques, *Chance and Necessity*, London, Fontana, 1974.

Murray, Charles, *Losing Ground: American Social Policy, 1950–1980*, New York, Basic Books, 1984.

Murray, Charles and Richard Hernstein, *The Bell Curve*, New York, Free Press, 1994.

Naess, Arne, 'The Shallow and the Deep, Long-Range Ecology Movement', *Inquiry*, 16 (1973).

Nietzsche, F., *Joyful Wisdom*, New York, Frederick Ungar, 1960.

Oakeshott, Michael, *Experience and Its Modes*, Cambridge, Cambridge University Press, 1933 and 1986.

Oakeshott, Michael, *On Human Conduct*, Oxford, Clarendon Press, 1975.

Oakeshott, Michael, *Rationalism in Politics*, London, Methuen, 1977.

Oakeshott, Michael, *On History and Other Essays*, Oxford, Blackwell, 1983.

Parekh, Bhikhu, 'Superior People: The Narrowness of Liberalism from Mill to Rawls', *Times Literary Supplement*, 25 February 1994.

Polanyi, Karl, *The Great Transformation*, Boston, Beacon Press, 1957.

Pollard, Stephen, *Schools, Selection and the Left*, London, Social Market Foundation, 1995.

Rawls, John, *A Theory of Justice*, Oxford, Oxford University Press, 1972.

Rawls, John, *Political Liberalism*, New York, Columbia University Press, 1993.

Raz, Joseph, *The Morality of Freedom*, Oxford, Clarendon Press, 1986.

Raz, Joseph, *Ethics in the Public Domain*, Oxford, Clarendon Press, 1994.

Rifkin, Jeremy, *The End of Work: The Decline of the Global Labour Force and the Dawn of the Post-market Era*, New York, G. P. Putnam's Sons, 1995.

Roemer, John, *A Future for Socialism*, London, Verso, 1994.

Rorty, Richard, *Philosophy and the Mirror of Nature*, Oxford, Blackwell, 1980.

Rorty, Richard, *Contingency, Irony and Solidarity*, Cambridge, Cambridge University Press, 1989.

Ross, Andrew, *The Chicago Gangster Theory of Life: Nature's Debt to Society*, London and New York, Verso, 1994.

Sandel, Michael, *Liberalism and the Limits of Justice*, Cambridge, Cambridge University Press, 1981.

van Creveld, Martin, *On Future War*, London, Brassey's (UK), 1991.

Walzer, Michael, *Spheres of Justice*, New York, Basic Books, 1983.

Wetlesen, Jon, *The Sage and the Way: Spinoza's Ethics of Freedom*, Assen, van Gorcum, 1979.

Willets, David, *Civic Conservatism*, London, Social Market Foundation, 1993.

Wilson, E. O., *On Human Nature*, New York, Bantam Books, 1979.

Wilson, E. O., *Biophilia*, Cambridge, Mass., Harvard University Press, 1984.

Wilson, E. O., *The Diversity of Life*, New York and London, W. W. Norton, 1992.

Wittgenstein, Ludwig, *Remarks on the Foundations of Mathematics*, Oxford, Blackwell, 1967.

Wooldridge, Adrian, *Meritocracy and the Classless Society*, London, Social Market Foundation, 1995.

INDEX

Compiled by Timothy Penton

Lightning Source UK Ltd.
Milton Keynes UK
25 August 2009

143076UK00001BC/68/P